www.hondamentalism.com

Simon Saunders is the man behind the Ariel Atom. Capable of 0-60mph in just 2.8 seconds it leaves bigger, more expensive road cars standing. But if you're looking for extras you've come to the wrong small workshop in Somerset. The frugal designer constantly asks: 'Is it necessary?' This process boosts the power to weight ratio. Simon calls it 'the Ariel diet.' It means luxuries such as seat upholstery and self-cancelling indicators go straight out of the non-existent windows. One thing you do get is a Honda Type R engine, chosen for both performance and reliability. Simon claims if you laid out every production car engine in the world and asked him to pick one he would 'always choose the Honda.' Which is nice of him to say.

170
F40 v ENZO: CLASH OF THE TITANS
ONE OF THESE CARS COULD JUST BE THE
GREATEST FERRARI SUPERCAR OF ALL

CONTENTS
Ferrari supercars 2007

♞ INTRODUCTION
60 years of Ferrari

You could be forgiven for thinking that the last thing the world needs right now is another book about Ferrari. You'd probably be right.

Fortunately, this isn't just another book about Ferrari. It's a collection of the best articles from the files of **evo** and *Octane* magazines, which means it's predominantly about *driving*. And whether it's a 1950s Formula One racer or the very latest roadgoing supercar, no one puts you in the driving seat quite like the road test teams at **evo** and *Octane*.

So while there's plenty here on Ferrari history and folklore, as well as a glimpse into its future and a catalogue of every roadgoing production Ferrari, it's mostly about the sheer excitement of driving some of the world's greatest cars.

We've a head-to-head between the 246 Dino F1 car of the late '50s and its Maserati rival, the glorious 250F. Then there's a memorable drive in not one but three 275GTBs, and a track test of the frankly terrifying 288 GTO Evoluzione, and a blast along the old Mille Miglia route in a 360 Spider, and... well, you get the idea.

But because even our writers appreciate a change of pace, we've also included features on restoring a 250 GTO, 60 facts about Ferrari, a look at the tragically short life of Alfredo 'Dino' Ferrari, and a fascinating round-up of some of the more obscure cars to wear that famous shield. Enjoy.

Peter Tomalin & David Lillywhite, co-editors

'It's about the sheer excitement of driving some of the world's greatest cars'

THE THRILL OF DRIVING

Octane
fuelling the passion

60 years of Ferrari
From the publishers of **evo** and *Octane* magazines

Editorial office
Tower Court, Irchester Road, Wollaston, Northants NN29 7PJ Tel 0207 907 6310 Fax 01933 663367
Email eds@evo.co.uk or info@octane-magazine.com
Websites www.evo.co.uk and www.octane-magazine.com

Advertising
Group advertising director: Des Flynn

evo advertising
Advertising manager: Duncan Clarke
tel 020 7907 6772 email ads.evo@dennis.co.uk

Octane advertising
Advertising director: Sanjay Seetanah
Tel 01628 510080 Email ads@octane-magazine.com

Co-editors
Peter Tomalin and David Lillywhite

Sub editor
Ian Eveleigh

Art editor
Dean Lettice

Designers
Rob Gould, Chee-Chiu Lee and Neil Carey

Dennis Motoring
Editorial director Harry Metcalfe
Publishers James Burnay and Geoff Love
Managing director Ian Westwood

Dennis Publishing Ltd
COO Brett Reynolds
Group finance director Ian Leggett
CEO James Tye
Chairman Felix Dennis

The publishers make every effort to ensure the contents are correct. All material published in this edition is copyright and unauthorised reproduction is forbidden. The editors and publishers give no warranties, guarantees or assurances and make no representations regarding any goods or services advertised in this edition.

evo and **Octane** are published under licences from Evo Publications Ltd and Octane Media Ltd respectively, subsidiary companies of Dennis Publishing Limited, United Kingdom. All rights in the licensed material belong to Felix Dennis, Evo Publications, Octane Media or Dennis Publishing and may not be reproduced, whether in whole or in part, without their prior written consent. **evo** and **Octane** are registered trademarks.

Printed by benhamgoodhead print Ltd

Distributed by Seymour

Scarlet fever

It has just four cylinders, it's more than 50 years old, but it will pull over 160mph and it's stunningly beautiful – the Ferrari 750 Monza is the archetypal 1950s road racer

Words: Mark Dixon **Photography:** Gus Gregory

The bloke in the control

tower is looking worried as the red Ferrari is unstrapped from its trailer. 'Is it properly silenced?' he asks. 'Only we have to be careful because some of the local residents start complaining if there's too much noise.'

'I'm sure it is,' say I reassuringly, trying to divert the guy's attention away from the drainpipe-sized exhaust that exits prominently from the Ferrari's nearside. And at that precise moment, its custodian Kerry McSwan fires up the three-litre, four-cylinder motor. Ka-boom!

Personally, I reckon that if you buy a house next door to a test track then you should expect a bit of noise, but I promise we'll keep the revs down on the straight beyond which all those sensitive (and wealthy) home-owners dwell. I don't say anything about the rest of the track, mind you.

After all, it would be criminal not to make the most of the chance to drive a 1950s Ferrari with Le Mans history. This 750 Monza was entered by Mike Sparken and Masten Gregory in the 1955 Le Mans and competed in numerous other international events around that time. Present owner Tom Walduck has driven it with Kerry in three Mille Miglia retrospectives so it's no trailer queen but it's still an exceptionally original car. Turns out it's an exceptionally well-sorted machine, too.

Ferrari's model range was bafflingly complex in the early 1950s as the company struggled to match engine capacities to racing formulae. In the years leading up to 1954, when the 750 Monza was introduced, there were no fewer than nine varieties of V12 engine and three four-cylinders. The 750 Monza – its number representing the cubic capacity in cc of a single cylinder, as was Ferrari's custom – had the biggest of the four-pot motors: a three-litre, twin-cam engine that could thrust this road-racer up to 160mph or more, depending on which final drive ratio was fitted.

So why make do with four cylinders when Ferrari had so much experience with 12? Partly because an in-line four can offer lots of low-down torque and partly because the smaller number of components means it can be lighter and more efficient. Aurelio Lampredi designed Ferrari's first four-

'Present owner Tom Walduck has driven it with Kerry McSwan in three Mille Miglia retrospectives so it's no trailer queen, but it's still an exceptionally original car. Turns out it's an exceptionally well-sorted machine, too'

'The name 'Sparken' is scratched on top of the gearbox casing, maybe by a Ferrari mechanic prior to the 24 Hours'

cylinder engine for the 1951 Formula 2 season and the three-litre used in the 750 Monza is an evolution of it, the new car taking its name from a one-two victory at Monza in June 1954 in the hands of Hawthorn/Maglioli and Gonzalez/Trintignant.

Chassis no. 0504M, which is causing our test track controller such anxiety as McSwan warms up the oil, was delivered in early 1955 to privateer Mike Sparken, the racing identity of a Frenchman whose real name was (and is, because he's still very much alive) Michel Poborejsky. On February 27, 1955, Sparken had immediate success with his new toy in the Agadir Grand Prix, which he won outright, and another win in the British Empire Trophy Race at Oulton Park a couple of months later. With various other races under his belt, he returned the Monza to the Ferrari factory so it could be prepared for the 1955 Le Mans 24 Hours.

In 1955 there were five Ferraris on the starting grid at Le Mans but none of them was to finish. In fact the Sparken/Gregory Monza was the first to retire, holing a piston in the third hour; but this disappointment was quickly put into perspective by the horrific accident that followed soon after,

Above
Without a helmet, driving the Monza is a breezy experience but otherwise it's a surprisingly relaxing machine — though the big, in-line 'four' is undeniably noisy

when Pierre Levegh's Mercedes ploughed into the crowd, killing 83 people and injuring 100 more.

Today, Sparken's Monza is still much as it was on that dreadful day in June, 52 years ago. Peer under the metal tonneau that covers the nearside of the cockpit and you'll see the outline of a hole, now neatly filled, cut for the filler neck of a supplementary fuel tank. The oil filler cap on the offside front wing has miniature holes for the lead seals that were threaded through by Le Mans scrutineers, and the name 'Sparken' is scratched on top of the gearbox casing.

That name may well have been scrawled by a Ferrari mechanic as he stripped the car prior to the 24-hour race, since a sheaf of invoices and correspondence reveals that Sparken spent a huge amount with the factory in the months leading up to June 1955. Ferrari hired out one of its mechanics to Sparken at Oulton and Goodwood, too, as well as taking care of transportation to the Agadir and Dakar grands prix in Africa and to Le Mans. Sparken clearly wasn't running his Monza on a shoestring.

Apart from the addition of an ammeter, the dash looks just as it did in 1955. You still fire up the big twin-cam in the same

Right and below
Three-litre, four-cylinder motor has twin camshafts, twin Webers and twin-plug ignition. Thin-rimmed wheel and chrome-gated gearlever are a joy to look at and use

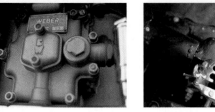

way, too, by turning the ignition key one click to the right and pulling on a lever deep under the scuttle, which acts directly on the starter motor. Already warm, the motor cannons into life, sounding loud and meaty. It'll oil its plugs if you leave it ticking over, so you must keep blipping the throttle while you prepare for take-off; as the revs rise and fall, vibrations percolate through the alloy-panelled bodywork.

Contemporary race reports often list 750 Monzas as having retired with clutch problems and Sparken's car was not immune at the time, so it's lucky I haven't done my research beforehand because the Monza's clutch makes an Austin Seven's seem nicely progressive. Smooth getaways are all but impossible because the multiplate clutch relies on metal-to-metal contact. 'Just keep the revs up and spin the wheels,' advises Kerry McSwan; 'the transmission can take it.' Well, if you insist...

With twin Webers partially open, the Monza fishtails lazily away and onto the test track, engine roaring in a thrilling if not sophisticated fashion – it sounds like any other big 'four', the harmonies of valve train and carburettors drowned out by the thunder of the exhaust. Snatch second, then third, and even the exhaust note starts to yield to the buffeting wind and the scream of gears in the rear transaxle.

The earliest Monzas had four-speed 'boxes but this 1955 model has the more usual five-speeder, with 'dog-leg' first out to the left of the traditional Ferrari chromed gate. There's no synchromesh but the faster you make changes, the better it works. Upshifts need nothing more than a good sense of

> **'Coming down through the 'box, your feet must tap the pedals with the rapidity of a Michael Flatley to whip through the double-declutching necessary for a clean change'**

timing but, coming down through the 'box, your feet must tap the pedals with the rapidity of a Michael Flatley to whip through the double-declutching necessary for a clean change.

Depending on which gears are housed in the diff' casing – which is mounted rigidly in the tubular chassis, and split vertically so that ratios can be swiftly altered – the Monza is good for anything between 113 and 164mph. That's not a theoretical top end, either. In 1955, journalist Hans Tanner recorded an electrically timed 163.06mph on the autostrada in a Monza identical to this one. That must have been fun for anyone pootling along the same stretch of road in a Topolino.

Mind you, Tanner also commented that 'at about 3500rpm [the engine] sounds like a boiler factory. In third gear there is a permanent vibration at all revs which makes you feel as if you've spent a day sitting on a secondhand pneumatic drill going full bore.' And Tanner's was a brand new car.

The Sparken Monza doesn't sound like a boiler factory – more like a busy repair shop, if anything. The engine was rebuilt by Hall & Fowler in the late 1990s and still feels fresh

> 'It soon gallops up to 110-120mph. With no race helmet and a Perspex screen that simply deflects the flies into your hair rather than your teeth, that feels very exciting indeed'

as a daisy: change down at 3500rpm from fifth to fourth and it shoves you in the back like the school bully. Safe maximum is 6000rpm but in practice there's not much to be gained by exceeding 5000; even in period, it wouldn't last long if subjected to very high revs. Remember, all five Ferraris retired from Le Mans in 1955.

With hemispherical combustion chambers and twin-plug ignition, the claimed power output is some 260bhp. Allowing a discount for period exaggeration that's still going some for a four-cylinder motor, if not quite up to the 100bhp per litre that Enzo Ferrari had hoped for (and that Norton had achieved with its motorcycle engines). The Monza has no speedo but, by my calculations from the revs showing on the tachometer, it soon gallops up to an easy 110-120mph. With no race helmet and a Perspex screen that simply deflects the flies into your hair rather than into your teeth, that feels very exciting indeed.

Exciting, but not scary. Your face may be being sculpted into Dali-esque shapes as it's pushed through a wall of air, and your ears assaulted by a combined barrage of wind noise, gear whine and exhaust blare, but there's no sense of hanging on to reality by your fingertips. For a race car, the Monza is almost relaxing. It's not jarred by the occasional missing chunk in the track and there's no kickback through the steering. As McSwan

points out, the Monza was built for racing at high speed for long periods over indifferent surfaces, including pavé, so it had literally to take the rough with the smooth.

It's helped in that respect by a de Dion rear axle – like the one used on Ferrari's GP cars of the period – which keeps the wheels vertical to the road surface when cornering but accounts for less unsprung weight, since the diff' is bolted to the chassis and not into the axle. Suspended below a transverse leaf spring, the axle tube is allowed to move up and down, but not sideways, by a square lump of bronze sliding in a vertical steel channel, while twin radius arms form a parallelogram with the axle hubs on each side and prevent them twisting under braking or acceleration. Given the choice of thrashing a Monza or a Mercedes 300 roadster over the Mille Miglia for days on end, I know which I'd choose and it would be red.

Running with half a tank of fuel, the handling feels reassuringly benign. The beautiful Borrani wires are currently shod with 6.00 x 16in tyres all round but Monzas often ran with 5.00s or 5.50s on the front, presumably to induce a measure of understeer to counteract the weight of a full tank at the rear. After all, the tank holds at least 30 gallons – how much more, McSwan doesn't know because it's never been completely filled... I get the impression the car »

Right
De Dion rear axle
helps put the power
down to the road
while reducing
unsprung weight.

'It drives as well as it did when new – maybe better, if Tanner's account is at all typical – and the odd minor dent or paint scratch only encourages you exercise it'

FERRARI 750 MONZA
SPECIFICATIONS

Engine
2999.6cc, four cylinders, twin overhead camshafts, 103 x 90mm bore and stroke, alloy crankcase with combined alloy head and block, screw-in iron cylinder liners, twin Weber 50DCOA3 carburettors

Power
260bhp @ 6400rpm

Transmission
Five-speed manual transaxle

Suspension
Front: independent, coil and wishbone, Houdaille shock absorbers
Rear: de Dion axle and single transverse spring, located by two radius rods on each side, Houdaille shock absorbers

Brakes
Hydraulically operated drums

Performance
Top speed 113-160mph depending on final drive

Weight
1680lb (760kg)

wouldn't bite you if the rear end did start to step out of line but I'm not stupid enough to tempt it when its value is about 20 times my annual income.

There's not much call to use the brakes on the circuit of the test track but the big, finned drums shrug the speed off well enough when required. The front drums were fitted for Le Mans and are bigger than standard – they're from a six-cylinder Ferrari – not for increased braking efficiency but simply because the greater surface area of the friction material meant it would last longer in a race. For a similar reason, the scoops ahead of the rear wheels are to cool the tyres, not the brakes.

Amazingly, despite a fairly energetic competition career when it was young in the hands of Sparken and, latterly Gregory, and at least occasional sporting use in the decades that followed, 0504M has remained totally original. The bodywork bears the scars of its 52 years and the front wings are slightly mismatched as the result of a shunt that happened back in the mists of time but otherwise it's exactly as Scaglietti's workshop turned it out in Modena in early 1955.

It is also quite stunningly beautiful, especially by the

standards of the mid-1950s. The first Monza prototype had a rather dumpy body based on a Lampredi design but all production Monzas were bodied in a much sleeker style that was the work of Ferrari's son, Dino. It's hard to believe that just a couple of years separate the 750 Monza from earlier, chunkier Ferraris such as the 340MM.

For a couple of years, 750 Monzas were the car of choice for privateers like Sparken, and could account for a third or more of a race grid. But Enzo Ferrari needed more cylinders to get the power outputs he demanded, and four-cylinder engines fell out of favour as quickly as they'd arrived. Ferrari reverted back to V12s (a new design by Lampredi) and the last incarnation of a four-cylinder Ferrari was the 2-litre 500TRC of 1957.

With a total of only 33 Monzas built, chassis no. 0504M is precious both for its competition history and its originality. Just as important is its sheer usability. It drives as well as it did when new – maybe better, if Tanner's account is at all typical – and the odd minor dent or paint scratch only encourages you not to worry about it but to get on and exercise the damn thing.

I hope that anyone who lives in the big houses behind the Surrey test track and whose afternoon nap may have been disturbed by the sound of a Ferrari engine pulling 5000rpm will forgive me. Honestly, it was worth it.

Thanks to Kerry McSwan and to Anthony Pozner at Hendon Way Motors. www.hendonwaymotors.com

THE SHAPE OF TECHNOLOGY.

CASE IN STEEL 45 MM Ø, AUTOMATIC
MECHANICAL MOVEMENT PANERAI
OP VIII CALIBRE, SECOND TIME
ZONE, POWER RESERVE 42
HOURS, C.O.S.C. CERTIFICATE,
SAPPHIRE CRYSTAL, SCREW-DOWN
CROWN, ADJUSTABLE BUCKLE.

Ferrari

Engineered by OFFICINE PANERAI

There's a well-worn

adage that if it looks right, it probably is. Think back through the history of man's mechanised movement and picture the first Supermarine Spitfire, the Bugatti Type 35, the Jaguar D-type, the Hawker Hunter, the Lotus 25. All of them effective, deadly even, and yet beautiful even to the non-enthusiast's gaze. Whether that matters is a good question, especially since all were tools required only to perform better than their opposition.

You can add to that list the front-engined Italian Grand Prix car of the 1950s. Long nose, tall boat-tail, big wheels and nary a straight line to be found, all blended into a perfectly proportioned whole. To a generation of wide-eyed youngsters, it was simply how a real racing car looked.

1950 had been the start of Formula One as a category, and if the decade of post-war austerity that followed will be better remembered for the cold war, civil rights and the bomb, it was nevertheless a glorious time for Grands Prix. The Germans who had dominated pre-war would not do it quite so easily this time; the English were gearing up for action later on and Maserati and Ferrari were already better organised and spurred on by a battle for Latin supremacy on the international stage. The men who drove any of them simply wanted to win. A list that includes Fangio, »

GRAND PRIX GIANTS

They were the last of the great front-engined Grand Prix racers.
Ferrari's 246 Dino locks horns once again with Maserati's 250F
Words: Mark Hales Photography: Matt Howell

Moss, Farina, Gonzalez, Ascari, Musso, Hawthorn and Collins is by no means complete, but certainly exclusive.

In 1954, the rules were changed and engines had to be 2.5 litres unsupercharged (or 750cc with a blower) and this was the cue for Maserati to make the seminal 250F, which retained some of the powerful purpose of the big pre-war cars, but shrank it into a more compact and elegant whole. The way the body's cigar shape sweeps and tapers along its length and the way the cockpit's opening peels its way from such compound curvature without spoiling it, is mesmerising. For me, the 250F is still the perfectly proportioned single seater.

Ferrari's Dino 246, which appeared four years later, was out of a similar mould but it was smaller and lighter, benefiting from progress in most areas. But the slightly more squashed look to the body and the prominent scoop on the bonnet to feed the downdraught carburettors does not allow it quite the same uninterrupted purity of line.

The two types would compete against each other – just. The 250F was probably nearing the end of its competitive life before the factory officially withdrew from Grand Prix racing in 1957 to concentrate on business. They continued engine development to assist the privateers, but the front-engined era was drawing to a close, too. Ferrari retired the Dinos in 1960 and a golden period gave way to the introduction of lighter and more nimble mid-engined cars. The two in the pictures are thus the perfect pair. The blood-red best that Italy could produce at the time.

The Maserati, which belongs to Pink Floyd musician Nick Mason, is a relatively late model – probably one of those converted by the factory for V12 engines in 1957 in an unsuccessful attempt to take on Ferrari, but later refitted with a six. The layout is conventional for the time; a long-stroke in-line engine sits tall beneath the bonnet, topped with twin overhead camshafts which also drive twin magnetos to feed twin

plugs per cylinder. This last is another period convention, necessitated by the hemispherical combustion chamber which was then thought optimum. The large hump on the piston to gain the required compression with this design compromises the flame travel in the chamber and the best defence was another plug on the other side to speed up the burning. Almost everybody used a similar arrangement and would do so for another ten years.

The length of the engine and the need to accommodate the driver immediately behind it led Maserati to put the gearbox in-unit with the rear axle and spin the propeller shaft – which runs between the driver's legs – at engine speed. Suspension is independent at the front with double wishbones and coil springs (telescopic dampers mounted separately), de Dion at the back via a transverse leaf spring pinned in the middle. Big 16in wire wheels complete the picture and are filled with simply huge aluminium finned drum brakes.

'The men who drove them simply wanted to win. A list which includes Fangio, Moss, Farina, Gonzalez, Ascari, Musso, Hawthorn and Collins is by no means complete, but it is certainly exclusive'

The Ferrari has been owned by the same family for over 20 years and was assembled out of spares in the 1980s, which makes it real, if not exactly official. At first sight it looks to have a similar layout to the Maserati's, but delve a little deeper and you see some more modern thinking. The engine is a V6 – unusually with an angle of 65 degrees rather than the more normal 60 and a concept pioneered by Enzo Ferrari's son Dino and designer Vittorio Jano, hence the soubriquet. The vee gets the weight lower and, because the engine is half the length, further back towards the centre – remove the bonnet and that long nose is filled with not much at all. The engine's layout is also why the carburettors and bonnet airscoop are where they are.

The 12 sparks are supplied by a single two-stage magneto driven from the back of one camshaft. It is exclusive to the engine and is now so rare that one changed hands recently for £20,000 – Dino ownership is clearly not for the faint of wallet. Transmission is also in the fashion of the time and lays at the back, in-unit with the axle like the Maserati's, but mounted across the car rather than in-line, which again helps shift weight forward. In addition, because drive goes to one end, the propeller shaft runs at an angle across the floor. That is why the engine is skewed under the bonnet.

The Maserati hangs its oil and fuel tanks right out the back inside that rivet-encrusted abdomen, which has to be the worst possible place to put them. Not only are they doing a fine impression of a pendulum, but it's an influence that will change as the fuel burns. Races in those days were long and cars might start with anything up to 40 gallons, which is a bit like riding a bike with a 270lb saddlebag.

The Ferrari moves that mass closer to the car's centre of gravity where it can't swing like a bobweight, putting the fluid inside panniers, one each side of the driver. On this car one is for oil, the other petrol, but depending on the length of the race Ferrari might have filled both with fuel and put a smaller tank for oil behind the driver. The science of weight distribution seems so obvious now and yet, at the time, requiring a driver clad in a polo shirt to sit in a bath of high octane petrol may not have seemed like obvious progress. It would be interesting to know whether Fangio or Musso or Moss really thought about such things.

Yet more modern touches are the Dino's big disc brakes inside smaller 15in wheels and the fully adjustable double wishbone suspension at both ends, all sprung by modern style coil-over spring/damper units. This was

the beginning of an exciting time in motorsport when the technology of design was about to gain ascendancy over complexity of engineering as a means to an end. Except maybe in the tyre department, where the very public nature of failure probably ensured a conservative approach. Ferrari would also try 16in wheels but the tyre section would remain, at 5.50 front and 6.50 rear, similar to those on the Maserati.

The Dino's driving position is another modern touch. The seat is much lower down than it is in the 250F and instead of splaying the knees to clear a big wheel, you stretch the arms to find it straight in front, level with your chest. Gearshift is then down and to the left and needs a moment's pause for thought; first gear is to the far left and back behind a spring-loaded detent, then it's right, all the way across the gate and forward for second, straight back for third, then back

across the gate to the left and forward for fourth. Fifth is then straight back. All of which is fine when you are thinking about it but easy to forget when you are busy.

GTO Engineering's John James says to stay where I am and he'll just roll the car forward. I turn the switch to both sets of plugs, let the clutch up at walking pace and the engine bursts immediately into life. Let it warm, then out of the paddock towards Cadwell Park's delightful collection of serpentine gradients. There's a slight judder from a clutch which is heavy underfoot and which sends a gentle jangling through the propeller shaft over which you sit, but it's easy enough and the engine is completely devoid of temperament. At least it is until you invite it to move a little faster...

The track is wet for the moment and any more than half throttle in any

gear sends the rear wheels spinning crazily, the needle on the big rev-counter flicking towards the 8500rpm limit and the tail waltzing one way or the other. I try and get a drift going by taking some more speed into the longer corners and holding it there with a gentle dose of that wonderful V6 urge, but the front doesn't point either, then the rear wheels spin anyway if you try and help it.

Probably it's too wet for the time being to feel the benefits of better weight distribution and, as ever, I can't help wondering whether it was like this for Fangio and Moss or whether the cars were set up differently. (I do remember reading how Fangio had made a pit-stop for tyres in which the mechanics had been hurriedly hand-cutting deeper grooves while he was on track.) A lap or two more just to savour the noise of the engine and the slickness of the right to left shift which, like all good dog-boxes,

Below
At Cadwell, Ferrari leads Maserati... The 250F's engine was equal to the Ferrari's by 1958, on paper at least. It doesn't feel it today

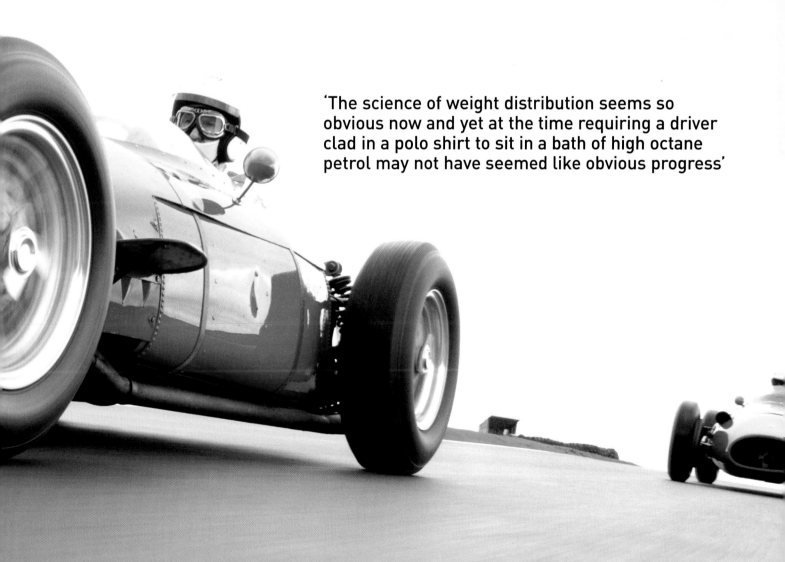

'The science of weight distribution seems so obvious now and yet at the time requiring a driver clad in a polo shirt to sit in a bath of high octane petrol may not have seemed like obvious progress'

'You sense the lower overall weight and the lesser inertia that makes the Dino feel quicker in its responses, but means the window of opportunity to get the car braked, pointed and the power on is narrower'

Above
Minimal gauges are harder to see on low-set Ferrari dash. Note angled propshaft running across floor

Far right
Network of pipes pump oil and fuel from the remote tanks. Leaks were a common source of retirement

gets slicker the faster you flick the lever. We resolve to let the track dry a little while we do some static photography.

That done and rain abated, it's time to try the 250F. There's a taller cockpit and a bigger vault to place a foot on the seat and step in – then a squat behind a much bigger wooden rimmed wheel which is closer to you and tilted forward at the top. The cockpit's sides are then further away and you sit higher, which somehow feels less intimate, more vintage. Gears are down on the floor to the right and the shift pattern is conventional H-pattern with a gate which also starts with a spring-loaded detent to the left-and-back for first. The straight six doesn't fire quite as easily and both Ten Tenths' Charlie Knill-Jones and GTO's James puff a little together before it catches, and then it isn't quite as smooth as the V6 when it does. There's a similar jangling from the prop although the clutch is lighter and so is the steering, but the 250F is just as simple to motivate.

Out on the circuit, which is now only damp in places, and the Maserati immediately feels lighter to the touch. The steering takes less muscle although the elbows move further with that big wheel, and you can feel the car rolling and pitching more in response to your inputs. I head for the driest patches, which are round the long corner at the top of Cadwell. The straight engine rasps and thrums through the seat, sending a hum through the propshaft.

Keep a good eye on the rev-counter now: the good guys used eight and more in the day, but we'll stick to seven-two like we're asked, by which time the engine is feeling a touch breathless anyway. Reach down towards the floor and cup a hand round the aluminium knob, kick the clutch pedal and flick the wrist. The shift is instant like a modern Hewland's but the lever moves further and it doesn't snick. There might be no gears at all in the box, so light is the action. It feels even slicker than the Ferrari's, which is saying something.

Meanwhile the car is surging forward, engine crackling and wailing and popping out of the long black pipe that trails behind my shoulder. Look up the road and remember the technique: don't brake, even though I want to, but keep the pedal planted hard to the floor. Ease the big rim and aim the front end at a point somewhere way up ahead.

Oh yes. The nose doesn't point and dive like it does on some of the older cars, but instead the whole body seems to swivel gently round a point somewhere in its middle, somewhere between your knees. Elbows and instinct catch the motion with that big wheel, but I mustn't slap it back into line as swiftly as possible, mustn't do what I've been doing for years, just rein it in to stop the yaw angle getting any bigger but let it all keep coming. Monitor the amount with little massages of that big rim and, whatever you do, don't lift off. We've found the zone and we want to stay there.

It's a joy in a completely different style to an aggressive, wheelspinning powerslide because it works the fronts almost as hard as the rears and as the road's sweep unravels, the car almost straightens itself. But then the tighter corners which follow are a little less homogenous. The big drums tend to grab and twitch the car one way and another until you have all the shoes squashed against all the drums, then you have to be careful not to let that energy dive on the laden front wheel and pivot the car round the front end. That will only give you a dose of snappy oversteer on the exit. Better to brake a little earlier and let the car settle, then power it through. Savour the crackle and the slick shift which soon follow. »

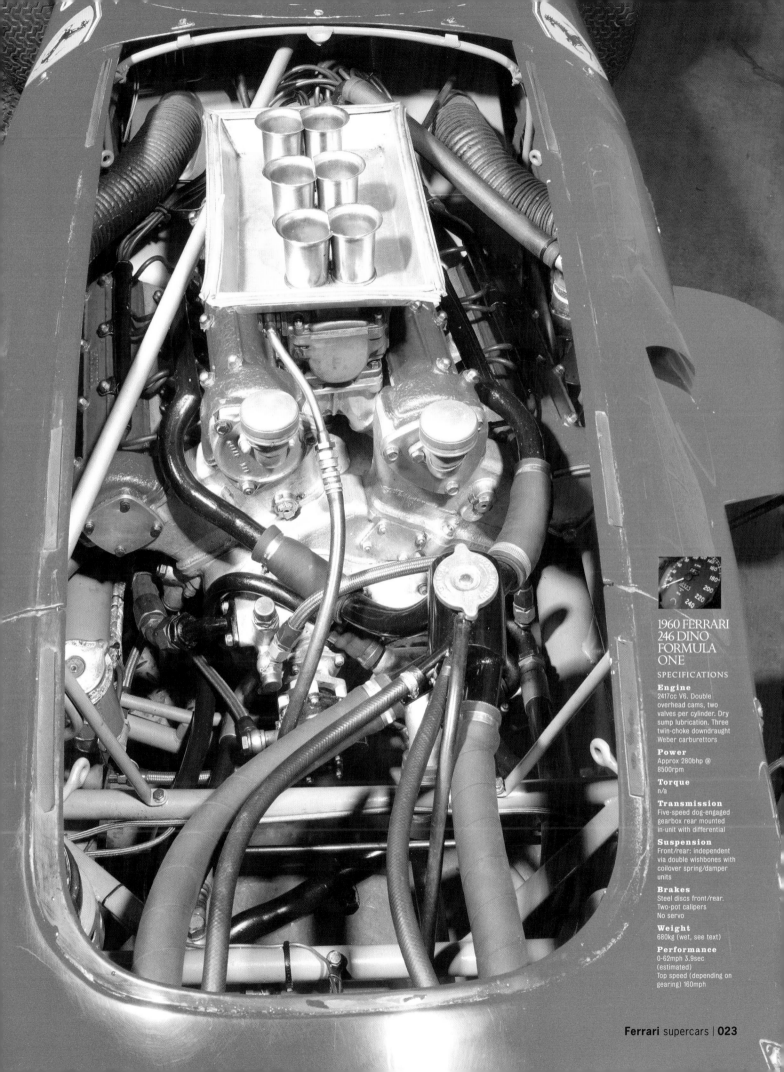

1960 FERRARI 246 DINO FORMULA ONE

SPECIFICATIONS

Engine
2417cc V6. Double overhead cams, two valves per cylinder. Dry sump lubrication. Three twin-choke downdraught Weber carburettors

Power
Approx 280bhp @ 8500rpm

Torque
n/a

Transmission
Five-speed dog-engaged gearbox rear mounted in-unit with differential

Suspension
Front/rear: independent via double wishbones with coilover spring/damper units

Brakes
Steel discs front/rear. Two-pot calipers No servo

Weight
680kg (wet, see text)

Performance
0-62mph 3.9sec (estimated)
Top speed (depending on gearing) 160mph

1957 MASERATI 250F FORMULA ONE

SPECIFICATIONS

Engine
2493cc in-line six. Twin overhead camshafts, two valves per cylinder. Dry sump lubrication. Three twin-choke sidedraught Weber carburettors

Power
Approx 230bhp @ 7200rpm (1954), 270bhp @ 8000rpm (1956), 290bhp @ 8000rpm (1958)

Torque
n/a

Transmission
Five-speed dog-engaged manual gearbox, rear mounted in-unit with differential

Suspension
Front: independent via double wishbones, coil springs and telescopic dampers. Rear: de Dion with transverse leaf spring and telescopic dampers

Brakes
Drum brakes with finned aluminium cladding. No servo

Weight
780kg (wet, see text)

Performance
0-60mph 4.3sec
Top speed (depending on gearing) 155mph

'Look up the road and remember the technique: don't brake, even though I want to, but keep the pedal planted hard to the floor. Ease the big rim and aim the front end at a point somewhere way up ahead'

Time for another go in the Dino, this time on a drier track and where hopping from one to the other highlights differences that are more subtle than you might expect. The steering is still heavier, but the driving position is more comfortable and you can brace the body better with legs outstretched and foot hard against a substantial footrest. The brakes you now find are firm underfoot, but they are tireless and accurate and allow you to place the car better.

You sense the lower overall weight and the lesser inertia, which makes the Dino feel quicker in its responses, but that does mean the window of opportunity to get the car braked, pointed and the power on is narrower. The tail-out oversteer that you can still have on the exit of the corner is more insistent and does need slapping firmly back into line. It's a more modern ambience and you drive it accordingly, using those discs late and hard then leaning on a front end which at first understeers quite strongly, but invites you to bring in the power of that sublime engine.

And sublime it certainly is. Harsh yet musical under load, crackling a fusillade every time you back off, you twist your head in an attempt to lessen the aural assault drilling its way from the underslung exhaust nearest

you and through the defence of helmet and earplugs. Utterly and completely smooth and ever more muscular as it sears through the mid-range, the V6 pulls and pulls, ever seamlessly towards eight-five with such eagerness you need to anticipate the shift, and think about which way to move the lever.

It's much revvier and bigger in the mid and upper ranges than the Maserati's in-line engine, but the exact numbers as ever depend on where you look. Maserati variously claimed 220-240bhp at 7200rpm in 1954, 280bhp at 8000rpm in 1957 and 290bhp in 1958. (The stillborn V12 was reputed to push out 320bhp at 10,000rpm). Ferrari claimed 280 or 290bhp at 8500 or 8300rpm for the carburettored 246 Dino throughout its two-year life.

Weight has a bearing on acceleration as well as handling, and here we encounter another potential revision of history. When we rolled Mason's car onto Cadwell's scales, the readout said 780kg. The Dino read 680 with exactly the same amount of fluids on board, which meant that on the day there was 100kg between them – a massive difference. I couldn't discover any official figures for Ferrari, but Maserati claimed 630kg dry for the 250F. Even allowing for fuel and oil, Mason's car is about 100kg more

than Maserati claimed. Like people, cars usually put on weight in later years but it's still difficult to see where the 250F might have gained that much.

Engine and brakes apart, though, the differences between them were not as clear cut as I had expected when I saw the respective layouts, and as I so often have, I began to wonder whether the intervening four decades had simply added some stiffness to the Ferrari's suspension. Or maybe this really was how they were at the time. Perhaps progress had already wrought its course and deliberate drifting as a means of gaining a handling balance on the hoof was about to be a thing of the past. Perhaps the two cars straddled the moment at which braking and pointing was about to take over, ready for the mid-engined revolution about to dawn.

There's no doubt, however, that on the day the Dino felt the lighter, more powerful car, more modern and faster round the lap. It wasn't, however, as much fun to drive as the older, heavier, less comfortable, slower Maserati, or at least, it was a different kind of fun. So let's just say that each had its own magic and that cannot necessarily be measured by the scales, the dynamometer or the stopwatch. Then, as now, there is just something about the red cars. △

Above
Gearchange in Maserati has conventional H-pattern and is a total delight.

Far left
Twin magnetos each feed one set of plugs per cylinder to promote better combustion.

Ferrari 250

The '250' simply represents cylinder size, but Ferrari's range of
V12s have star quality, from the first Mille Miglia to the last Lusso

Words: David Lillywhite Photography: Michel Zumbrunn

250 SW

If ever there was a line-up of models that managed to be both highly evocative and deeply confusing, it's those from the prancing horse with '250' in their designation. So here we bring ten landmark models, from the first to wear the '250' moniker, through GTO to the last-of-the-line Lusso. We've kept away from the out-and-out racers, like the 250 Testa Rossa and the 250LM, but brought together examples of all the major road cars.

This is a range that encompasses a staggering variety of body styles, built by masters of coachbuilding such as Vignale, Pinin Farina and Zagato. There are clear links between the models, but chassis changed, wheelbases altered and levels of trim varied enormously. Surprisingly, given that the cars are named '250' by the cubic capacity of a single cylinder of their 3-litre V12s, there are even two different engines used in the range.

Ferrari 250s are associated with greatness. Some represented firsts in Ferrari history, others have achieved legendary status through race victories or simple beauty. Curiously, few actually show great innovation, but that doesn't stop a 250 of some sort featuring in most people's lists of their most desirable cars.

»

250 Mille Miglia

In the early 1950s, the fledgling Ferrari company was a constructor of competition machinery, with a small sideline in road cars, and already establishing a reputation for race track domination – Formula One and Le Mans victories had been chalked up in 1948 and '49 respectively.

To deal with the variety of race disciplines being attacked, the company had developed two engines, the original Gioacchino Colombo-designed 'short-block' V12 and the later, larger-capacity Aurelio Lampredi 'long-block' V12. Gradually the smaller engine was enlarged from its original 1.5-litre capacity, through 159, 166, 212 and 225 (2.7-litre) designations. Meanwhile, the large, torquey Lampredi engines, as used in the 4.1-litre Ferrari 340 for example, were gaining a reputation for troublesome behaviour; not so much due to shortcomings in the design, but because their high torque was breaking transmissions.

The answer was to enlarge the Colombo engine once more, to 3 litres, and to change the cylinder head design from siamesed to individual ports. This gave the engine a new lease of life and set it up for use in the following 250s.

Using this more compact engine in the lighter chassis of the smaller-engined cars resulted in the very first 250, a Vignale-bodied coupé that was initially named the 250S. This was the car that Ferrari entered in the 1952 Mille Miglia, driven by Giovanni Bracco who, legend has it, chained-smoked and brandy-swigged his way to a heroic win. The result was so important that Ferrari named all subsequent versions of the 250S as 250 Mille Miglias.

A total of some 32 of these cars were subsequently produced, some as Berlinettas (pictured) built by Pinin Farina (plus-two from Vignale), others as open-tops. The chassis were typical of Ferraris of the time, with oval tubing, a transverse leaf spring at the front, leaf springs at the back and Houdaille lever-arm dampers all round. A new four-speed gearbox was developed too, in place of the existing five-speeder.

The 250 Mille Miglia went on to score a number of important victories, particularly in America in the hands of Phil Hill.

'Ferrari entered the 250S in the 1952 Mille Miglia, driven by Giovanni Bracco who, legend has it, chain-smoked and brandy-swigged his way to victory'

250 **Europa**

It might not be one of the better known 250s, but really the Europa, introduced in 1953, is the true start of the model line, because it was the first of the Gran Turismos, aimed at fast cross-country touring. Surprisingly, though, it used the Lampredi V12, which was a good engine but not necessarily as suitable for road use as the 'short block' Colombo V12.

The way this came about is simple, if a little illogical in hindsight. Ferrari had built its first real road car, the 166, in 1947, based around a 2400mm wheelbase tubular chassis and the 2-litre Colombo V12. It was an expensive, sometimes troublesome machine that nonetheless rewarded those who could match its abilities.

As explained in the 250 Mille Miglia section, the engine was enlarged over the years to give the 195 (2.3-litre), and the 212 (2.5-litre), while the bodies were supplied by an array of coachbuilders. The chassis remained virtually unchanged, although wheelbases changed, with two versions of the 212 built, the Inter and the Export, the latter with a shorter wheelbase.

When the time came to develop the next stage of road car, the 3-litre version of the Colombo V12 was still being experimented with for the 250 Mille Miglia, and it seemed a safer option to use the Lampredi V12, which was already doing sterling service in the 4.1-litre 340 and 342 models. The result was the shortlived 250 Export and the more popular 250 Europa.

Although Michelotti and Vignale styled the first Europa, Pinin Farina dominated production. The basic, long-serving chassis continued, now stretched to 2800mm (Export 2400mm) and, with the addition of a better appointed interior with extra soundproofing, weight was up a fifth on previous road cars. The pay-off was that the Europa was by far the easiest Ferrari to live with so far and capable of 135mph and 0-60mph in under eight seconds.

However, it was clear that Ferrari customers needed a little less in the way of thoroughbred behaviour from their Grand Tourers, and the Europa was phased out by the similarly named but otherwise quite different GT Europa.

'The pay-off was that the Europa was by far the easiest Ferrari so far to live with, and capable of 135mph and 0-60mph in under 8 seconds'

250 GT

The 250 Europa established Ferrari as a maker of serious, upmarket grand tourers – but the quality of the ride, the standard of the trim and the reliability of the all-alloy Lampredi engine left a little to be desired.

The Colombo engine – more responsive, lighter and shorter than the Lampredi unit – was better suited to a relatively compact Grand Tourer. So, for 1955 the car was revised, using the 3-litre Colombo engine from the 250 Mille Miglia and independent coil spring front suspension instead of Ferrari's traditional transverse leaf set-up. The shorter engine also allowed a reduction in the wheelbase, down to 2600mm.

The new car, confusingly named GT Europa, was a massive improvement and, at 140mph, even faster than the outgoing Europa. After 28 had been made, the Europa tag was dropped, and the model became known simply as 250 GT. But there's little simple about the range of styles that the 250 GT was available in...

Ferrari had settled on Pinin Farina as its coachbuilder of choice by this time so, predictably, of the 28 GT Europas built, 27 were from Pinin Farina. The other car was a one-off special by Vignale for Princess Liliane de Rethy of Belgium.

There were also seven lightweight 'Berlinettas' built in alloy by Pinin Farina – and three of these cars had an unusual rear wing treatment with a very prominent kick-up line from sill to sail panel (like the Tour de France on page 32).

For the 250 GT, Pinin Farina once again got the ball rolling, continuing the distinctive rear wing styling of the previous three GT Europa Berlinettas. But the company was struggling to keep up, its workshops packed and order books overflowing, so work was farmed out to local Carrozzeria Boano, where 250 GTs (with flush rear wing styling) were produced until mid-1957.

Then Mario-Felice Boano left to become chief stylist at Fiat, and his business partner Luciano Polla was joined by Boano's son-in-law, Ezio Ellena. The company's name became Carrozzeria Ellena but production of 250 GTs continued for another 12 months, unchanged except for an almost undetectably higher roofline for better headroom This period of 250 GTs are known as Boano and Ellena models, with the former company's cars called 'low roof' and the latter 'high roof'.

Pinin Farina, meanwhile, had been building a new factory to enable production of the 250 GT to return 'home'. To mark the change, a new design was launched with clean, notchback styling, 2600mm wheelbase, the best appointed interior so far and performance of 150mph and 6.7 seconds for 0-60. This is the model you see above.

The 250 GT Pinin Farina, or PF, as it became known, was launched in 1958, gaining twin distributors and then the 'outside-plug' engine (referring to the position of the spark plugs) in 1959, disc brakes, telescopic dampers and revised steering in 1960. It went on to sell more than 350 examples, all in left-hand-drive.

'It was massively revised, using the 3-litre Colombo V12 of the 250 Mille Miglia and coil springs instead of Ferrari's traditional transverse leaf'

250 GT Cabriolet

Usually when we think of road-going 250s, we think of muscular, coupé styling. But there were several versions of lithe, sexy, open-top 250s built too, which started with a one-off convertible from the Boano era.

Once Pinin Farina was back on the 250 scene, an open-top version was quickly produced. Initially there were four prototypes, each featuring unique body and interior treatments.

The first was chassis number 0655 GT, which was built for Ferrari racing ace Peter Collins. It featured a cut-down driver's door, a crackle-black dashboard and unusual styling creases in the wings. The windscreen did without a chrome top rail and Collins later equipped it with Dunlop disc brakes and alloy wheels (Borrani wire wheels had always been a 250 staple).

Another of the prototypes was built with a cut-down windscreen and a faired driver's headrest (like a D-type's). The third was built for the 1957 Paris Salon and the fourth was sold to the Aga Khan.

However these four cars were simply interesting experiments ahead of a run of 36

open-top 250 GT Cabriolets, which are now known as Series 1 (pictured).

The kicked-up rear wings of the earlier coupés remained, perfectly suiting the svelte styling, but all but the very last of the Series 1 models featured headlights equipped with gorgeous perspex cowls.

In the meantime, the California Spider had been introduced (see page 33), based heavily on the competition variant of the 250, the Tour de France. Ferrari needed to differentiate between these two models which, although produced by different coachbuilders, looked remarkably similar. The solution was unfortunate in many ways, for the Cabriolet was revised with more sober styling – and no headlight cowls. This was the Series 2.

By way of compensation, the Series 2 was made more practical, with a more accommodating interior and improved boot space for grand touring. It was first shown at the 1959 Paris Salon but production didn't start until 1960, lasting until 1962.

Despite the improved comfort, many find the Series 2 a little too soft, and few disagree that the Series 1 is easily the best looking.

'Another of the prototypes was built with a cut-down windscreen and a faired driver's headrest, like a D-type'

250 Tour de France

Trading on the success of the 250 GT, Ferrari produced a handful of tuned, lightweight competizione versions. They used Pinin Farina-designed bodies built by Scaglietti in aloy, and entered them into International GT racing. Quite a turn-around from previous policies of producing road cars merely to finance the racing...

In 1956, the prestigious Tour de France was dominated by 250 GT Competiziones, with one winning in the hands of de Portago and third place being taken by the very car that had been displayed at the 1955 Paris Salon.

This success prompted Ferrari to name subsequent Competiziones with the Tour de France moniker. Initially they followed the style of the 250 Mille Miglia (some with Plexiglass cowled headlights), based around the 2600mm wheelbase chassis with drum brakes, coil spring front suspension and a leaf sprung axle at the rear. Power outputs initially varied between 230 and 240bhp.

Some of these early cars used plastic sliding side windows, others had wind-up glass, and all eight Scaglietti built cars of the Series I Tour

de France received varying numbers of vents in the rear sail panel behind the side windows. Inside, appointments were basic.

For 1957, a Series II was introduced, which featured 14 vents in the sail panels, an extended nose, bonnet scoop (supplying air into a carburettor surround pan) and heavily re-profiled rear wings. Customers could specify a Testa Rossa specification engine, with lightweight pistons and con-rods and six oversize downdraught Weber carburettors.

Over the following years, until 1959, Ferrari continued to evolve the Tour de France. The Series III brought headlights set further back in the wings and covered by Plexiglass covers, rear wings with prominent fins and a three-vent sail panel. The Series IV moved to a single vent and power output crept up to between 240 and 260bhp, while the Series V (pictured) lost the headlight cowls.

All this for fewer than 100 cars, even including the handful of Zagato-built models. And yet, the Tour de France is now known as the finest long-wheelbase Ferrari GT that was ever produced.

'Ferrari produced a number of Competizione 250 GTs. Quite a turn-around from previous policies of building road cars merely to finance the racing'

250 Califomia

It's the late-1950s, and Ferrari's 250 GT Tour de France is beginning its now-legendary domination of GT class competition. There's a drop-top version of the 250 on the way but, in California, dealer Jon von Neumann (of Ferrari Representatives of Hollywood) has an idea that just won't go away. He wants Ferrari to build a convertible version of the Tour de France. Crucially, North American Ferrari importer Luigi Chinetti backs his idea.

Of course, the result is the 250 GT California Spider, a more focussed, more hard-core drop-top than the GT Spider Pininfarina. Compare this California with the Cabriolet on page 31, and you'll see they that look similar. However, the California was not just built by Scaglietti of Modena (which produced many of the Pininfarina designs), but designed by Scaglietti too.

The California was initially based around a 2600mm wheelbase chassis and equipped with a 240bhp engine, and in this form was given its formal debut in late 1958. Customers could specify all the options that buyers of a Tour de France were offered – from race-spec camshafts to full Competizione set-ups – plus the additional extra of an elegant glassfibre hardtop. Some Californias were fitted with cowled headlights, some were left uncovered, but what's now known as the long-wheelbase California (pictured) continued until 1960.

In tandem with California production, though, Ferrari was developing a new short-wheelbase chassis. This would lead to the replacement for the Tour de France, referred to as the 250 GT SWB (see the next page) and, unsurprisingly, the new 2400mm chassis founds its way to the California Spyder.

This ushered in a new era of Californias, which tended to appear to sit lower, with a more aggressive stance. Like the long-wheelbase Californias, the SWBs were built with both open and closed headlights, so the best way to differentiate is to count the vents behind the front wheelarch – a LWB should have three, while an SWB has only two.

Fittingly, the highest-specification 250 GT California ever built was ordered by Luigi Chinetti for the 1960 Le Mans. With 280bhp it was as quick as a tin-top SWB.

'In California, Jon von Neumann has an idea that just won't go away. He wants Ferrari to build a convertible version of the 250 Tour de France'

250 SWB

Ferrari's lightweight GTs were always known as Berlinettas which, between 1956 and '59 were well represented by the all-conquering Tour de France models. But in the last days of the Tour de France 250s, seven 'Interim' Berlinettas were produced to a new, more modern style.

These cars performed well in racing in 1959 but they were replaced by a new model that looked near-identical but would go on to even greater success and admiration. That model was the 250 GT SWB, the last three letters standing for short wheelbase.

The SWB was based on a new chassis with a wheelbase of 2400mm, 200mm shorter than before. Pininfarina (renamed from Pinin Farina around this time) simply chopped out the extra length from the middle of the Interim's body, losing the quarter windows and in the process producing what is arguably the car with the finest combination of good looks and muscular aggression ever seen.

Between late 1959 and early 1963 the SWB was produced in two forms, the Competizione and the Lusso (or 'street' specification). As the former, it was built by Scaglietti in aluminium,

usually with a 275bhp engine, a strengthened version of the familiar four-speed gearbox, bucket seats and sliding side windows.

The Lusso, not to be confused with the later 1962-64 Lusso featured on p38, was produced in steel except for an aluminium bonnet, doors and bootlid and was more opulently equipped inside. With a lower compression ratio and smaller carburettors, a Lusso engine typically produced 240bhp. Specifications were often mixed around though, so steel-bodied cars came with competition engines and vice versa.

But to give itself the best chance of winning the coveted International GT Championship, Ferrari produced a batch of 21 special SWBs for 1961. These were the SEFAC Hot Rods with smaller diameter chassis tubing for reduced weight, ultra-thin aluminium panelling and an engine equipped with Testa Rossa cylinder heads and bucket-sized carburettors that gave 285-295bhp.

These cars were good for 160mph, and won at Spa, Mille Miglia, Monza, Le Mans (GT class), Riverside and Tour de France. And yes, Ferrari won the GT Championship.

'Pininfarina simply chopped 200mm from the middle, losing the quarter windows and producing a car with the finest combination of looks and aggression'

250 GTE

If any model demonstrates Ferrari's changing attitude towards commerciality, as well as the public's acceptance of Ferrari as a serious manufacturer of road cars, it's the 250 GTE. Other than a few special order 195s, 212s, 340s and 342s, the GTE was the first of the marque to be equipped with anything in the way of rear seats.

The car was a commercial success too, with more than 950 GTEs sold between 1960 and '63, while the profits were usefully put towards the increasingly high-budget Ferrari race team.

The GTE kept to the 2600mm wheelbase of the 250 GT and the Tour de France but the cabin was made more roomy by moving the engine forward in the chassis by 200mm and widening the track of the front and rear wheels. Engine output was an impressive 240bhp at 7000rpm, which took the GTE from zero to 60mph in just over seven seconds, with a top speed of almost 140mph – not bad for a four-seater.

Rear seats aside, the GTE represents the archetypal spec for a 1960s Ferrari: Pininfarina steel body with aluminium bonnet, doors and

boot, disc brakes, Nardi steering wheel, leather-covered seats and transmission tunnel, chrome-rimmed Veglia instruments and Borrani wire wheels. It pushes all the right buttons...

It was revealed as a new model at the 1960 Le Mans 24 Hours where a prototype GTE was used as a course car, before being officially launched five months later at the Paris Salon, Ferrari's favourite show. Little changed during the car's first two and a half years, even when the Series II was launched, the main update being the dashboard.

For the 1963 Series III a number of changes were phased in, some of them seen during Series II production. The rear leaf springs were changed for more responsive coils, the rear wings reprofiled, the rear lights changed and the driving lamps moved from the grille to directly under the headlights.

During production, an overdrive operating on fourth gear was also introduced and this, with the disc brakes and suspension improvements, made the GTE the most useable 250 thus far. Now it's one of the most affordable of the range.

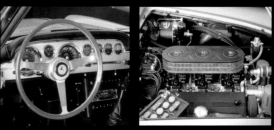

'The car was a commercial success, with the profits usefully put towards the increasingly high-budget Ferrari race team'

250 **GTO**

In a line-up of iconic, highly collectible and astonishingly capable machines, the GTO is the version of the 250 that stands above the rest. It's the 250 that most enthusiasts think of first, the 250 that's deservedly at the top of every wish list.

As successor to the great 250 SWB Competizione (and the SEFAC Hot-Rods in particular), the GTO was aimed fair and square at the important GT championship. The 'O' of GTO stands for 'Omologato' (homologation) which, in hindsight, is an ironic nod to the FIA's qualifying rules – these stated that 100 cars had to be built for homologation to be granted. Ferrari got around these rules by convincing the FIA that the GTO was really a slightly modified 250 SWB. In many ways, that was true, although within the terms of FIA rules it was stretching the truth.

At least the evolution was there to see. The chassis of the GTO was little different from the SWB's, despite some extra bracing around damper and engine mounts and various other minor mods to stiffen the chassis. The engine, too, was the same Colombo V12 built to Testa Rossa specifications as used in the SWB Competizione. But larger valves and higher lift cams brought power up to around 300bhp (later, one of two 4-litre GTOs would

produce a stunning 390bhp). With a new five-speed gearbox, the GTO was capable of over 170mph, and the acceleration was as vivid as five seconds from 0 to 60mph.

But the biggest difference of all between the GTO and its SWB predecessor was its bodywork. Despite the dominance of Pininfarina designs throughout the 250 range (and indeed all Ferraris of the era), the GTO was styled by Giotto Bizzarrini. He worked closely with experts at the university in Milan, using their wind tunnel to reduce drag produced by the new body.

The cowled headlights and low front all helped the low-drag cause, while weight was pared to a minimum with thin aluminium panelling, Plexiglas side windows and rear screen and a stripped-bare interior. Bizzarrini had done a superb job, but fell foul of Enzo Ferrari's famous cull of top employees and was sacked in November 1961. This left 25-year-old Mauro Forghieri in charge of the GTO project.

Forghieri didn't quite get the GTO ready for the first race of the next season, at Daytona in February 1962, but the SWB/GTO development mule, driven by Stirling Moss, finished first in the GT class and fourth overall. When the genuine GTO was ready,

Phil Hill and Oliver Gendebien finished first in class and second overall at Sebring, and the wins kept on coming; Ferrari won the GT manufacturers' championship with GTOs in 1962 and '63.

For 1964, the GTO's body shape was revised to reduce drag still further. The '64 car was shorter, wider and lower, with more vents around the body, a flatter rear deck and a less curvy front end. Some prefer it, others feel the original was best. The changes worked, though, for Ferrari won the championship once again.

In all, 37 250 GTOs were built between late 1961 and early '64, three of which were to 1964 specification. Now the GTO is known as the car to have fetched the highest ever price at auction (£6 million in 1990) but it's best to think of it as one of the greatest GT cars ever built.

> 'Bizzarrini fell foul of Enzo Ferrari's famous cull of top employees and was sacked in November 1961, leaving 25-year-old Mauro Forghieri in charge of the GTO project'

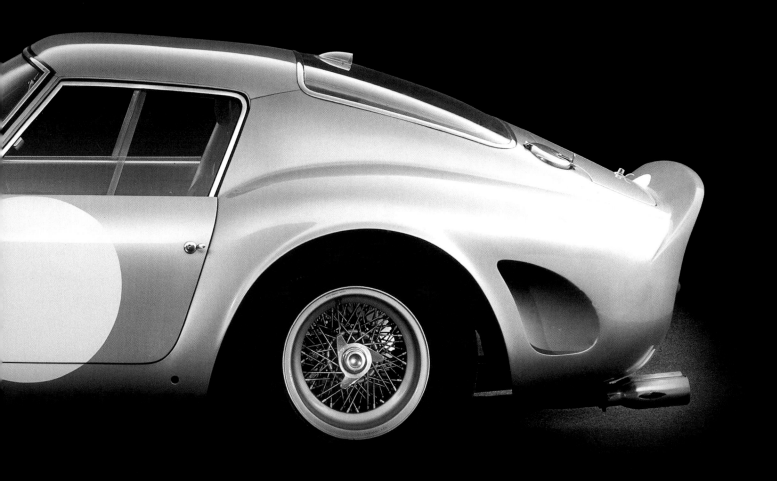

'The GTO was styled by Giotto Bizzarrini, who worked closely with the experts at the university in Milan, using their wind tunnel to reduce the drag of the new body'

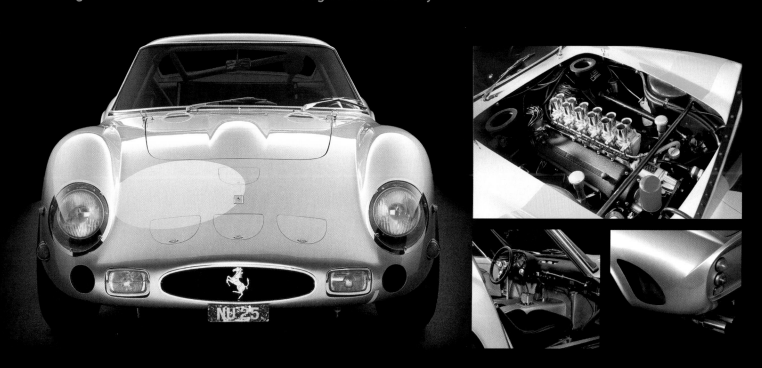

250 GT Lusso

Take the bare bones of a 250 GTO and re-clothe it in an elegant body of more civilised intention, and the result is the 250 Lusso – often said to be the best-looking 250 ever produced.

The Lusso is an incredible machine, with similar levels of comfort and performance to the 250 SWB. Chassis were to the same design as the GTO's, but the engine was placed slightly further forward to aid cabin space. Pininfarina penned the style, introducing a simple Kamm tail with neat circular rear lights and a wonderfully simple front end with a tiny bumper and separate overriders.

Lusso engines were generally ordered with outputs of 240bhp, which was enough to give performance figures of 150mph and a sub-seven second 0-60. Coil springs and disc brakes all-round were by then the 250 norm, but the interior of the Lusso set a new standard for the range. The bucket seats were trimmed in high-quality leather, as was the transmission tunnel and the doors, while the luggage area behind the seats was trimmed in vinyl with leather straps. The dashboard was also leather-trimmed, but the real point of interest here is its unique Pininfarina styling, with a large speedometer and matching revcounter mounted in the centre, cocooned in sweeping cowls, and the five minor instruments ahead of the driver, visible through the aluminium spokes of the gorgeous Nardi steering wheel.

There were 362 Lussos produced, 23 of which were right-hand-drive.

As the last 250 road car to be introduced, the Lusso represents the results of ten years of development, which took the Ferrari GT from being a sometimes temperamental, haphazardly produced road-racer to a sophisticated, predictable (in the best sense of the word), high-performance grand tourer.

Funny, though, that in all those years, the outright performance didn't change significantly and the sense of style and character never diminished. That's why all 250s are, and always will be, so special.

Thanks to Ferrari specialist Paul Baber (www.250swb.com), Justin Platt of THRE, all the car owners, Lukas Hüni and photographer Michel Zumbrunn.

'...a significant step forward in comfort from the 250 SWB 'Lusso' and yet only a small step down from the performance of a GTO'

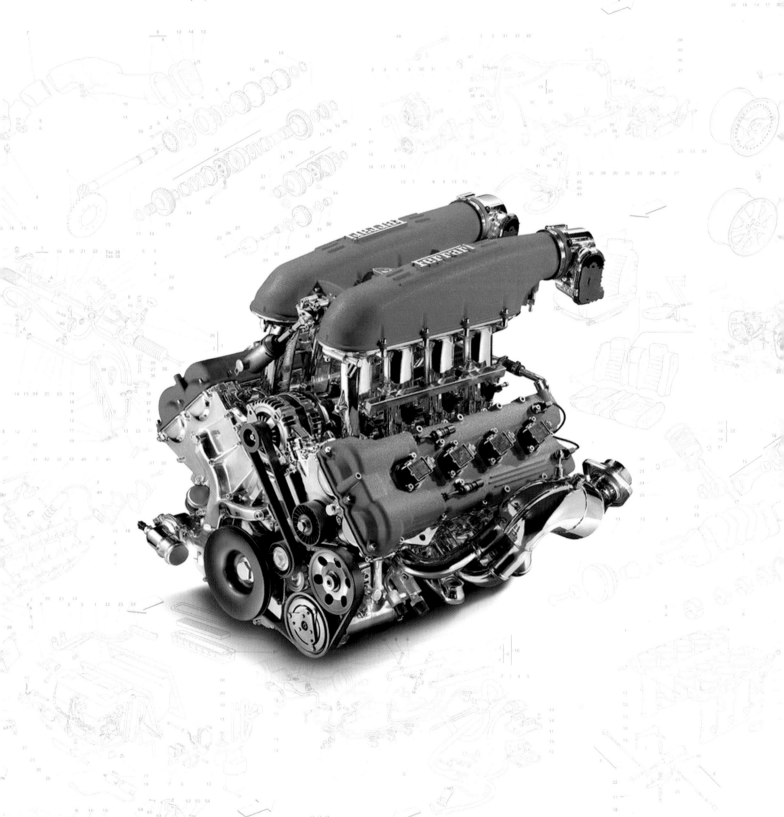

Words: Robert Coucher
Pictures: Michael Bailie

RUBY MAX

Competition Ferraris of the Sixties have
long eclipsed the 250GT Lusso in terms of
value and image, but Robert Coucher is still
impressed by this elegant grand tourer

The most desirable

classic Ferraris have always been those models that have seen action in competition. These 'comp' cars, like the Tour de France, SWB, GTO, 275/GTB4 and – stretching it – Daytona, have all at some point benefited from Ferrari's racing provenance. It's the road cars that have tended to languish in dealer showrooms. But now that the best Ferraris are in huge demand for historic racing and rallying, prices have rocketed. More recently, some of the road cars have come to focus and they too are being appreciated for what they are, rather than being ignored because of their lack of racing prowess.

The Ferrari 250GT Lusso is a case in point. A cousin of the GTO and SWB, the Lusso was designed purely as a road car. Yet it remains very exclusive, with only 350 examples ever built. When the 250 SWB was *the* model to have a decade or so ago, the Lusso was ignored like Cinderella before the ball. Lusso, meaning luxury, has long been a turn-off for the weekend warriors, but the Lusso is now, at last, desired as a thing of beauty, if not a snorting road racer. Some prospective owners in this market have also matured. They now realise that thoroughly sorted road racers are great on a track or on a timed run up the Stelvio Pass, but they can be highly strung and downright unpleasant on a Sunday drive to the nearest gastro-pub.

Many of you will know John Mayston-Taylor of Lynx Motors International. Renowned for his beautiful lightweight Jaguars and Ford GT40s, Mayston-Taylor is a perfectionist's perfectionist. His cars are always 'minters', but when I first glance at his Ferrari Lusso, sitting in the bright sunshine at the Lynx works in St Leonards on Sea, the exquisite coupe is so dazzling I have to put on my sunglasses.

Recovering from the visual onslaught, my next thought is 'thank goodness it's not red'. Finished in ever-so-deep Rosso Rubino, the car is simply beautiful, a full 100-point show car. The luscious plumy hue is set off by twinkling polished stainless steel and aluminium 72-spoke Borrani wires with their chariot-style knock-ons. Mayston-Taylor explains how these spinners are correct because the centres curve inwards. Many Ferraris are fitted with the slightly later and incorrect spinners, but who would know? Mayston-Taylor does.

Walking around the Lusso I feel undressed. The car has such an expensive and tasteful mien. The fresh tan leather upholstery is again in perfect harmony with the exterior colour. The trim is the correct Connolly 'Luxan', a specific grain originally supplied to Ferrari. Mayston-Taylor called

'It has a bit more chrome and flourish than the stripped road racers, but it is an elegant grand tourer and the overall shape is beautifully proportioned and graceful'

Left: knock-ons are correct for the Lusso because the centres curve inwards. It's all in the details...

Jonathan Connolly of Connolly Brothers, who researched the archives to find the precise replacement hides. Rob O'Rourke at Moto-Technique, who is regarded as the best in the business, then re-trimmed the interior.

Open the driver's door and you are enveloped by that lovely smell of proper Connolly leather. Slip into the fixed-back bucket seat and you feel like you've climbed into one of those impossibly expensive Hermes handbags. From the piped seats to the leather-covered transmission tunnel and quilted rear deck with its luggage straps in place, just sitting in this Ferrari's interior is an event in itself.

The cabin is light and airy with slim pillars and good visibility in all directions. The instrument layout – long regarded as plain odd – is now just quirky and not unattractive. The Veglia speedo and rev counter are located in the centre of the dash, aimed at the driver, with the lesser gauges straight ahead. The tall gearshift lever is a little less macho than usual, with a nice two-finger indentation on the leading edge, and it does without a racy exposed gate. The large wood-rimmed steering wheel feels cool and is beautifully lacquered. I notice that the chrome ashtray is slightly patinated. Mayston-Taylor says he decided to leave it original, as with the Ferrari badge on the bonnet, to retain a link to the car's rather unique past.

This 1963 Ferrari 250GT, chassis number 4411GT, is the 26th Lusso built. It was ordered by French actress Mylene Demongeot but she never took delivery. A Parisian gentleman bought it and used it for long drives down to his second home, in the South of

Above right: Colombo V12 rebuilt to original specification. Said to be good for an 'honest' 230bhp

'The engine is the classic Colombo-designed, short-stroke 60deg V12. The displacement is 3 litres and each cylinder has a capacity of 250cc – hence the Ferrari nomenclature of 250'

France, until the early 1980s. He then garaged the Lusso until it was sold in 1996 to an Englishman who stored it in London until 2003. Now registered 4411 RU, the Ferrari has only covered 59,000km. what a find.

Later, looking at the photographs of the car in its original, unrestored and fine condition, I feel a pang of sorrow that it had not been left as it was: a slightly threadbare, careworn old Italian aristocrat with lots of drives and adventures under its Borranis. Mayston-Taylor felt the same, but on close inspection the 40-year-old Ferrari was evidently tired and in need of refurbishment. So, in true Lynx style, 4111GT has been transformed into arguably the best Lusso in existence.

The Lusso was styled by Pininfarina but built by Carrozzeria Scaglietti. It is very stylised, particularly its three-piece front bumper: a main centre section and two corner overriders curved under the sidelights. Some aficionados view the Lusso as excessively fussy. Certainly it has a bit more chrome and flourish than the stripped road racers, but it is an elegant grand tourer and **»** the overall shape is beautifully proportioned and graceful, from the low aquiline nose to its purposely kicked-up Kamm tail.

The engine is the classic Colombo-designed, short-stroke 60° V12, with two valves per cylinder and a single overhead cam per bank. The displacement is 3-litres and each cylinder has a capacity of 250cc – hence the Ferrari nomenclature of 250. Power was quoted at 240 (Italian) bhp at a high-revving 7000rpm, with a maximum of 192lb ft of torque reached at a heady 6000rpm. With the engine rebuilt by Lynx, to standard spec but using modern components, Mayston-Taylor reckons it is now putting out an honest 230bhp. And the engine is a thing of beauty. Slung low in the frame it displays all the best Ferrari signatures: 12 cylinders topped by crackle-black cam covers, a smart line-up of Weber carbs running down the centre, and two bright orange filters standing to attention at the front. Naturally there are twin distributors, twin coils and a Flamm air horn to clear the way. Interestingly, it still retains a special French chassis plate next to the Ferrari one.

At last it's time to head out and drive. The key is switched on and pushed against the spring loading. That unique Ferrari whirr from the starter motor leads to a crackle and roar as the V12 catches. The three, twin-choke 36DCS Webers snaffle and pop as the fuel fills the bowls and soon the engine is running smoothly. It emits that special Ferrari V12 wail that grown men pay a fortune to listen to. It sounds urgent and busy and you can tell there is a lot going on under the bonnet. Talented engineers have worked hard to ensure the myriad

'That unique Ferrari whirr from the starter motor leads to a crackle and roar as the V12 catches'

of mechanical components mesh and coordinate in syncopation – and they want you to hear about it.

The throttle is a bit stiff, as are the gearshift and clutch pedal, but the Ferrari moves away with ease. All the controls are linear and allow for smooth progress, but in today's power-assisted world you do have to re-adjust to using some old-fashioned muscle power. The thought that you might have to rev this engine hard to get any response is soon banished. Low-end torque is ample and the car has a gentle fluidity. The power comes through in a steady swell as the revs rise. Ambling through the villages of Sussex, the Lusso is a co-operative companion. The driving position is good for a driver of average size, but those with long legs might suffer the close-set pedals.

The steering wheel is set high, and while the low-geared worm and sector system is not as sharp as a good rack-and-pinion, it is perfectly accurate for fast road use. The suspension is the standard 1960s Ferrari set-up. At the front there are the usual coil-sprung double wishbones and at the rear the perfunctory live axle suspended by coil-assisted leaf springs and two radius arms for additional axle location.

As the countryside opens up, the Ferrari sharpens. The engine sounds glorious and it feels strong but not massively powerful. Mayston-Taylor has resisted the urge to turn it into a hot-rod, and the sound that emanates from the four Ansa exhaust pipes is tastefully strident. With its beautiful controls and lovely ambience, the Ferrari reminds you of a delicately refined Lancia Flaminia – and that's no put-down. Then, cresting a rise, you feel the solid rear axle thump, akin to an Alfa Romeo Giulia. The

Top: care was taken to ensure the interior was retrimmed in the correct Connelly hide. Smells lovely

'All the controls are linear and allow for smooth progress, but in today's power-assisted world you do have to readjust to using some old-fashioned muscle power'

Lusso has Girling disc brakes all round, assisted by a servo, and they are more than up to the job but, as with the other controls, they do require a shove.

All the while the engine is zinging along happily, and when the road becomes a fast dual-carriageway you change down into third and let the Ferrari off its leash. As it's new the engine can't be maxed, but as the revs rise you feel the power muster. As Derek Bell noted when he raced a Ferrari at the Goodwood Revival, albeit with a slightly different and race-tuned engine, you have to rev all Ferraris hard to access the last reserves of power that reside right at the top end. That means about 8000rpm, which is not going to happen here.

Pushing along a bit in fourth gear, your brain tells you to go for fifth, but it's not there – this is one of the last Ferraris fitted with a four-speed gearbox. Many owners have upgraded to a five-speed but Mayston-Taylor has left this car original. Yes, it can get a bit fussy on the motorway, but the mechanical sound should be savoured. Some purists mutter that the engine is too heavy and the engine, positioned well forward in the chassis, is »

**FERRARI
250GT
LUSSO**

SPECIFICATIONS

Engine
2953cc V12, single
overhead cams,
triple Weber 36DCS
carburettors

Power
230bhp @ 7000rpm

Transmission
Four-speed manual

Suspension
Front: double wishbones,
coils springs; rear: live
axle, leaf springs assisted
by coils, two radius arms

Brakes
Servo-assisted discs

Performance
Top speed 145mph

Value
£230,000-£250,000

not as well placed as in the 250SWB. Maybe so, but driven as intended the Lusso does not succumb to understeer and the 230bhp engine is well up to hauling it along at quite a lick. Undoubtedly the lavish trim adds a bit more weight, but the bonnet, doors and boot lid are all aluminium. Each skin is hand fitted and no skin from this car will fit another without a lot of fettling.

Becoming more familiar with the Lusso, we peel off the main roads at Rye and head out across the Walland Marsh towards Dungeness. While this is no track test, it is possible to trot along at a fair old clip. The period Michelin XWX tyres are 205 section, although they do look fatter on the very offset wheels, and they do what it is expected. Their adhesion is not high but the Ferrari's handling is benign in the real world. The car feels smooth and tracks as straight as an arrow, devoid of any nervousness. Over badly broken tarmac the ride does suffer and transverse ridges can cause choppiness, but this is a car of 1960s vintage and it is up to you to 'drive' and control it. That's the fun part.

In the distance we see a huge shape rising out of the mist, the Dungeness nuclear power station. Pulling up to the beach front we are met by the sight of the largest shale beach in Britain. Along the flat and almost deserted expanse of beach are numerous small wooden houses. They resemble beach houses but without any of the frivolity or fun. The whole area is like a weird David Lynch film set, the Rosso

Rubino Lusso looking like an impossibly large ruby washed up on the dull white shale. An extraordinary sight.

With photographer Bailie still taking pictures, Mayston-Taylor and I talk Ferrari over lunch at a local inn. I learn that this car is now valued at £230,000-250,000, a doubling of its worth in the past three years, but still only a third the cost of a 250SWB, so all things are relative.

Mayston-Taylor is a seasoned historic racer and it is very encouraging that he and many other Ferrari enthusiasts have realised that the 250GT Lusso is a fine piece of kit. Sure, it's not the fastest Ferrari on the block, but it is a pleasant way to motor down to the beach for a light lunch. In 2003, Susan Mayston-Taylor took 4411GT to Paris for the Louis Vuitton Classic where it was awarded the Prix de l'Elegance. Then she and John were invited to take part in the Italia Classica where only special examples of a marque are eligible. This Lusso made the draw and the car behaved perfectly, totally at home in the beautiful Italian countryside.

So here we have a Ferrari for the grown up grand routier. The 250 Lusso is now appreciated as an ideal machine for those long and genteel drives we all feel we deserve at some point in our rat-race lives. It offers an attractive blend of elegance and languid insouciance as well as a good dose of panache. The Lusso is a full-blooded Ferrari but one that has sufficient brevity to offer you the chance to enjoy the poetry as well as the motion.

'Last year, Susan Mayston-Taylor took 4411GT to Paris for the 2003 Louis Vuitton Classic where it was awarded the Prix de l'Elegance'

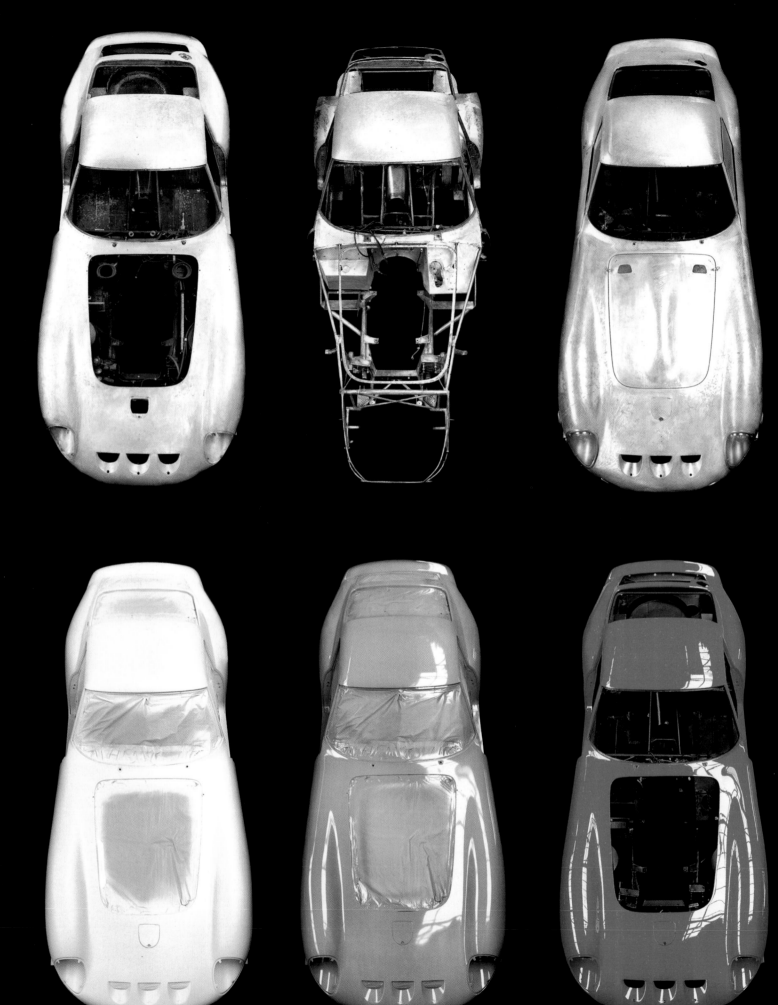

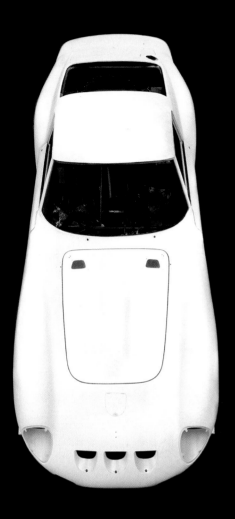

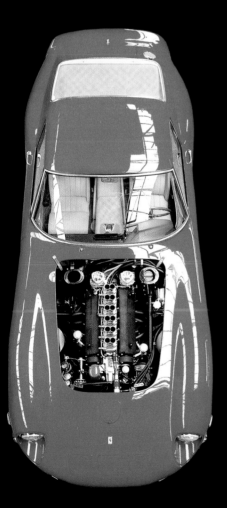

Reborn...

How do you set about restoring one of the most valuable cars in the world?
Octane charts the progress of 2450 hours in the life of a Ferrari GTO
Words: Robert Coucher   Photography courtesy of Kevin O'Rourke

There is a fair old debate

going on in the world of historic cars at the moment. Should cars be restored or preserved? In Britain and Europe we grumble when some of our American cousins completely rebuild their historic cars, chroming the cam covers and wire wheels in the process. We profess to liking our historics careworn and patinated. The best proponents of this 'fit for purpose and nothing more' ethos are the lovely old contraptions found at any VSCC meeting in Britain. Or the scruffy vintage Bugattis enjoyed by the elegant drivers in the French Bugatti Club. Every grease nipple is oozing but the paint is wretched and chrome has been wantonly rubbed through to the brass!

The Americans have responded with a special Preservation Class at Pebble Beach, and with the Pebble Tour which, rather shockingly, encourages entrants to actually drive their cars. The good news is that most do, with gusto. Other top-flight concours events have followed suit but, to be fair, these genteel motor cars in the Preservation arena are usually vintage automobiles that have led a ridiculously sheltered life doing little or no mileage, let alone having had to face the ravages of Driving Miss Daisy... Stored in sympathetic conditions, a mere wipe of »

Above
3527GT in good company
at Mototechnique's
workshop: experience
counts for everything

'With a motor car of this magnitude, the best in the business were called upon to work their magic'

Ferrari 250GTO

SPECIFICATIONS

Engine
2953cc V12, sohc per
bank, two valves per
cylinder, six twin-choke
Weber carburettors

Max power
290bhp@7500-8000rpm

Transmission
Five-speed manual,
rear-wheel drive, LSD

Brakes
Servo-assisted discs

Weight
1050kg (2314lb)

Performance
0-60mph 6.5sec
Top speed 170mph

Value
£7,000,000-plus

Duck Oil and some of this century's air in the tyres sees them ready for the judges on the lawn.

Of course, this sort of debate intensifies when a tremendously rare and important historic machine like the Ferrari 250GTO here is concerned. As with all 39 Ferrari GTOs constructed, chassis number 3527GT's history has been detailed in various books. The previous owner, Stephen Pilkington – obviously a proper car chap who enjoyed his GTO properly and fast – had owned the special Ferrari since 1984. It has long been regarded as a 'lovely original car', which Pilkington drove on many Ferrari and GTO events in Europe. Quickly.

Purchasing the car in 2005, the new owner was faced with a quandary. Leave it as is or restore it. A tough decision, made more so when you consider a GTO is worth north of £7 million, if you can ever persuade one of the owners to sell. If this were a Ferrari that had been cossetted and gently exercised from new, then the decision would have been simple. Leave it alone. But the reality check is that Ferrari GTOs were built as racing cars, to last one season, over 40 years ago.

So, while 3527GT was a lovely original car, it had survived a tough racing life. It was sold new to Gottfried Koechert in May 1962 and was promptly entered in the Nürburgring 1000Km but retired. In September it was entered in the Tour de France, piloted by Lucien Bianchi and Claude Dubois, who led the fierce road race until the last day, when they collided with a milk lorry. The lightweight aluminium nose of the Ferrari was stoved in but, with victory within their grasp, the pair leapt out and cut most of the front of the car clean off. Unfortunately they could not manage better than seventh overall.

The car continued to race, winning the Angolan GP in Luanda in 1962 with Bianchi at the wheel. Then in 1965 it retired from racing and Graber, the Swiss coachbuilder, exacted some modifications, turning the old racer into a more comfortable tourer. 'One big advantage of the GTO is the noise level inside. It doesn't allow the passenger to speak and this leaves the driver in peace to savour the permanent and unique pleasure of driving the GTO on the road,' said GTO expert Jess Pourret. Quite.

In order to quieten the interior din, Graber soundproofed and carpeted the cabin, fitted panels to most exposed inner surfaces, replaced the Perspex side windows with wind-up glass and reupholstered the racing seats in leather. Rather optimistic little nerf bars were fitted to the front and the rear lights were replaced with assemblies from a Volkswagen camper van. Ouch. Pilkington returned the exterior to original but kept the sensible Graber-modified interior, enjoying the GTO as such for 20 years.

The current owner, a successful individual and amateur historic racing driver, wanted a GTO as a touring car to add to his collection. With its history, 3527GT was just the car, a

»

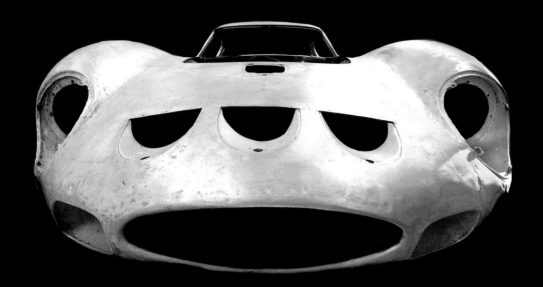

'As with most old racing cars, the nose and tail sections needed some love and attention, but overall the GTO was in remarkably good condition'

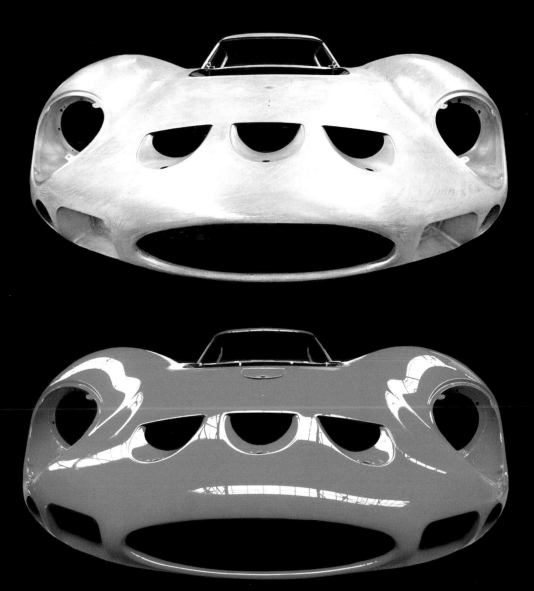

The restoration

'The non-original paint was micro-blistered and cracking, so it had to come off. We applied stripper and discovered the extent of all the repairs that had been necessary over the years'

This page
Specialist work such as trimming was contracted out to known and trusted friends and colleagues

straight and original example in need of a little refreshing. And with a motor car of this magnitude the best in the business were called upon to work their magic: Kevin O'Rourke of Mototechnique in West Molesey near Richmond, son Rob (Rorky) O'Rourke of O'Rourke Coach Trimmers in Cranleigh near Guildford, and Martin Greaves of Classic Performance Engineering in Northamptonshire. The engine had previously been rebuilt by Ferrari specialist Greypaul and was in fine fettle, so the GTO went into O'Rourke's for a fresh coat of paint. But, as we all know, the real problems materialise once you scratch the surface...

'The non-original paintwork was micro-blistered and cracking, so it had to come off,' says Kevin O'Rourke. 'But first the body and chassis were digitally measured and recorded: both proved to be remarkably close to tolerance but not perfect. So we applied paint stripper and, once the car was in bare aluminium, discovered the extent of all the repairs that had been necessary over the years.

'Unfortunately, there was evidence of electrolytic corrosion where the aluminium skin wraps around the steel spaceframe. We would need to cut out this corrosion and let in new ally in numerous places. At this point it was decided to remove all the body panels so we could make an informed judgement as to

'With the panels removed we were able to gain full access to all inner panels, spaceframe and chassis tubes, to strip, straighten, repair, paint and protect the inner areas properly. It is imperative you have clean welds throughout the process to ensure none of the flux gets trapped in the ally, to burst through later,' says O'Rourke. 'And as with most old racing cars, the nose and tail sections needed some love and attention. But overall the GTO was in surprisingly good condition,' he continues.

Once everything was lined up, a roll protection cage was designed and fabricated. At the request of the owner, this carries adjustable mountings for inertia-reel seat belts, while concealed mountings for three-inch racing harnesses are incorporated elsewhere in the car.

With the chassis refurbished, the original, carefully repaired body panels were refitted utilising all the factory rivet holes. These panels were all prepared and pre-painted internally to prevent any future electrolytic reaction. Next, a polyurethane primer was applied and baked at 90°C for an hour, then abraded and made ready for the polyester primer filler. This was hand sanded and shaped before a further grey sealer primer was applied. Grey is the best base for a red finish.

'The GTO was originally finished in Rosso Cina, which is

Above
Stripping
bare meta
only way t
the true c
of vulnera.
and tail se

The GTO was originally finished in Rosso Cina, a Fiat colour. We gave the owner a number of swatches and he went for this lovely deep burgundy. It's known as Rosso Kev...'

client a number of swatches to choose from and he went for this lovely deep burgundy. It's known as Rosso Kev,' he laughs. Four coats of base colour were applied and then coated in clear two-pack lacquer for protection. The Ferrari was then sanded and polished and underbody stone protection applied.

With the GTO's bodywork renovated, re-assembled and painted, the car went up to Martin Greaves at Classic Performance Engineering for the rebuilt mechanical components to be refitted. 'Our intention was to make the GTO safe, reliable and great to drive,' says Greaves. 'We knew the engine was in fine condition with good oil pressure but, just to be sure, we removed the cam covers and sump for a quick look-see and rebuilt all the ancillary components. The gearbox was stripped and crack-tested and we found third gear was cracked. Gears are not generally available but I eventually sourced one through our contacts.

'With the engine out we discovered the linkages operating the six twin-choke Weber carburettors were worn and had to be rebuilt and rebushed. These GTOs are renowned as being balanced and lovely to drive so we did not alter the camber or suspension settings. We simply stripped, crack-tested, rebuilt and refreshed everything, then reassembled it all carefully.'

The exhaust system had to be replaced because it had been patched up rather too often, and special heat-shields were inserted between the pipes and the passenger floor. All tanks were stripped, acid dipped and repainted. The rear ally fuel tank – now foam filled – is a work of art, as are the beautiful Borrani wire wheels, which were reshod with correct Michelin XWX tyres. The original Koni dampers were overhauled and the entire braking system was refreshed.

'The owner intends using the Ferrari for fast road events so we carefully engineered in some heating and cooling fans. They are completely hidden in the existing cooling ducts and do a good job of increasing the flow of cool air, or hot, at the flick of a switch. On the Tour Auto, for example, a properly demisted windscreen is more important than an extra 50 horsepower,' adds a knowing Greaves.

With fresh mechanicals and wiring loom, the Ferrari was sent down to O'Rourke the younger in Cranleigh. 'As it had been converted to road use years ago, my brief was to do the same but add a few improvements and subtle upgrades to the interior: the sort of thing Ferrari would have done itself,' says Rorky. 'We unpicked most of the Graber interior and wrapped up all the sections for storage. Then we soundproofed the cockpit and made up new ally panels for the door cards and interior. The ones for the roof were fine so we reused those.'

Graber had panelled-up most surfaces, leaving precious little interior storage space. O'Rourke opened up all these little **»**

binnacles, covering any exposed chassis tubing with hand-stitched and Connollised tan leather, using diamond-pattern stitching where appropriate. GTOs have fixed racing bucket seats, which are not a realistic option for long runs down to the South of France. Modern adjustable seats were sourced which Rorky retrimmed in sumptuous leather and mounted on runners. They look simpatico and are very effective.

With the interior beautifully appointed and the original rear Perspex windscreen polished and refitted, the GTO went back to Mototechnique for final assembly of doors and side windows, bonnet and boot lid. Detailing complete, it made a last trip to Martin Greaves for final setting-up.

At this point, real patience is required from both the owner and engineer. Little progress is visible for the hours of workshop time required to get the myriad of detailed components to work in harmony. Things like the windscreen wiper action, the heating and demisting, properly bled and adjusted brakes, damper settings and all the other small details that turn a good car into a special one.

The final thing to do was to run up the V12 engine, debug it and get the carburettor tuning spot on. Initially there was a slight misfire at high rpm; however, optimising ignition and carburation settings ensured clean running to 7500rpm.

'The Ferrari is fabulous on the road,' says Greaves. 'Running on original-spec Michelins, you drive the GTO through the seat-of-your-pants and it responds beautifully. The engine is remarkably tractable and, being a V12, it's lovely and smooth. But, saying that, it does like about 3000rpm showing on the clock and above five-thou' it really comes alive. It's one of the best GTOs I have yet driven,' he adds.

So how much does a project like this cost? Well, it would be rude to discuss money but think along the lines of 1500 hours in the bodyshop, 200 with the trimmer and 750 hours for mechanical work and set-up. Considering the magnitude of the task, this seems entirely acceptable.

On completion, 3527GT was presented at Goodwood House, making its first appearance at a special function hosted by Lord March. Martin Greaves then delivered the Ferrari to Ashford for collection by its new owner. 'He had a quick look around the car as I pointed out various controls, then popped his bag and laptop into the boot and disappeared off to the Channel Tunnel. No tentative drive around the car park, he was straight off to France! We didn't hear from him for a while and were all sick with worry,' says Greaves.

Two days and over 1000 miles later, the O'Rourkes and Greaves each received an e-mail from the owner: 'I have just completed a rather-too-warm trip to the South of France, arriving Friday lunchtime in the GTO. The car drove faultlessly throughout the trip (including very heavy traffic in Paris) and arrived in perfect order... Everything about the car is splendid. And I am certain much, much better than when it left Modena. Your teams have done a cracking job and I am very grateful. The Ferrari is perfect...'

'On completion, 3527GT was presented at Goodwood House, making its first appearance at a special function hosted by Lord March'

Three 275s, all with

differing specifications spanning the model's five-year life, and the possibility to drive them on the same day and on the same pieces of road. It seemed like an opportunity which couldn't be allowed to pass. Would progress inevitably make the later car a better drive? That hasn't always been the case. Would the difference between them – if any there was – be obvious or subtle? Ferraris are nothing if not bewildering in their detail differences and, as I've said on several occasions, sometimes it's hard to know what Enzo was after. Would the passage of time and the revisions of various owners render comparison irrelevant? This last is a perennial problem. Perhaps we should just look and drive and see what we might find.

Before we do that, we should recap a little. The 275GTB – or Berlinetta – fixed-head coupe arrived in 1964 and appeared rather more sophisticated mechanically than the 250 series that it replaced. The 250s of the early 1960s »

THREE DIMENSIONS

Ferrari's 275 combined the power of a 3-litre V12 with a rear-mounted transaxle for race-car handling. How do the three different versions compare?

Words: Mark Hales Photography: Paul Harmer

had all featured a simple beam back axle hung on a pair of cart-type multi-leaf springs, while at the front were simple double wishbones with upper and lower pans locating a pair of large-diameter coil springs. Even the hallowed GTO had the same, an entirely conventional layout which did service for a great many cars, not least the Mk3 Ford Cortina. Up front was a 3-litre engine with 12 cylinders, each displacing 250cc and fed and exhausted by two valves operated by one chain-driven overhead cam for each bank. Ferrari denomination is often bewildering, but in this case the 250cc displacement denotes the model; the same classification was used for the 275, which featured a slightly larger bore that, times 12, gave a total swept volume of 3286cc. The rest of the engine was, essentially, similar and it breathed through three or six twin-choke downdraught Webers, depending on, well, I'm not quite sure what. Probably whatever the customer ordered.

The 275 did away with the beam axle and cart springs and instead utilised independent suspension together with a rear-mounted five-speed transaxle. Along with many others like Maserati and BRM, the rear gearbox had been seen on Grand Prix cars – usually together with de Dion rear suspension – but this was the first time Ferrari had put a box in the back of a touring car. The location means the propeller shaft always spins at engine speed, so aligning the two accurately in a hand-built car assumed a greater importance – hence Ferrari connected the engine and transmission via a large-diameter tube that guaranteed alignment and housed the propeller shaft.

To accommodate all this unfamiliar technology, Pininfarina drew a curvaceous body with its host of signature cues: the gently bulging flanks under the chop-top cabin, the long snout that juts way beyond the front wheels, the parabolic screen with its steep rake, the quartet of air vents in the flanks ahead of the doors. All are essential ingredients in the 275's visual appeal and they combine seamlessly to create the car's neat and uncluttered appearance. Some of the bodies were made in steel, some in aluminium, and some in thinner aluminium, of which more in a moment.

In 1966, the 275GTB/4 appeared, the suffix denoting that the engine boasted four cams. It also came as standard with the dry-sump lubrication from the earlier competition model. The GTB/4 is the most sought-after and revered of the 275s, but the only visual difference is a full-length bulge on the bonnet, to create airspace for the sextet of downdraught Webers, you assume, although they look to have plenty of clearance to me. Less than 300 of the four-cams were made, and about 450 of the two-cam cars. The aforementioned thinner aluminium was for the lightweight 275GTB/C competition models, and only a dozen of these were made, in 1966, all but one powered by a dry-sump version of the two-cam engine. The sole exception was fitted with the first of the four-cam power units and came to England for Ferrari importer Ronnie Hoare and his Maranello Concessionaires team. They took it to that year's Le Mans 24 hours where Piers Courage and young Formula Three hopeful Roy Pike drove it to eighth place.

Our trio, which are all owned by the same enthusiast, is comprised of an early, 1964 two-cam 3.3-litre 275GTB, one

Right: 1964 275GTB is the oldest and least powerful of our trio, with 280bhp.
Middle: GTB/4 from 1969 has another 20bhp.
Far right: extremely rare 1966 GTB/C model – just 12 were built – gets its performance advantage by being the lightest of the 275s

of the GTB/C two-cam lightweights of 1966, and one of the last GTB/4s, made in 1969, by which time the 365GTB/4 (the Daytona) had already succeeded it. But if the difference between the 250 and 275 was more significant than usual in Ferrari touring cars hitherto noted for their conservatism, the differences between this trio are, on paper, not that great. The older 275GTB is a six-carburettor car with a claimed 280bhp output, the GTB/4 four-cam also has six carburettors but only another 20bhp, while the two-cam GTB/C, which should be quicker than either of the others, turns out to have three carburettors. The books say it should have six – the three-carburettor spec was for the lower-compression GTS that produced about 260bhp. Yet chassis number 09041, the car in front of us, is fitted with the correct dry-sump lubrication. This is beginning to make my head ache. Whether the engine has been fiddled with at some point, or a lower spec one installed and equipped with dry-sump equipment, is hard to say, but as it turns out there are more significant factors likely to affect the assessment.

Before that, though, we have the unusual and interesting freedom to park all three cars close to each other and mooch between them, looking for picky little differences. Independently we all reach the conclusion that the original GTB definitely has a shorter nose than the other two, so out comes the tape measure and... they're all identical. The difference, we then decide, has to be the car's slightly orange shade of red and how it reflects the light, and, on the GTB/C, the larger-diameter 15-inch Borrani wire wheels with 70-profile tyres, and the white circles on the doors. The other two both have slotted 14-inch Campagnolo aluminium wheels with the traditional balloon-profile XWX Michelins. Uncanny, though, how all of us – including the guys who look after the car – all made a similar assumption about the dimensions.

Open the door of the GTB and there's a familiar waft of Italian leather as you prepare to lever yourself in, but the windscreen's base comes a good way along the top of the door, the rake of the screen places the top edge even further back, and the vestigial, laid-back bucket seat is bolted low in the aperture, so supporting your body weight while you miss the sharp edges is a trick you need to learn lest you look like a geriatric – and to avoid banging your head on the roof's edge any more than once... Once in, the driving position is

'To accommodate this unfamiliar technology, Pininfarina drew a curvaceous body with its host of signature cues: the gently bulging flanks under the chop-top cabin, the long snout that juts way beyond the front wheels, the parabolic screen, the quartet of air vents ahead of the doors'

traditional Italian of the period; if your legs are comfortable you can't reach the wheel properly, and in the GTB/4 you definitely can't operate the oh-so-skinny handbrake lever when the belts are tight. You can in the older car because it has inertia reel belts.

Check out the airtex roof lining and the cable-operated window winders, which are light to operate but need a deal of twirling. More clues that would give away the country of origin and the period, if not the prancing horse on the bonnet. The wheel that's just out of reach is the traditional wood-rim with broad, flat, polished aluminium spokes, and there is the row of period-fashionable piano-key switches in the centre of the dash while, down in the tunnel below the screen, your feet find a set of pendant pedals. This too was another departure, because the more traditional mounting was to hinge them on the floor. Crank the engine and, no matter how many times I do it, somehow I never get used to the shimmering whirr of the starter or the way the engine stumbles into life amid the traditional haze of oil smoke and petrol fumes.

Ease the gearlever across left and back against a hefty spring for the dog-leg first, make sure the engine is clear of excess fuel that might make it hunt and shunt, and you can move gently away. It's not highly strung exactly, but you're never in any doubt that this is a thoroughbred with more than the usual number of camshafts and carburettors. The steering, you already know, is hard work at parking speeds. It's low-geared too, which requires you to use a lot of lock for relatively shallow turns, but once on the move the effort doesn't lessen as much as you would expect because the weighting is replaced by a strong amount of self-centring. This varies with lock, speed and cornering effort – all welcome messages that power steering can hide. Apparently, promotional literature for the 275 had promised a rack and pinion, but when the car appeared there was a traditional steering box. Whatever – it feels pretty good even if it is hard work. The 275 is not a car you drive with one hand, which presumably is why there's a foot-operated switch for the wipers.

I also know that, at first, the 275 can feel as if it's not with you. It takes a while to anticipate the steering's weight, to shuffle the rim a bit to suit the approaching corner and get the hands opposite each other to deal with the weighting. Takes a while to get the gearshift smooth, to time the drop in revs to meet the next gear and to get the movement of the lever and the dip of the clutch in harmony – the more so when you want to rev up for the downshift. This gearchange is slicker than the Daytona's and the slotted gate is easy to navigate – only the first-to-second dog leg needs any conscious direction. Then you have to get used to the way the car takes a set before the corner. It's a kind of yaw which – unconsciously – you anticipate and time so that the angle is settled just before the apex. It's very much a rear-gearbox Ferrari trait and it has to be managed correctly. Use it to lessen the work at the wheel and the car will begin to work with you. Provoke it, brake into the corner, lift off suddenly in the middle or sling the car at the turn and the yaw will become a swing. That needs a very swift reaction that involves a lot of muscular arm twirling.

The engine, meanwhile, is smooth and willing, not to mention loud. The thrash of mechanicals comes hissing back from the front, blending with the yowl resonating in the silencer boxes underneath before rasping from the multiple pipes at the back. And yet this one isn't the wailing tenor that I was, once again, expecting. Funny how preconceptions so easily become reality when the evidence isn't there, which is why it's good to have the three together. The two-cam V12's sound has a rattle to it, a little like an American V8's but not quite so offbeat, and it's a soundtrack to some very fast progress, make no mistake – 280bhp is a lot even by today's standards, and the ease with which the GTB can reach 100mph in third as it flashes through the trees lining the narrow test facility is startling, as is the width of

Left: GTB/C proves to be the trickiest to handle of our group, but that may be down to its set-up. Other two are softer but easier to work with

'You have to get used to the way the car takes a set before the corner. It's a kind of yaw which – unconsciously – you anticipate and time so that the angle is settled just before the apex'

»

'280bhp is a lot even by today's standards, and the ease with which the GTB can reach 100mph in third as it flashes through the trees lining the narrow test facility is startling, as is the width of the power band'

Above right:
275 not the easiest car to get into and out of – note how far round the windscreen wraps compared to where the seat base starts

the power band, which stretches all the way round the dial to 7500rpm and seems to keep on pulling and pulling.

The GTB/4 is next up, and apart from the colour and some minor details in the switchgear, and of course the long strake on the bonnet, you would be hard pressed to tell without lifting the lid. Then you see the different heads and distributors, and the bunches of tiny exhaust pipes winding their way past the ancillaries, the drives and castings, pipes and heatshields, and you note that it looks busier and bigger, even if the bore and stroke within is similar. Crank it all up, though, and after the familiar whirr the difference is immediately and startlingly obvious. The four-cam is revvier, spinning up at the touch of the pedal as if there is half the inertia to the mechanicals. It suddenly makes the two-cam sound lazy, an impression which carries on and up through the gears. The increase is supposedly only 20bhp, but the engine's midrange feels twice as big and the extra revs (between 500 and 1000 depending on who you talk to) have been utilised to make the final drive shorter and the ratios closer. All the corners are a gear up on the two cam and the revs die away more quickly when you back off, so not only are you busier at the lever, the car is harder to drive smoothly.

The midrange punch and the extra revs make the GTB/4 feel disproportionately quicker, but when you come to apply the brakes (which on either car are barely up to the performance of the engine) you find the speed is real; you really are approaching the corners that much faster. Then you notice

the steering is less pointy, or perhaps the car responds better for less work at the wheel. It still rolls a lot, but it does so more gently and the yaw is more restrained – you don't have to second-guess the impending set of the tail. Less of a hinge feeling and more like a modern car, which of course it was, by five years. Engineers being what they are, those at Ferrari must have revised spring and damper rates and fettled the set-up as the car evolved. That said, it is 80kg heavier than the older car.

That leaves the C-model, and the prospect that it will be sharper still to drive, even if the engine might be less powerful. Visual differences are left-hand-drive, 15-inch wires, a big aluminium gearknob instead of a small plastic one, and a prominent footrest. Big, wide full-harness belts are a recent addition, but history says that the suspension was supplied 'race tuned' and that the whole car is 80kg lighter than the B-model (making it 160kg lighter than the four-cam), mainly thanks to the thinner gauge aluminium. Eighty kilos might not sound much, but it is nevertheless a lot to lose, and as you poke around the car you notice hosts of little details intended to save weight: the bumpers are lighter and the brackets that attach them smaller; inside there are various economies of trim and the side windows are plastic. The bonnet is lighter to lift and there are rows of holes drilled round its strengthening webs. Meanwhile the two-cam engine, with its bigger, simpler cam covers and triple carburettors, looks way down low thanks to the dry sump underneath. That, of course, is the ➤➤

FERRARI 275GTB/C
SPECIFICATIONS

Engine
3286cc V12, single overhead cams, two valves per cylinder, three twin-choke downdraught Weber carburettors, dry sump lubrication

Power
260bhp @ 7000rpm

Transmission
Five-speed synchromesh gearbox rear mounted in-unit with limited-slip differential

Suspension
Front/rear suspension: independent via double wishbones coilover spring/damper units

Brakes
Steel disc brakes front and rear. No servo

Performance
Top speed 160mph
0-60mph 6.4sec

FERRARI 275GTB
SPECIFICATIONS

Engine
3286cc V12, single overhead cams, two valves per cylinder, six twin-choke downdraught Weber carburettors, wet sump lubrication

Power
280bhp @ 7500rpm

Transmission
Five-speed synchromesh gearbox rear mounted in-unit with limited-slip differential

Suspension
Front/rear suspension: independent via double wishbones coilover spring/damper units

Brakes
Steel disc brakes front and rear. No servo

Performance
Top speed 160mph
0-60mph 6.5sec

FERRARI 275GTB/4
SPECIFICATIONS

Engine
3286cc V12, double overhead cams, two valves per cylinder, six twin-choke downdraught Weber carburettors, dry sump lubrication

Power
300bhp @ 8000rpm

Transmission
Five-speed synchromesh gearbox rear mounted in-unit with limited-slip differential

Suspension
Front/rear suspension: independent via double wishbones coilover spring/damper units

Brakes
Steel disc brakes front and rear. No servo

Performance
Top speed 166mph
0-60mph 6.7sec

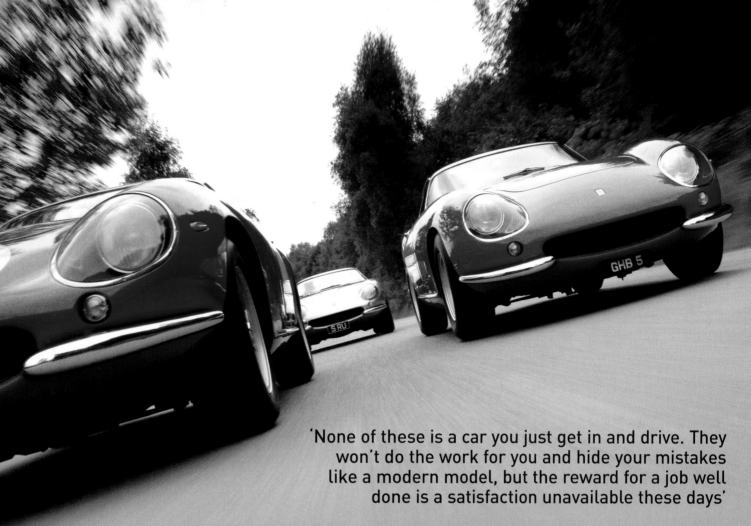

'None of these is a car you just get in and drive. They won't do the work for you and hide your mistakes like a modern model, but the reward for a job well done is a satisfaction unavailable these days'

main reason they did it, to get the centre of gravity lower as much as to guard against oil surge.

Firing it up sadly provides the first disappointment, because the thumping rattle in the engine's beat sounds lumpier still and its response to the accelerator is hoarse and lazy. Maybe it isn't firing on all 12. I haven't helped matters by leaving on the boost pump, thus forcing fuel past the float needles, but a few gentle laps on a light throttle followed by some harder ones on a heavier one cleans up the plugs while trailing a distinct haze of blue. But the engine still sounds unhappy. It could just be that this is how they feel when they have three carburettors and 260bhp, but I think compressions are low and more oil than usual is finding its way into the combustion chambers. The guys speculate that one of the distributors may be incorrectly timed – they have only recently inherited the car and it arrived exactly as it finished the last event.

How the driver made it to the end, though, I really don't know. Never mind the engine – the brakes, which started out with a wooden pedal, disappear towards the floor after a short while, and the hinged feel of the chassis that was incipient in the B-model is decidedly more insistent on the C. All the 275s hate being in the corner off the power, and you really have to settle then drive them through each turn, but this one will snap suddenly in the middle of the corner even when you try to avoid it. That means frenzied and messy wheel winding and the sense that this is all pretty pointless – the chassis is not right for whatever reason and the engine is sickly, so there's no point in risking someone else's million-pound car when we aren't going to learn anything. A pity, but the comparative element was once again useful because, even if the engine's poor health was obvious, it would be easy to conclude that the handling was always like that.

It's always interesting, when you have driven a bunch, to get back in the first one and see how it feels with the benefit of experience, and it's good to have the freedom to do that. The GTB's engine still feels the least revvy, and the car is definitely not the quickest, but having become more used to the breed, the slightly slower responses and taller gears feel more relaxed and easier to manage. The chassis, meanwhile, feels more involving because it moves about more, and the steering feels more responsive as a result. And the more you get a rhythm going – and the confidence to float the car through a series of bends – the more that yaw and set work for you and the less work you have to do at the wheel. A racer this might not be, but you can see how it might be a very entertaining way to travel along French D-roads when you're in the mood for such things. Rhythm is the key, and the 275 and I are now together, so I'm no longer just along for the ride. It's surprising, too, how settling into the drive means that ordinary, restrained B-road travel becomes easier too; the co-ordination of clutch and gears and the anticipation that gets it done in time so you don't fumble at T-junctions or sharp corners. The ride is also surprisingly supple. The chassis and body is not stiff by modern standards, but only on really rough surfaces does the car give away its vintage construction.

They do grow on you, but maybe, just maybe, the older car, which at first had seemed less exciting, is actually more accessible and has a simpler charm. None of these, though, is a car you just get in and drive; you have to learn some new techniques and some different co-ordination. They won't do the work for you and hide your mistakes like a modern model, but the reward for a job well done is satisfaction unavailable these days. And you know what? After a while even the driving position seems more natural...

$61 MILLION* TWO-NIGHT TOTAL

errari 250 GT California

**Charlie Ross and David Gooding sell the
1959 Ferrari 250 GT LWB California Spyder
at the 2007 Pebble Beach Auction**

SOLD – $4,455,000

ID $

S $
	4,455,000
	2,249,296
	3,307,423
FRANC | 5,384,402 |
00) | 5,096,221 |

**GOODING
& COMPANY**

goodingco.com   310·899·1960

GOODING
& COMPANY®

PEBBLE BEACH AUCTIONS

1959 F

FINAL B

DOLLAR

GBP £

EURO €

SWISS

YEN (x

GOODING
& COMPANY

Dino

'I am convinced that when a man tells a woman he loves her, he only means that he desires her, and that the only perfect love in this world is that of a father for his son.'

These words were written by Enzo Ferrari in 1961, five years after the death of his son, Alfredo, known affectionately as Dino.

Dino's tragically short life – he was just 24 – was soon woven into Ferrari folklore, while a series of racing cars and road cars were named in his honour, the most famous being the gorgeous Dino 246 GT.

But what was Dino, the man, really like? And does the 246 GT deserve its iconic status? Peter Tomalin went to Modena for answers and was granted rare access to the people and places at the heart of the Ferrari legend.

This, then, is the story of Dino Ferrari and the cars that carried his name

Pictures: David Shepherd

Dino 246 GT looks as pretty today as ever. Some owners added Ferrari shields, but a totally original 246 has only Dino badges

Boy, it's warm in here. Warm and *very* noisy. Just a few miles south of the Ferrari factory, the road climbs rapidly into the hills, stringing together the sleepy villages of Montagnana, Montardone and Serramazzoni. The tiny silver sports car howls between the corners, its V6 engine revving close to 7000rpm before each upshift. To my left, in the driver's seat, owner Massimo Cecchi is clearly enjoying wringing every last drop of speed from his wonderful little Dino. 'It's a great engine, no?' he shouts above the raucous exhaust note and the rush of the wind – both side-windows are fully down to draw some air into the cockpit, yet our shirts still cling to our backs when we pause,

elated, in a lay-by a few minutes later. Massimo grins and points a finger at me. 'Now your turn.'

It's always slightly nerve-wracking, driving someone else's supercar, especially when they're sitting alongside, and even more so when it's as achingly beautiful and totally pristine as this gorgeous Dino 246 GT. And I want so badly for it to be great, because this is a car I've loved since I was a boy. For me, this is so much more than just another road test.

In fact this story is something I've been wanting to write for years, ever since I read Brock Yates' biography of Enzo Ferrari, which includes a number of evocative passages about the young Dino: how he became wracked by a mysterious

illness before dying at the age of just 24, how his father came almost to deify his memory, and how he inspired a series of 'baby Ferrari' racing cars and road cars.

I wanted to drive a 24 6 GT on the roads around Maranello. I wanted to ask the people at the factory whether we would ever see another Dino road car, as has been rumoured in sections of the press. Most of all, though, I wanted to know what Dino the man was like, and to try to get to the truth of some of the stories about him. Did he really design the first Ferrari V6 engine, the first engine that would carry his name, or was that all part of Ferrari mythology?

Dino's short life was dogged by debilitating

'It's nerve-wracking driving someone else's supercar, even more so when it's as achingly beautiful and totally pristine as this Dino'

illness, but he did have one blissful means of escape. He forged a close friendship with a young test driver at the factory, Sergio Sighinolfi, and the two of them would spend hours ripping along these very hill-roads above Maranello in whatever was the latest Ferrari model – a 212 Inter, perhaps, or a fearsome Mondial.

The Modena region in summer can be stiflingly hot, the temperature frequently in the mid-30s; it's only late-April now, but already it's in the high-20s. As Massimo brings the howling 246 GT to a halt in the next sleepy village and we swap places, still grinning, it's not very hard to imagine what it must have been like for Dino and Sergio. I blip the throttle; the revs fly again. Italian

hill-roads, Ferrari sports cars, baking sunshine – some things seem almost eternal.

REWIND TO THE MORNING, and the quiet, leafy back-streets of central Modena, 15 minutes up the road from smaller Maranello. Modena is where the Scuderia Ferrari was formed, where the Ferrari family lived – and where they were laid to rest. We've been brought here by Ferrari press officer Roberto Casolari to meet a man who was as close to the family as perhaps anyone has ever been.

We park near an imposing, stone-built 19th century apartment block; Roberto thumbs a numbered button on the intercom panel, the door

clicks open and we step off the pavement into a cool, marble-floored hallway. Two flights of stairs up, we're greeted with a warm handshake by an elderly man who seems strangely familiar (only later does it click that I must have seen him in numerous photos with Enzo Ferrari). 'Peter,' says Roberto, 'May I introduce Franco Gozzi...'

Inside the apartment it's dimly lit, the windows mostly shuttered, but we're ushered into a small sitting room which is flooded by soft late-morning sunlight, the high-ceilinged walls covered in photos and memorabilia. Everywhere you look is Ferrari.

Franco Gozzi's life first became entwined with Ferrari in 1958 when, fresh from university, he

secured a work placement at Maranello. He must have made an immediate impression, because one of his first assignments was drafting the thesis that won Enzo Ferrari an honorary degree in engineering. In 1960 he joined the payroll, initially as assistant to the sales director, later as head of the press office, in which role he was for many years Enzo's filter, spokesman and confidant. For several years he was also director of motorsport (it's all there in his book, Memoirs of Enzo Ferrari's Lieutenant). Basically, Gozzi was at Enzo Ferrari's side for three decades and was still at the heart of the company when Luca di Montezemolo began his reign. Franco Gozzi *is* Ferrari's history.

But there's more. By one of those almost spooky twists of fate, Franco Gozzi was born in 1932, the same year as Enzo's first-born. The young Franco actually went to school with the young Dino Ferrari.

So I ask him to tell me about Dino. Some reports suggest that, even as a small boy, he was frail and sickly. Not so, says Franco. 'I knew him from school, we were classmates, and he was a normal boy till he was a teenager. Tall, average build, active, just another boy...

'After we were at secondary school together, he went to technical school while I studied humanities. When I saw him later he was quite different. Very stiff and awkward in his movements. By the time he was about 19 it was obvious something was not right...'

Dino, it would transpire, was showing the classic symptoms of muscular dystrophy, a genetic condition that causes muscle-wasting, resulting in increasing weakness and disability. 'For many, many years nobody really understood why he died,' says Franco. 'Muscular dystrophy wasn't really understood. But I have no doubt that's what it was. Later Mr Ferrari made many donations to muscular dystrophy research.'

There seems to be no question that Enzo was genuinely devoted to Dino. In fact the boy influenced his father's life even before he was born. Enzo had vowed he would give up motor-racing if he had a son, and he was as good as his word. When Laura Ferrari gave birth to a boy on January 19, 1932, Enzo called time on his driving career, turning instead to team management, first with Alfa Romeos (under the Scuderia Ferrari banner) and, after the war, with his own cars. The boy was named Alfredo, after Enzo's late brother, though everyone called him Alfredino (little Alfredo), which was later shortened to Dino.

The family lived in a tiny two-bedroomed apartment over the Scuderia at 11 Viale Trento

Trieste in Modena. They weren't wealthy, but Ferrari made sure Dino had the best schooling available. After high school and technical school, he studied economics at Bologna then mechanical engineering at a Swiss university. In fact, although he gained a degree, it was only a two-year course, Ferrari perhaps being mindful of his son's failing health. 'In Italy to have the title of engineer would take five years,' says Gozzi, 'but for the father, this was enough – enough to call his son an engineer. The father was so proud of the son...'

And with good reason. Dino was certainly bright, passionate about cars, and with a good eye for styling as well as an aptitude for engineering. Even after he started work in the engine design department at Maranello, he also spent many hours at the Scaglietti coachworks, which was just across the road from the factory, and he is widely credited with the design of the pretty 750 Monza, one of the definitive mid-'50s sports-racing Ferraris.

Of his involvement in the design of the engine that would be named in his honour, there is more doubt. Ferrari legend has it that as Dino's health deteriorated and he spent more time confined to his bed, he would sketch engineering concepts that he and his father would later discuss with engineer Vittorio Jano. One of these, towards the end of his life, was for a 1.5-litre V6 engine.

Franco Gozzi, having spoken to most of the people who were around at the time, thinks it unlikely that Dino actually designed the engine. But did he have some input into the design? A long silence. 'It's... possible. He was involved in the discussions, yes, but how much was his idea we'll never know for sure.

'What is certain is he had a great passion for engines – everyone I spoke to told me this. He was like his father in this regard. Ferrari himself was only interested in the engines, never chassis and bodywork. I remember he would speak of Dino as his *technical* son. My technical son...'

Despite his illness, Dino put on a brave face for the world. Franco Gozzi's wife, Gabriella, also knew the Ferrari family well – her father, Antonio, ran the barbershop that Enzo Ferrari would visit first thing every day, for a shave and to catch up on all the Modenese gossip (old man Ferrari was an inveterate gossip). Gabriella doesn't speak English, but through Franco she tells us how she would visit Dino when he was confined to bed, either at the apartment above the Scuderia or at the local hospital. He was, she says, always smiling, always positive.

I ask Franco how Mr Ferrari remembered Dino when they spoke of him. 'He was already an icon, a myth. There were pictures of Dino in the factory, in his office, everywhere. I remember he asked me to write that Dino was his *total* son. »

Left, from top: Franco Gozzi at home, surrounded by Ferrari mementoes; nine-year-old Dino with his dad; Gozzi makes a point; Dino cuts his engineering teeth; lunch at the Montana with Massimo Cecchi

Tomalin enjoys the 246 GT on the old Ferrari test routes. Below: a teenaged Dino at the wheel of a 166 Inter, which had a 2-litre V12. One of his greatest pleasures was driving these same roads

'The little Dino is wonderfully light on its feet... and bursting with energy'

Total son. It seems strange now, although for a long time of course it was not widely known that there was a second son...'

It would emerge only years after Dino's death that Ferrari had another son, Piero, by his long-time mistress, Lina Lardi. Born in 1945, Piero Ferrari is now 62 and has long since taken his place in the Ferrari company hierarchy – today he is vice president of Ferrari and retains a 10 per cent stake in the company. It's highly unlikely the two brothers ever met, says Gozzi. 'Dino died in 56, and until 1960 it was absolutely secret that there was a second son. In 1961 Mr Ferrari brought Piero to me to find some work for him...'

It's said Enzo planned and hoped that Dino

would inherit and one day run the company. Franco Gozzi shrugs, turns down the corners of his mouth; he is not so sure. 'The business was evolving, everything changes... Mr Ferrari himself, he would tell me, "I am not an industrialist, I am not a car manufacturer. I am an artisan." His life was here in Modena. He was the right person at the right time. If you look at the business now, it requires a different sort of character. I am not sure Dino was that person.'

We leave Franco and Gabriella Gozzi in the apartment they have shared since they married in 1964, an apartment that is both a family home and a repository of so much of Ferrari's past, its essence. I could listen to Franco all day, but we have

a lunch appointment – at the famous Montana restaurant that nestles alongside the Fiorano test track back in Maranello – with Florentine businessman and car collector Massimo Cecchi and, of course, his beautiful little Dino.

The iconic Dino road car appeared 40 years ago as the 206 GT, a miniature exotic with an aluminium body and an all-alloy 2-litre V6 engine. Better known is the later 246, which had a more powerful, 2.4-litre, iron-block version of the V6, albeit with heavier steel bodywork to push along. Heavier and notoriously rust-prone, though there's no sign of the Italian tin-worm on Massimo's flawless 1971 example.

There's no Ferrari badge on the 246 GT – Dino was launched as a separate brand; in fact the only prancing horse is on the chassis plate tucked away inside the engine bay (below). But you know within an instant of turning the ignition key that this car has the heart and soul of Ferrari. That isn't just a V6 behind you – it's half of a Ferrari V12 – and it revs with such energy and such presence that you soon forget the unexceptional 195bhp power-peak, instead savouring the intake roar through the three Weber carburettors and the exhaust's bark through the four chromed tailpipes slung beneath that perfect Kamm tail.

Massimo, of course, knows that this engine thrives on revs. I'm not expecting the Dino to feel quick – contemporary road testers recorded 0-60 in a little over 7sec – but when he pins the

throttles wide open through second and third it sprints with affecting vigour. You just need to keep it above about 3500 – it can occasionally stumble on part-throttle at the bottom of the rev-range, but at the top-end it feels like it'll happily pull all the way to the 7800rpm red line and keep doing it for hour after hour – just like a race engine would.

It's a real event, this little car, even from the passenger seat, looking out through the deeply dished windscreen, the sensual curves of the front wings rushing past the greenery as we climb into the hills just south of Maranello. The seats themselves are tiny, the backs barely reaching your shoulders and fixed at a semi-reclined angle. When it's my turn I find the driving position initially odd – not only am I semi recumbent, but the steering wheel is a real stretch away; it also seems to be angled towards the headlining,

while my knees are slightly splayed around it and the pedals are heavily offset to the right. Oh, and the five-speed gearbox with its exposed gate has first on a dog-leg, across towards me and back. Helping stabilise my accelerating heart-rate are an encouragingly progressive clutch and quite brilliant visibility for a mid-engined car, helped by amusingly thin screen-pillars. Directly ahead is a lovely little oval-shaped instrument pod that's packed with gauges, the important ones clearly visible under the slim, leather-wrapped rim of a tiny, three-spoke steering wheel.

Everything about the Dino speaks of lightness, subtlety and delicacy, and having watched Massimo deftly palm the chromed, ball-topped gearstick around the gate, I'm surprised at the sheer physicality of driving it. The unassisted steering feels initially light once you're on the move – you almost nudge it into a corner – but once it's in there it loads up massively, so much so that in tighter turns you want to haul yourself up straighter in the seat to get more leverage. The pedals and gearshift need firm applications too, and the downshift from third to second requires you to match the revs perfectly – ideally by double-declutching – to avoid a most indelicate scrunching sound. Get it right and it's hugely satisfying. I managed it, ooh, at least twice, eliciting a cheer from the ever-encouraging Massimo alongside.

The faster you go, and the more you tune into

DINO 246 GT
SPECIFICATIONS

Engine
65deg V6, 2418cc, dohc

Location
Mid engined,
rear-wheel drive

Max power
195bhp @ 7600rpm

Max torque
167lb ft @ 5500rpm

Weight
(kerb) 1079kg

Power-to-weight
183bhp/ton

0-60mph
7.2sec

Top speed
146mph

Production
1969-73 (total 2487)

Price new
£5485

Price now
£60,000-£80,000

the chassis, the more fun it gets. The Dino rides fluidly, no doubt partly thanks to the tall sidewalls of its 205/70 V-rated Michelin radials which sit on 14in(!) Cromadora alloys. They also no doubt contribute to its malleability at the limits of grip. This car feels as if it's constantly moving around a central axis, its attitude dictated largely by your right foot. It'll power-oversteer too, as Massimo ably demonstrates later, smearing the tail wide as we exit some of the tighter corners. The controls might be heavy, but down at the road surface the little Dino is wonderfully light on its feet.

Best of all, though, the engine feels as if it's bursting with energy, just like it must have done when it was new. It sounds quite marvellously throaty when you hold the throttle flat, all the way through four, five, six thousand revs, while on the over-run there's a micro-fusillade of pops and coughs. Just as well we've got the windows down, all the better to hear it. In fact I'm so absorbed with driving the Dino that after 30 minutes I'm not even aware of the eccentricities of the driving position. That's how good it is. At one point we pass a stationary 599 GTB wearing 'Prova' plates, the factory test driver pausing to log an observation; I glance at the car, at the wonderful scenery and at Massimo, who genuinely seems to be enjoying himself despite the occasional syncro-defeating downshift, and it feels as if these roads could have been made for the Dino – or maybe it's the other way round...

That night we eat out at the Cavallino restaurant, just opposite the factory gates back in Maranello, and wash down some more first-rate pasta with some Ferrari-branded Modenese lambrusco, which tastes surprisingly good, for lambrusco. You can see why some people live and breathe the marque – round here you can even eat and drink Ferrari.

SPEAK TO ANYONE WHO KNEW DINO and a clear picture emerges, of a bright, personable, enthusiastic young man with a genuine love of cars. Carlo Benzi, who worked on the admin side at the Scuderia, can remember being driven from Modena to Maranello on several occasions by the young Ferrari. 'Dino had a lot of passion for cars, for both engines and design,' he says. 'In fact he often used to advise his father about these things.' Dino was never fit enough to race, but his father did provide a number of road cars which he drove with enthusiasm, initially small Fiats but later a 2-litre Ferrari that Dino and the young test driver Sighinolfi would take into the hills.

Doug Nye, the leading Ferrari historian, has spoken to a number of people who knew Dino. 'Everyone recalls him as having been a very pleasant and engaging young man – obviously

Cars called Dino. Going clockwise from below, 'sharknose' 156 F1, 206 GT, 196 S at Watkins Glen in 1961, 246 Tasmania down under in '68, 1973 308 GT4, 206 S at the Ring in '66, 166 F2 at Monza in '68, 156 F2 chasing a Maserati 250F in the '57 GP di Modena; 1969 206 SP and 246 S at Sebring in 1962. Opposite above: 246 F1 in the Galleria

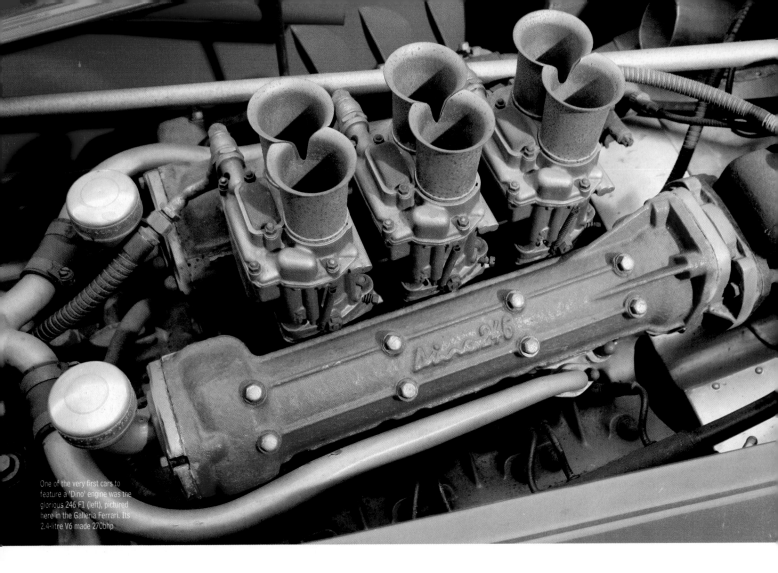

One of the very first cars to feature a 'Dino' engine was the glorious 246 F1 (left), pictured here in the Galleria Ferrari. Its 2.4-litre V6 made 270bhp

pale, awkward in his movements and increasingly fragile – a useful ally with his father's ear – but straightforward and open, not a politician...' As Franco Gozzi says: 'Everybody says he was a good, normal boy – not a genius maybe, but it is impossible to find someone who speaks against the boy.'

American Carroll Shelby spent many hours with Dino during the summer and autumn of 1955; in Brock Yates' book, Shelby recalls Dino as being shy around strangers but open and affable with friends. He also remembers him losing weight quite noticeably in this period, while his legs became so stiff he had difficulty walking. By the end of the year he was mostly idling the days away with the mechanics and customers who packed the old Scuderia, which was by then a car

delivery building. The young Ferrari spoke pretty good English, something his father never did, which meant he got on well with the Americans and Brits who were by now regularly frequenting the Scuderia. 'Dino was a good guy,' says Shelby, 'always smiling.'

But he was also a very sick young man. By early 1956, with Modena shrouded in the winter fog typical of the region, Dino's health was deteriorating rapidly. He was spending more and more time in bed, tended by his mother, visited after work by his father, and – possibly – sketching his proposals for a new V6 engine.

The end came on June 30. Although there was for many years a degree of mystery surrounding his illness, most who have since studied his case history agree that as well as suffering

with muscular dystrophy, Dino also contracted nephritis, a disease of the kidneys, which his debilitated system could not fight. Eventually his kidneys gave out. His life had spanned just 24 years, five months and eleven days.

WE'RE ON THE VIALE TRENTO TRIESTE, standing at the exact spot where the Scuderia Ferrari used to be, where Enzo and Laura and Dino used to live. It's mid morning, the second day of our visit. These days there's a commercial bank on the site, and an engineering business owned by Piero Ferrari, independent of Ferrari SpA. There's also a multi-storey car park – in

Below from left: site of the Scuderia today, and as it was. Enzo and Dino with 'Nando' Righetti, gentleman racer and valued customer – if he crashed his new Ferrari he bought another! Above: early Dino V6 engine in 246 F1

fact the only clue that this is the birthplace of the whole Ferrari legend is a nondescript sign for the car park: 'Garage Ferrari'. Look across the wide, busy road, however, and plenty of the old street remains. We're met by Giancarlo, another retired Ferrari employee, who points to what used to be a car repair shop, a cafe, a Lancia dealership, another garage, apartments, shops... Trento Trieste was (and still is) a noisily bustling thoroughfare.

A few days after Dino's death, the funeral cortege formed up just here and made its way first to the local Sant'Agnese church, for a service attended by around 1000 mourners, and then out of town to the San Cataldo cemetery where his body would be placed in the family crypt. And it's Dino's final journey that we retrace now, with press officer Roberto Casolari as our guide.

On the way we pause at a rather grand apartment block a couple of streets away in Garibaldi square – this was Enzo's home in his later life – and further on we pass the site of the disused Modena racetrack, now the Park Enzo Ferrari. After a drive of 15 minutes or so, just as the outskirts of town give way to scrubby countryside and allotments, we arrive at the San Cataldo Cemetery. It's vast – ever since the middle of the 19th century, this has been the last resting place of the great and good of Modena. The perimeter wall seems to run for almost a mile, but eventually we find an entrance, park in a dusty courtyard and make our way to the administration office.

Problem. We can look at the outside of the Ferrari family crypt, but we can't go inside, and we can't take any photos, at all. Roberto puts a call through to his bosses back at Maranello. Nothing doing. So we wander around the impressive Romanesque central square and look at the outside of the crypt – and then just as we're about to leave, something very wonderful happens. A call comes through from the office of Piero Ferrari himself: we've been granted access; his driver is on his way with the key to the crypt. Twenty minutes later he's here.

With a combination of mounting excitement and due reverence we crunch down the gravel path, climb the steps, and watch as the key is turned in the lock and the big, heavy iron gates are swung open. And then we step inside.

It's cool, quiet, serene, rather like a small chapel. The walls are granite and marble, carved with latin inscriptions, and there's a high, translucent, domed ceiling; around us are the tombs of Enzo Ferrari, his father, his mother, his brother... all bearing little enamelled portraits of the deceased. And over to our right, alongside that of his mother Laura, Dino's tomb, with a small portrait of that now-familiar smiling face. Ing. Alfredo 'Dino' Ferrari, 1932-1956.

There's a bouquet of what look like dark red roses placed on the floor; and on the shelf above Enzo Ferrari's tomb, a small, slightly dusty model of an F40. No-one says a word for several moments, the silence eventually broken by Shep's camera. *Schlick*. It's been quite a morning.

LESS THAN A YEAR AFTER DINO'S death, the first V6-engined Ferrari appeared. It was a Grand Prix car, the 156, built to the then-new F2 regs, and cast on the cam covers of the 1.5-litre V6 was the legend 'Dino'. It debuted in the Gran Premio di Napoli on April 28 1957 – 50 years ago almost to the very day of our visit – and finished third. So began a line of Dino engines and cars, some of which can be found at our next destination – the excellent Galleria Ferrari in Maranello.

It has been an unforgettable two days, but the most vivid memories will be of the hill roads and that fantastic 246 GT, a car that – if you're lucky enough to drive a really good one, as I did – fully deserves its reputation. It's a totally engaging baby supercar with a sweet balance, a cracking little engine and a big, big character.

Ferrari, of course, has emphatically denied that there will be a new Dino, and there's no deviation from that line during our visit. But as an enthusiast, of course, you can't help dreaming... So imagine a small, beautiful, lightweight, mid-engined car, with a charismatic 3-litre quad-cam V6 or V8. Imagine it in aluminium with a Dino badge and a price tag of around £60K.

The story of Dino the man is inevitably a sad one. But when I think of him now, it'll be on those test routes, ripping along in a Ferrari sports car in brilliant late-spring sunshine, smiling broadly. As Franco Gozzi says, Dino wasn't a genius. But he was a proper enthusiast, a talented designer and a promising engineer. He was also a much-loved son. He was a good guy. △

Horses for Courses

A Ferrari wouldn't be most people's choice as the ideal rally car – but in the early-1980s this solitary 308GTB competed on some of Europe's most gruelling events

Words: Jacques Vassal Photography: Matthieu Heurault

It must have seemed

a strange decision to enter a Ferrari on the Monte Carlo Rally. The prancing horse had never been at home on snowy roads, let alone icy ones. Yet in 1982 this Ferrari 308GTB competed on the 'Monte', towards the end of a short but intensive career as a rally car that had at least the tacit, if not explicit, approval of Enzo himself.

The story begins in October 1973, when Ferrari launched the 308GT4 at the Salon de l'Auto in Paris. It was its very first V8 road car and, after the V6 Dino (206 and 246GT or GTS), only its second model with ❯❯

'GIVEN 300BHP AND LESS WEIGHT, A 308GTB

a transverse rear-engine. More surprisingly, it was also its first rear-engined 2+2. The 308GT4 engine produced 255bhp and the car, labelled Dino (not Ferrari), was bodied by Bertone – not Pininfarina. The design was angular and made the GT4 look rather like a bigger Matra Bagheera. Not very exciting at first sight. However, when driven quickly on a club circuit or a mountain road it showed excellent roadholding and reasonable performance (from 1976 the GT4 was eventually labelled as a Ferrari – as if old Enzo had decreed that it was worthy of his name after all).

Next off the line was the 308GTB, which was launched at the Salon de l'Auto two years later, in October 1975. This was a true Ferrari (or so the prancing horse on the bonnet warned us), boasting a smooth two-seater body by Pininfarina, which brought it all back home.

The 308GTB engine was borrowed from the Rocchi-designed 308GT4's: a 90°, all-alloy, 3-litre V8, which initially fed by four downdraught Weber carburettors. Those first 308GTBs later turned out to be the best in terms of efficiency: their bodies were mostly made of glassfibre – quite a departure from the traditional steel and

Above:
from this angle, the similarity to a Stratos – Michelotto prepped those, too – is notable

aluminium, but with the advantage of lighter weight. From 1981 the cars had steel bodies and K-Jetronic fuel injection, but back in 1980 the only 308GTB on the market was the glassfibre-bodied car with the carburettor-fed motor.

Now the Pozzi-Ferrari team and its most famous driver come into the picture. Jean-Claude Andruet was a very useful race driver, on both track and road. He may have been better known for his rally achievements but he was also an exceptional performer in endurance races such as the 24 Hours of Le Mans. His race record included victories at the 1972 Tour de France with a Pozzi-entered Group 4 Ferrari Daytona, the 1973 Monte Carlo with an Alpine A110, 1974 Tour de Corse with a Lancia Stratos and 1977 San Remo with a Fiat-Abarth 131.

Andruet had the ability typical of the best rally drivers to improvise in ever-changing conditions – wet or dry, night or day, snow or gravel. His only flaw was his unpredictability. One day he might lose his temper, the next day he might fall into a depression which would then affect his results. But when he was in the right mood, he was able to deliver incredibly quick drives.

Left and below:
lots of extra knobs
and switches, but that
traditional chromed
Ferrari gate
survived...

COULD PERHAPS WIN THE MONTE CARLO RALLY'

Since the early 1970s, Charles Pozzi, the French Ferrari importer, and his new manager Daniel Marin had been entering Ferraris in various events, notably the Group 4 Daytonas at Le Mans and on the Tour de France, which Andruet had won. They later entered 512BB/LMs at Le Mans, where Andruet raced for them too. Based on his vast experience of rear-engined cars, Andruet remarked to Marin that 'Given 300bhp and less weight, a Ferrari 308GTB could shine and perhaps even win the Monte Carlo Rally and other road races.'

On one of his trips to Maranello, Marin talked to Enzo Ferrari about it and asked the old man if he would support the plan. The Commendatore reacted in typical fashion by not giving a clear 'yes' or 'no'. He just remarked that his firm now belonged to 'an industrial group which raced factory rally cars', implying Fiat and Lancia without actually mentioning them by name. But he added, 'Marin, you are a free man...'

After his conversation with Enzo Ferrari, Marin spoke with Gaetano Florini, who was in charge of the customers' racing department. Florini reassured the young French manager that, if he did not say 'no', the old man really meant 'yes', and

Above:
transverse-mounted
3-litre V8 was
tweaked to deliver
310bhp thanks to
fuel injection

he suggested that Michelotto from Padua could be the right man to turn a standard 308GTB into a rally car. Michelotto had successfully done the same thing to the Lancia Stratos and had also made the first racing 308GTB – to Group 4 specifications.

After being introduced to the press in March 1978, that car, chassis number 20951, competed in several Italian rallies, recording a few discouraging retirements before 'Lele' Pinto finished third on the Monza Rally. The following year, the same car and driver would win the Monza.

In 1980, 20951 was driven by Andruet on the Targa Florio, and he dominated the event until a fire forced him to retire. The car was repaired and subsequently sold to Pozzi, then during the Hunsruck Rally in Germany, Andruet and his female co-driver survived a terrifying crash: 20951 flipped upside down and its crew could only wait helplessly for rescue as they listened to the sound of petrol dripping down beside them...

In 1983, 20951 was sold to popular cartoonist Albert Uderzo of Astérix fame, who used it in many club meetings the following years. Uderzo eventually sold it in 1998, through a sports car dealer in the South of France. **»**

'SNOW WAS SCARCE ON THE MONTE IN 1982 AND ANDRUET AND MARIN KNEW THAT, GIVEN THE POWER AND ROADHOLDING OF THE 308 ON DRY SECTIONS, THEY STOOD A CHANCE'

Chassis 26713 – our feature car – was delivered to Pozzi in 1981. It was much lighter than standard, weighing 950kg instead of 1200, and power was boosted to a healthy 310bhp thanks to a new fuel injection system. Since the regulations didn't allow a full race gearbox to be used, the standard gears were modified by removing every alternate tooth. This made smooth gearchanging tricky, but Andruet and, later, his colleague Guy Chasseuil got used to it.

In 1981, 26713 was entered on several rallies, wearing the colours of Entremont, a specialist cheese company from the Alps. Andruet started with a pair of wins, on the Quattro Regione in Italy and then, in Belgium, at the 12 Hours of Ypres. On the Tour de Corse, Andruet led for much of the event until he was stopped by mysterious fuel line blockages; the mechanics later discovered that an unusual mixture of petrol had dissolved the inside of a plastic filter.

Andruet managed to win another favourite rally of his with 26713, the Cévennes Rally in the South of France, but on the Madeira Rally, in Spain, he was again betrayed by a poor petrol feed. He still believes that, on this occasion, the fuel problem was no accident but deliberate sabotage.

On the Tour de France in 1981, Andruet drove another 308GTB Group 4 for Pozzi. He won, even though a stone took out the belt driving the water pump at the start of a special stage. Andruet had a comfortable lead and Marin knew that, after a stop to cool down the engine, it would make it to the finish. Which it did. 'They were unbelievably reliable engines', he comments today.

Andruet drove 26713 again for Ferrari-France in the

Above: yellow headlamp lenses date this Ferrari perhaps more than any other feature...

1982 Monte Carlo Rally. The car had by then been repainted with Pioneer livery, since the French importer for the Japanese hi-fi manufacturer was also a racing enthusiast. Andruet started with poor odds against the Renault 5 Turbos and Audi quattros that then led the World Championship and had much bigger, works-sponsored budgets. But snow was scarce on the Monte that year and Andruet and Marin knew that, given the power and roadholding of the 308 on dry sections, they stood a good chance.

As fate would have it, a loose wire cost them three minutes on one of the early stages. Then, underestimating the extent of an ice patch, Andruet stuffed the car into a wall. That was the end of Ferrari's Monte venture, but it wasn't the end of 26713's racing career. The car was entered again in the Targa Florio, where Andruet finished second. For most of the remaining season it was driven by Andruet's mate Guy Chasseuil, an excellent former Porsche driver, but mechanical failures caused him to retire from the 24 Hours of Ypres, Tour de Corse and Tour de France.

In 1983 Group 4 disappeared from the rally regulations to be replaced by Group B. The 308GTB was no longer eligible and, while Ferrari had a formidable successor up its sleeve – the twin-turbo 288GTO of 1984, which might well have been used for rallying – Group B itself did not survive the terrible accident that cost the lives of Henri Toivonen and his co-driver on the Tour de Corse.

The writing was on the wall. A Ferrari would never again be entered on a World Championship Rally – but 26713 remains safely in a French collection to this day.

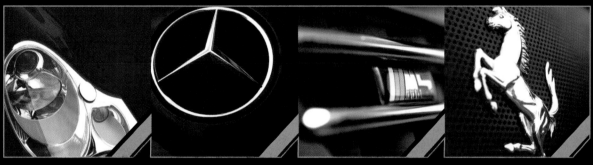

Factor 12

Three classic 12-cylinder Ferraris, three price brackets. Any one of them is currrently an excellent buy. So will you have Testarossa, Daytona or 550M?

Words: Dale Drinnon **Photography:** Paul Harmer

409K

V12 WSR

'V8s DO THEIR JOBS ADMIRABLY, BUT THERE'S SOMETHING WONDERFULLY HEDONISTIC ABOUT HAVING THOSE FOUR EXTRA EXPLOSIONS. IN A PERFECT WORLD, WE'D ALL HAVE A FERRARI 12 FOR PURE MENTAL HEALTH REASONS'

Isn't it funny, I think, standing over the gently idling Daytona, waiting patiently for some engine temp, how every consideration of Ferraris comes around to the wonderful sound, but all they ever mention is the thrill when you bottom the throttle? Never this, never the smooth, seamless murmur through all those pipes at tickover, never the soft hissing of great masses of air sliding toward waiting cylinders or the faint background whirr of rotating parts warming to their task. Never the lovely anticipation of it all. Shame, that; the pleasure is never as intense without the anticipation.

Legend has it that Enzo himself once defined a Ferrari as an automobile with 12 cylinders. And if he didn't, please don't tell me. Even though the V8s do their job admirably well, there's still something wonderfully hedonistic about having those extra four explosions. In a perfect world, we'd all have a Ferrari '12' stashed away for pure mental health reasons. It's a theme that Ferrari constantly turns to for its highest flyers, and the biggest, baddest production Ferrari in the neighbourhood is the just-launched 599GTB, with six litres of V12 mounted right up front.

Alas, the new 599 is in the region of £160,000, and getting into a first-class example of most of the two-seater, genuine 150mph-plus Ferrari 12s that preceded it will now swallow damn near that much on the classic market – or more. Of course, finding the best price on the fastest Ferrari has long been shooting at a moving target, so photographer Paul Harmer and I went to a specialist with a rep for dealing in the very fastest to find out where the true values are these days. Bob Houghton Limited has sold, serviced, raced or restored virtually every type of car Ferrari ever made; price guides have their place, but sometimes you just have to go talk to the people at the front.

»

Paying for it

The cheapest way to buy anything, of course, is always cash, but for most of us it's nice to know that a growing number of specialist car dealers are offering access to financing.

Bob Houghton arranges its services through Car Finance 4 Less, a lender that specialises in finance packages above £25K for prestige and exotic cars. Loans available include the traditional hire-purchase plan of equal monthly repayments calculated on a fixed interest rate, as well as a variation wherein the interest floats with prevailing bank rates. Both plans can also be had with the option of a final large 'balloon' payment at the end.

Balloon payments allow you to make smaller payments on the principal than a conventional loan permits, then settling up the outstanding balance in one go, by refinancing, payment outright, or other mutually agreeable means. For further details, call 0845 070 1324 or go to www.car-finance4less.com

IN THE SPACE OF A DEEP BREATH THE LANDSCAPE IS INSANELY FLASHING BY AND THAT NEEDLE RUSHING ACROSS THE TOP OF THE DIAL ISN'T THE REV COUNTER, IT'S THE SPEEDO'

512M feels too wide for many British minor roads but, when you have the room, it's devastatingly quick

TESTAROSSA (1984-1996)
SPECIFICATIONS

Engine
4942cc all-alloy 180-degree flat-12, dohc, four valves per cylinder, Bosch fuel injection

Power
390bhp @ 6300rpm
(F512M: 440bhp)

Torque
361lb ft @ 4500rpm
(F512M: 369lb ft)

Transmission
Five-speed manual, rear-wheel drive

Suspension
Coil and wishbone, telescopic shocks, anti-roll bars; double springs/shocks at rear

Brakes
Four-wheel vented discs with servo assist

Weight
1506kg (3313lb) approx

Performance
0-60mph 5.2sec (F512M: 4.7sec) Top speed 181mph (F512M: 195mph)

Value
£18,000-65,000

The Testarossa Series

Remember one thing when it comes to Ferrari prices: they're not cars, they're collectors' items, and collectors quite understandably rarely want something there's plenty of. Which makes anything with slotted sides a veritable snip. The flat-12 Testarossa series was Ferrari's best seller ever; from the beginning in 1984, badged simply as Testarossa, through the renamed 512TR and on to the final F512M, almost 10,000 were built. By way of comparison, total production of the Daytona coupé was some 1300 units.

From a collectable standpoint, the Testarossa is therefore the Ford Fiesta of Ferraris, and basically subject to ordinary mortal market forces. Older models sell for less than newer models, and you can shop around for price and condition. Outstanding examples of the early Testarossas can be had for around £35K, surely the cheapest possible way to go 180mph-plus regardless of brand, and the gorgeous late F512M from Bob Houghton we're driving here is bang on sixty thousand.

Maintenance and repairs, however, can be a major trap for the unwary; the Testarossa's mid-mounted engine and tight drivetrain packaging make any job back there a pain, and cambelt changes are an engine-out procedure – to the tune of about two grand every three years. I know you've heard this before, but for God's sake don't get sucked into a 'needs minor work' in an effort to save money. It never turns out that way on anything, much less a Ferrari, much less still a Testarossa. On the upside, Russell Smith, service manager at Bob Houghton, says a sound example with a clean service history usually makes a pretty reliable vehicle, and continued regular maintenance should keep it so. Ignore those cambelt changes, though, and you'll be the one trying desperately to flog on a 'needs minor work'.

Driving a Testarossa is very much an '80s supercar kind of experience – Götterdämmerung performance levels are design priority one, and oh yeah, now where shall we put the people? The old AGIF (Arse Goes In First) rule of thumb doesn't work so well when entering one of these, and the Italian driving position is too pronounced for even my normally Italo-sympathetic tastes, although I should add that the accommodation changed several times during the series, so your experiences may vary, and the interior was typically miles ahead of its contemporary competition. That still won't give you any more headroom, though, or put the pedals in front of your feet instead of the passenger's.

Not that any of it matters after I turn the ignition key. First there's the patented zing of Ferrari starter motor, then the engine catches, going instantly from nothing to effortless baritone hum. Click the shifter through the slotted gate into the dogleg first, bring clutch and throttle together gently and I'm off to a surprisingly easy start. So easy, really, that I might as well just nail it and see what happens... In the space of a deep breath the landscape is insanely flashing by, the polite wee hum is now a manic bellow immediately behind my left ear, and that needle rushing across the top of the dial as the rear tyres fight for grip isn't the rev counter, it's the speedo. Umm, think I'll back off a bit now, enjoy the comfy seats, maybe try out the radio.

While I'm waiting for my heart rate to stabilise, I learn that exploring country lanes isn't exactly the Testarossa's strong suit; factor in the marginal rear quarter visibility and it isn't really a town car, either. Find yourself an open road, though, **»**

550's dramatic shape is every inch a Ferrari, but interior – chrome gear gate aside – fails to excite

and there is no doubt it's the fastest thing available for anywhere near the price. Unless, that is, Miami Vice makes a comeback. Now let's try that loud pedal again, shall we?

550 Maranello

The 550 Maranello premiered in 1996 as a V12 replacement for the F512M, and was Ferrari's first big front-engined GT in 20-odd years. If the 512 isn't wild enough for you, the 550 has 45 more bhp and cuts almost a half-tick off the already infinitesimal 0-60 time – and the real essence of the car is obvious from merely my first 20 seconds with it.

From behind the wheel of Paul's Mercedes estate I hop straight into the 550, square up to the edge of the road, and, having never driven the model before, pull out with hard right-hand steering lock and what doesn't feel like a lot of throttle at the time. Oops. Wrong. The car launches with a vengeance, kicks the rear end out in a pendulum-swing attempt at a 180, and as the traction control warning starts flashing I counter-steer, short-shift to second, collect up a small side-step to the opposite side, and press on down the road grinning, never letting off the power the whole time.

The moral of the story? Any car that not only saves a stunningly ordinary driver from his own silliness but also flatters his ego in the process has got to be a fantastic piece of machinery. In retrospect, I'm fully aware that what I deserved was an embarrassing 10mph half-spin and stall; what the 550 gave me instead was a bail-out so neat and subtle that it felt as though I did it all myself. A big part of that, of course, was thanks to an unobtrusive and sensitive

550 MARANELLO (1996-2002)
SPECIFICATIONS

Engine
5474cc all-alloy V12, dohc, four valves per cylinder, Bosch M5.2 engine management system, variable inlet and exhaust manifold geometry

Power
485bhp @ 7000rpm

Torque
419lb ft @ 5000rpm

Transmission
Six-speed manual or four-speed automatic, rear-wheel drive

Suspension
Coil and wishbone, driver adjustable shock absorbers, anti-roll bars, electronic traction control

Brakes
Four-wheel vented discs, servo-assisted, ABS

Weight
1690kg (3718lb)

Performance
0-60mph 4.3sec
Top speed 199mph

Value
£50,000-70,000

traction control system; more importantly, though, the car has such a sense of balance and overwhelming competence about it that you feel capable and at ease from the moment you take the controls. Good as the 512M is, drive it and the 550 back to back and the difference in confidence-factor stands out like a sore thumb.

Too bad then about the Buick Riviera interior styling. The Maranello may have the Testarossa beat on comfort and ergonomics (the heel-and-toe is to die for) but, when it comes to fighter pilot fantasies, the 550 doesn't have a clue. Worst yet, the car we're driving has those miserable four-point 'racing' harnesses and as always they're complete bollocks: hard to get into and impossible to adjust, so I usually wind up getting bitchy and sitting on them; how safe is that? Sadly, they're part of our test car's otherwise desirable World Speed Record option package, along with stiffer suspension and the carbonfibre seats; it could have been worse, they could have given the WSRs a wretched paddle-shift gearbox.

Where the Maranello shines, though, is in driving refinement. This is a remarkably civilised automobile, and that statement doesn't have to be qualified with 'for a car capable of 200mph'. Potter around the village at a walking pace or blast from that to 100 before you can finish this paragraph, it's all the same to the 550, and come to think of it, the car would probably do either in sixth gear. Unlike the Testarossa, it's actually comfortable with normal everyday driving, and never gives the impression you've got too much car for the circumstances. Furthermore, the service ▶▶

'THE 550 HAS SUCH A SENSE OF BALANCE AND OVERWHELMING COMPETENCE ABOUT IT, YOU FEEL CAPABLE AND AT EASE FROM THE MOMENT YOU TAKE THE CONTROLS'

Servicing and repairs

Predicting any car's repair bills is a thankless task, so let's just say that any major repairs on any Ferrari can be extremely expensive. Fortunately, the models we're considering are rugged customers, and the most common non-scheduled service is a run-of-the-mill clutch replacement. For a Testarossa, that's a £1000 job; for the 550 it's £1600, and on a Daytona you'll pay £1300. Both of the newer models require an annual service at £550, plus another service package every 12,500 miles for roughly £1000. Cambelt replacements on the 550 are £800. Daytonas, with no package requirements and chain-driven cams, are somewhat more 'as and when', but Russell Smith recommends budgeting about £1000 per year for purely routine maintenance.

Insurance

The mere idea of insuring a Ferrari is enough to bring out a cold sweat, but the real figures are less painful than you'd think.

A quick call to Aon Classic Car Insurance (01483 706000) listed the following factors for a policy: a second-vehicle F512M worth £60,000, garage-kept at the author's home in Oxfordshire, usage rate of 3000 miles per year, driver with a clean record and aged sufficiently, shall we say, to have been holding a full licence when the Daytona was new.

The annual payment quoted was £1142.30, provided a Thatcham approved alarm/immobiliser and a 24-hour pro-active tracking device are fitted. If your car doesn't have the former (and most cars of this type already will), expect to pay from around £325 for a Thatcham Category One; trackers start at roughly £500, usually plus an annual subscription charge of £100 or so.

'IT'S CLASSIC PININFARINA, AND EVERY TINY DETAIL IS PERFECT, RIGHT DOWN TO THE SWEEP OF THE REAR WING AROUND THE TAIL LAMPS AND THE HEARTBREAKING CURL OF THE DELICATE DOOR HANDLES'

Without doubt the best-looking of the trio, Daytona doesn't give much away in real-world speed, either

techs at Bob Houghton, who have seen it all, use terms like 'bulletproof' in connection with the 550; engine builder Peter North says it's the best production Ferrari engine ever.

The bottom line: the 550 is one of the fastest and most usable Ferrari 12s to date, and being plentiful and just barely out of production is priced seriously low for its performance level. Expect to pay in the mid-50s for a good one, but be aware that very short-mileage cars loaded with goodies have recently sold in the 60s, and this rare right-hand-drive WSR with its cherished registration number is over £70,000. Very collectable, that.

365GTB/4 Daytona

So exactly how is a car that costs three times as much as a decent Testarossa still a good buy? Well, when it comes to classic V12 Ferrari GTs, it's getting hard to find any for less. To be honest, a better question would be how come the Daytona is so inexpensive; it is, after all, the fastest and most powerful of the traditional front-engined Ferrari coupés, and the company's last such design before the Commendatore died. Iin the '80s, those very factors drove the prices to staggering levels as speculators beat each other with sticks for the opportunity to invest in them. After the sharks moved on, prices took a tumble, and then more or less went stagnant; there are, in the end, a helluva lot more Daytonas than 330 Spyders or 250 Lussos.

That analysis may have changed, however, even in the

365GTB/4 DAYTONA (1968-1973)

SPECIFICATIONS

Engine
4390cc all-alloy 60-degree V12, dohc, two valves per cylinder, six 40mm Weber DCN carburettors

Power
352bhp @ 7500rpm

Torque
318lb ft @ 5500rpm

Transmission
Five-speed manual, rear-wheel drive

Suspension
Coil and wishbone, telescopic shocks, front anti-roll bar

Brakes
Four-wheel vented discs, servo assisted

Weight
1600kg (3520lb)

Performance
0-60mph 5.8sec
Top speed 175mph

Value
£80,000-105,000

interval before you read this: Daytonas have enjoyed a slow rebound over the last few years and enough market experts consider the car undervalued to place it at the top of our 'Cars to Watch' list for 2006. Bob Houghton sales manager Simon Jordan says good ones are currently at £95,000 or slightly above, and an additional 10 percent increase this year would not be at all out of order. If you can see a 365GTB/4 in your future (in reality, the nickname Daytona was a motoring journo thing), it might be wise not to dither.

Just don't count on buying this one; it's the property of long-time Houghton customer Dick Young, and it's not for sale. It's interesting to note that Dick has owned lots of Ferraris over the years, and while he presently also has a 550 Maranello, it's the Daytona he takes along to trackdays. He's been doing it since he bought the car in 1999; the car remains bog-standard and has suffered no mechanical breakdowns at all.

Now, to be fair, there's something I should probably mention: I think the Daytona is the most beautiful mechanical object ever created. It's classic Pininfarina, of course, and every tiny detail is perfect, right down to the sweep of rear wing around the tail lamps, the alloy-spoked steering wheel, and the heartbreaking curl of the delicate door handles. Do not even think about reverse parking the thing, however, because not a single one of those artistically sculpted corners is visible from the driver's seat. Not that you'd be tempted – the low-speed steering really is as stiff as you've heard, and although it does lighten up appreciably once in motion, all of the Daytona's

controls are high-effort by modern standards. No surprise: they were by '70s standards too, if memory serves. They are, on the other hand, fabulously precise, and at the speeds the car was designed for, that's what matters.

On paper against the two newer cars the Daytona doesn't look quite as fast as it used to; on the road in the real world it's a different matter. The six big Webers don't flow very well at low revs, and off the line the car is a bit flat, but keep up the revs and it's a monster. To be honest, though, I didn't expect the handling to be so impressive anymore, but there must be some magic in tall tyres and chassis compliance: on surfaces where the others felt slightly jiggly at speed, the old Daytona was poised, relaxed... and faster than dammit.

In fact, I have to admit I cheated just a touch with the Daytona. After the photos were all done, the notes taken and the day was officially over, I ducked out for one last drive down our quiet side road. I ran it up the gears and gave it its head, letting it wind on through the long, fast corners, listening to the sweet V12 howl and drinking in the moment. Those who would not call this car a bargain, as the saying goes, know the price of everything... and the value of nothing.

So, 365, 512 or 550? When it comes to sheer performance and entertainment for your money, the Testarossa is a winner, hands down, and if they weren't good cars to boot, Ferrari wouldn't have sold so many when they were new; trust me, they weren't giving them away. Testarossas were supercars then and still are, so let the classic car market's Inverse Law of

> 'REMEMBER ONE THING WHEN IT COMES TO FERRARI PRICES: THEY'RE NOT CARS, THEY'RE COLLECTORS' ITEMS, AND COLLECTORS RARELY WANT SOMETHING THERE'S PLENTY OF'

Supply and Demand work in your favour for a change.

Think of the 550M as the next logical step up. It's faster, more user-friendly and cheaper to maintain – if a tad less visceral, too, it must be said.

The Daytona? Well, it isn't often that you get the chance to own a true masterpiece, is it? At any price.

Thanks to Dick Young, and to Bob Houghton, Simon Jordan and Russell Smith at Bob Houghton Limited. For more information on the dealership, visit www.bobhoughtonferrari.co.uk, or call 0870 90 40 430. △

THE MISSING LINK

No celebration of Ferrari's ultimate supercars would be complete without a track test of the fearsome and incredibly rare 288 GTO Evoluzione, the car that linked the GTO and the F40. Tony Dron drives it

Photography: Phil Ward

There are rare and

exotic Ferrari supercars, and then there's the 288 GTO Evoluzione, the rarest – and fiercest – of them all. The idea was to create a Group B racer from the 288 GTO. Although the gorgeous-looking GTO had been built to Group B regulations, it never had serious potential as a competition machine. The 288 GTO Evoluzione, on the other hand, most certainly did. This was the car with which Ferrari intended to take on and beat Porsche's high-tech 959 Group B racer. Unfortunately we shall never know how that contest might have turned out.

Though it was probably too fierce for rallies, even tarmac events, the Evo looked a winner as a circuit racer. The trouble was that Group B rally cars were proving alarmingly lethal and the regulations were changed. Group B racing just fizzled out, leaving this beast all dressed »

up with nowhere to go. A handful were sold to appreciative private collectors and the model was then quietly forgotten by most of the world, though it led directly to probably the most famous Ferrari supercar of all, the F40.

It remains a staggering machine. The standard 288 GTO, with its 400bhp V8, was quick enough but the heavily modified Evoluzione produces a breathtaking 650bhp and has a brutally functional, carbonfibre racing body. The whole

thing weighs a mere 940kg dry. Much lighter than that of the GTO road car, the Evoluzione's bodywork can be lifted away in seconds, giving racing mechanics instant access to the vital parts. And that brutal, purposeful look resulted from a ruthless quest for effective race-circuit aerodynamics. It contrasts startlingly with the soft, flowing grace of the standard car.

Ferrari experts at Auto Italia magazine, who have been trying to pin down the full story for

some years, conclude that six 288 GTO Evos were made between 1985 and 1988. The first, they say, was a modified version of the original 288 GTO prototype. Two more completely new cars were made before the racing programme was officially abandoned.

The design was then adapted to create the F40, and it was only after the F40 had gone into production, the experts claim, that three more 288 GTO Evoluziones were made to satisfy the requests of individual collectors. One thing is beyond doubt: the 288 GTO Evoluzione is a genuine missing link in the chain of Ferrari supercar development.

Work had begun on race-tuning the GTO's engine in 1983, altering valve timing, fuel injection settings and the compression ratio, which was raised from 7.6:1 to 7.8:1. Turbo boost pressure was raised from 0.8bar to 1.7bar and all of that lifted the 2885cc V8's power output to 530bhp.

The next step included the use of larger IHI turbochargers, still running at up to 1.7bar. The turbos themselves were water-cooled and there were also large intercoolers. In this form the engine was known as the F114CK and produced that stunning figure of 650bhp. The suspension was given the racing treatment but the fundamental design was unchanged. Probably the biggest chassis alteration was the

Evoluzione ain't pretty, but it's certainly functional, and it's still brutally quick. You can almost see the F40 bursting out from within the prettier GTO shape, as the focus turned to aerodynamics and downforce. Evo was also used to test the latest composite body materials.
Left: do you get the feeling that cooling was a major issue?
Bottom left: cockpit is pure racecar

'What really gets your attention, though, is the devastating acceleration'

use of spherical bearings instead of bushes for wishbone location.

When the programme was canned, Ferrari decided to use the Evo as a basis for a no-frills road car, which became the F40. The basic engine and transmission layout were retained, but power was reduced to 478bhp (the 650bhp engine wasn't suitable for road use). Apart from being very much prettier than the car we see here, the F40 was also bigger, about 160kg heavier and a great deal more civilised. That's fair enough: the Evo was pure racecar, whereas the F40 was also intended for road use.

Some years ago, when this car (serial number 79887) first came into the care of Tim Samways' company, Sporting & Historic Car Engineers Ltd, I have to admit that I hadn't a clue what it was. I knew it was a Ferrari, obviously, but like almost everyone else I hadn't noticed the existence of the 288 GTO Evoluzione back in 1985. As far as I'm aware, no track test had appeared anywhere. Until now, that is.

Because I race several cars prepared by Tim, I was lucky enough to be invited to some RMA trackdays – two days at Spa and two at the old Nürburgring – back in November. And this was one of the cars I drove, along with a Porsche GT1, a Ferrari F50 and other good things.

This ended some years of frustration over the Evo. I had been offered a drive in it several

times but something had always gone wrong, usually the circuit being red-flagged because of someone else's accident. At least after one such outing at Silverstone we had a decent batch of photographs to show for our efforts.

But this time it finally happened.

Spa-Francorchamps is one of the world's great, superfast road circuits and the ideal place to enjoy a real blast in a device like this. And right away the excitement starts to build. The Evo is

left-hand drive and has a proper racecar cockpit – purely functional with no sound-deadening or unnecessary trim. The doors are incredibly light and flexible; from the inside they open by tugging on plastic-sheathed cables. There's a small hole in the Perspex side windows with a sliding panel for ventilation.

The driving position is excellent, with plenty of headroom and large pedals designed for accurate use. The seat holds you firmly in place »

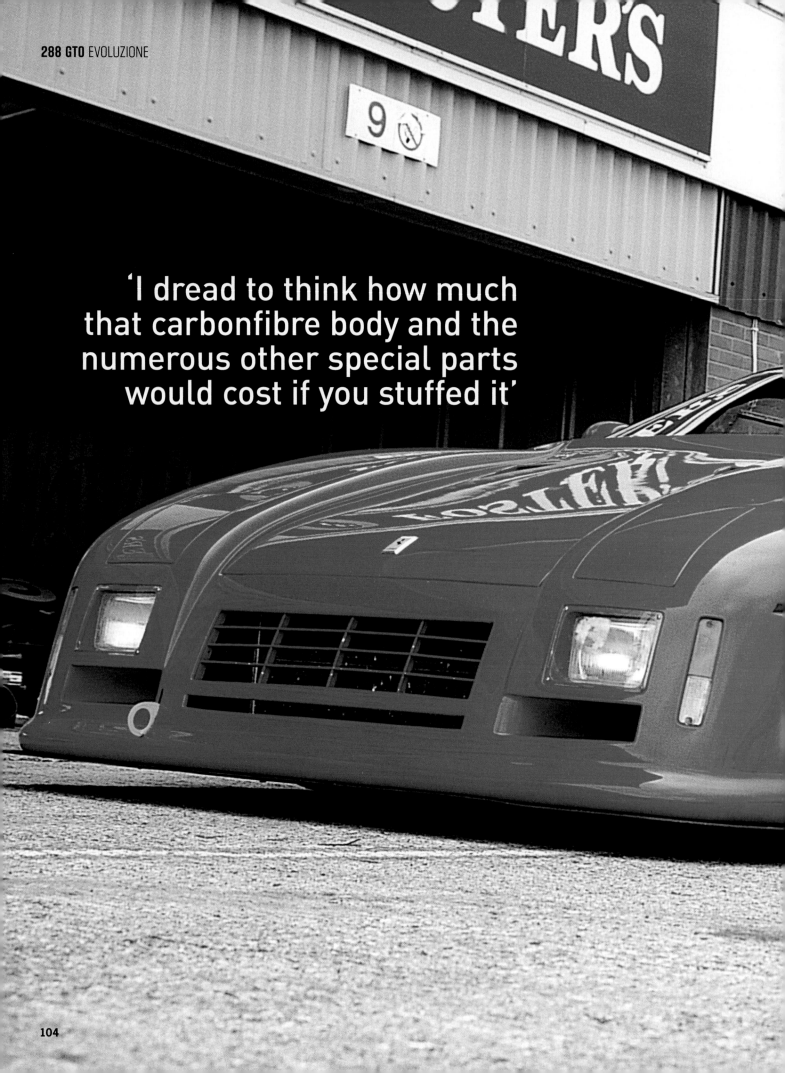

'I dread to think how much that carbonfibre body and the numerous other special parts would cost if you stuffed it'

and the steering wheel is ideally positioned. The instruments are small and there's no speedo.

The steering feels great, the brakes have good feel and reassuring bite, and as I pick up the pace, the body holds the whole thing down. The gearbox, however, is pretty horrible: smooth, quiet changes require a firm, positive, practised hand. You can shift cleanly eventually, but the 'box is not a source of pleasure.

What really gets your attention, though, is the devastating acceleration, coupled with an incredible howl from the engine on full throttle. The Evo is eye-wateringly quick and we're getting the full 650bhp today. (A fault in the turbo adjustment means we can't reduce the boost from its maximum setting even if we want to!)

And it's the sudden rush of power that demands you take the 288 Evoluzione seriously. The chassis is capable of high cornering forces but you need to concentrate hard on opening the throttles accurately. Put your foot down hard a moment too early and all hell could be let loose. You can make sense of it on a circuit but it demands a very highly-developed sense of throttle control.

This car and Spa's famous Eau Rouge ultra-fast S-bends make an interesting combination. Get halfway close to what it can do through there and the first word that comes to mind is 'terrifying'. Quickly followed by 'awe-inspiring'.

Pulling 7500rpm in top – 165mph – quite easily on the following straight, I ease off before the red line. It would have hit 172mph at 7800rpm (with different gearing, 230mph is very much on) but I didn't want to risk breaking it. Running a car

**FERRARI
288 GTO
EVOLUZIONE**

SPECIFICATIONS

Chassis
Tubular steel frame, braced by composite side pieces and aluminium floor

Body
Carbonfibre composite

Engine
90deg V8, 2855cc, biturbo

Cylinder head
Dohc per bank, 4v per cyl

Max power
650bhp @ 7800rpm

Max torque
450lb ft @ 4000rpm

Transmission
Five-speed manual gearbox, rear drive, ZF lsd

Suspension
Double wishbones located by spherical joints, coil springs over double adjustable gas dampers, anti-roll bar

Brakes
330mm diameter ventilated discs, front and rear

Weight
(dry) 940kg

Power/weight
702bhp/ton

0-60mph
n/a

Max speed
230mph (est)

'You can shift cleanly eventually, but the gearbox is not a source of pleasure...'

like this is a pretty daunting prospect. Thing is, it's worth a huge amount of money. I dread to think how much that carbon-fibre body and numerous other special parts would cost if you stuffed it.

Speaking to Tim Samways, he has been pretty impressed by the GTO's basically robust qualities. The weak point has proved to be the gearbox. It's a racing dog 'box, relatively crude and heavy in use, and the gearchange can knock itself out of adjustment, requiring fairly regular fettling. Tim has also had to change the original electronic fuel injection and ignition kit. It had become unreliable with age so he chose to replace it with Motec equipment and that has banished a persistent misfire problem.

He had to change the wheels too. When new, the GTO had 16in wheels but original-type Pirellis are no longer available in that size. Tim went for 17in wheels of the same width, fitting lower profile Dunlop slicks, which maintain the same rolling radius. It was a successful switch, because this Evo handles really well.

It's just that rapid surge of power that needs watching. Put it like this: the 288 GTO Evoluzione made the F50 I drove seem overly civilised, almost easy by comparison, and I never thought I'd see myself writing that.

Engine is a development of the GTO's V8 with twin IHI turbos. At full boost, it produces 650bhp from just 2855cc – that's over 225bhp per litre! Just six examples of the Evoluzione were built, only five are still believed to be in existence, and one of those is retained by the factory. Ferraris don't come any more special than the Evo

Dark Horses

In among the iconic Maranello machines that we know and love, there
are one-offs and special-bodied cars that only true enthusiasts
recognise. These are a few of our favourites...
Words: Jack Carfrae

» P4/5 by Pininfarina

Ferrari Enzo not quite distinctive enough for you? Then why not have it rebodied with the flavour of the glorious late-60s 330 P3/4 sports-racer? That's what one super-rich American enthusiast did. Car collector James Glickenhaus located the last remaining box-fresh Enzo, still shrouded in white plastic and undriven, and had it shipped to Pininfarina, where it was fitted with a Jason Castriota-designed body.

Little separates the car from the Enzo mechanically. The 660bhp V12 and F1-style six-speed gearbox remain. However, the P4/5's kerb weight is lower than that of the Enzo, and the revised body is both lower and more aerodynamic, as well as being arguably more attractive.

Glickenhaus has a deep love of the P3/4 and P4 Ferraris – he owns chassis no 0846, worth £6 million. Which explains why he was willing to part with more than £500,000 for an Enzo and an additional £2.4 million for its conversion...

'Volpi commissioned Bizzarrini to cannibalise
his 1961 Ferrari 250SWB and build
something that would be faster than a GTO'

250 Breadvan

The Breadvan came about largely as a result of Enzo Ferrari's famous bloody-mindedness. Count Giovanni Volpi di Misurata was its instigator after Enzo refused to deliver a pair of 250GTOs. Enzo's argument was that the Count financed the company ATS, which employed ex-Ferrari types such as Bizzarrini, Chiti and Gardini. So Volpi commissioned Bizzarrini to cannibalise his 1961 Ferrari 250SWB and build something that would be faster than a GTO.

Bizzarrini's flair for aerodynamics resulted in the deep curves, knife-edged nose and high, truncated tail. The engine was moved back much further than in a standard 250SWB to sit behind the front axle, improving the handling. The number of carbs doubled to six dual-throat Webers, which required an unusual teardrop-like clear cover to house them. Suspension was tweaked, GTO wheels and tyres were added and the whole car sat much lower than in standard form. In competition it proved as fast as the GTOs but unreliable.

» 575 GTZ

Zagato's long-standing association with Ferrari was reignited in 2005 after a 12-year hiatus. The Milanese coachbuilder is renowned for producing striking and distinctive bodywork and the GTZ is no exception.

It was Japanese collector Yoshiyuki Hayashi who contacted Zagato with the commission. Hayashi already owned a standard 2004 Ferrari 575M, which became the platform for the Zagato body. Noriko Harada, head of design at Zagato, took the responsibility of penning a new body for the 575.

The brief was simple: to make a completely individual car, and this allowed Zagato free rein with the design. The 575 was inspired by the hallowed Ferrari 250GTZ, arguably one of Zagato's best looking cars, which just happened to be approaching its 50th anniversary. The 575 GTZ has Zagato's trademark 'double bubble' roof and two-tone paintwork.

» 375 America Agnelli Speciale

Whilst it is difficult to identify the most valuable or exotic of Gianni Agnelli's cars, almost certainly the most *individual* is the Ferrari 375 America. The 375 was far from his only Ferrari, or even his only coachbuilt one. He bought a 166 MM Barchetta, bodied by Touring of Milan in 1950, and a 212 Inter coupe by Vignale two years later.

However, the Speciale was Agnelli's first truly bespoke Ferrari. Easily the fastest of his collection, the Speciale was revealed on Pinin Farina's stand at the Turin Motor Show in 1955. Agnelli ordered 'a Ferrari that doesn't look like a Ferrari'. The deep green and dark red colour combination, sloping pillars and clear roof panel are all unique.

The Speciale was easily the most elaborately styled of Pininfarina's Ferraris, and had the blistering performance to back up its appearance with a 0-60 time of 6.5 seconds.

'The Speciale was easily the most elaborately styled of Pininfarina's Ferraris, and had the blistering performance to back up its appearance'

'Robert Jankel claimed to have used only the windscreen, A-pillars and doors from the donor vehicle. Of all bespoke Ferraris, this was the most outlandish'

» Daytona Shooting Brake

Over a decade after the original 250SWB Breadvan, Luigi Chinetti Junior, son of the renowned New York Ferrari dealer, decided to turn his hand to automotive design. He found a willing backer in Florida property developer Bob Gittelman, who liked Luigi's design for a 330GT estate but wanted it adapted for a Daytona chassis.

To build the creation, they turned to the Surrey-based Jankel Group, a subcontracting coachbuilder for Rolls-Royce and also home to Panther Westwinds. The finished article was an unusual but impressive piece. Robert Jankel, the craftsman behind the car, claimed to have used only the windscreen, A-pillars and doors from the donor vehicle, while the interior was completely reworked with unorthodox but tasteful use of wood and leather. Of all the bespoke Ferraris, this was probably the most outlandish.

THE FIRST TIME

Nothing quite matches the anticipation and sheer thrill of
driving your first Ferrari, as Jethro Bovingdon reports

Pictures: Andy Morgan

Ask the average car nut why Ferraris are special and you'll probably hear a lot of stuff about unrivalled motorsport heritage filtering through to the road cars; the famous recipe of race-it-on-Sunday sell-it-on-Monday. It's a great notion to conjure with, but I grew up in a time when the Ferrari F1 car's only chance of obtaining any silverware was to ram-raid the McLaren or Williams pit garage and scream off into the distance. That's assuming it would actually make it down the pit-lane – never a certainty in the wilderness years.

So much for that theory. Then there's the aura that surrounds all those exquisite looking and fantastically capable road cars. Well, when I was 10 years old, Ferrari's flagship was the unwieldy Testarossa. Then there was the Mondial – not one of Pininfarina's greatest designs, I

think you'll agree. The 328 GTB looked gorgeous but was getting a bit long in the tooth, and the 288GTO, a rare '80s highlight, had been and gone. Ferrari simply weren't delivering the goods on road or track for the vast majority of my childhood.

And yet I love Ferraris. Nowadays I can appreciate the glory years of sportscar racing and we're in the midst of a Ferrari-dominated era in F1. But I haven't suddenly started dreaming about owning a car wearing the Prancing Horse. From an early age I've imagined myself at the wheel of a Ferrari – made my Dad stop if one was parked on the street, or driven to Ferrari garages just to steal a few precious minutes poring over the cars in the showroom and on the forecourt.

Countless other kids my age no doubt did the same – and very few of them would have known much about the racing history, nor would they have known much about Enzo as the architect of a legend. To be honest, like me at 10 years old, they probably didn't care that much. When a low-slung bright red Ferrari pops and bangs past you on the over-run it captures the imagination. It's an emotional thing, pure and simple. F1 had nothing to do with it – and even if somebody more enlightened had told me that Ferrari road cars were trading almost exclusively on the badge and the noise, I'd still have wanted one. Testarossa in white, sir? Yes please.

Fortunately as I got a bit older and a bit wiser Ferrari was turning the corner. The 512TR brought the Testarossa bang up to date, and with the 288GTO's replacement, the F40, Ferrari

reasserted itself as the maker of the ultimate road car, complete with that 202mph maximum. You can keep your 959, I thought. And now I'm in the privileged position of working on a motoring magazine in an era when Ferrari road cars can be counted amongst the very best in the world. Game on.

Now, there are only a limited number of magazine articles that you can base around a Ferrari and I reckon I must have flogged every last one of them to the bossed at **evo** in an effort to get behind the wheel of one of the red cars. The closest I came was when we had a 360 Modena booked for a couple of days for a feature about gearboxes back in issue 37. But insurance problems meant a drive wasn't on the cards.

Still, good things come to those who wait and now that I'm here standing next to a 355 Spider outside Ferrari dealer MHT in Gloucestershire the length and frustration of the build-up seems perfectly fitting. This is a moment to savour and I realise now that jumping into a Ferrari on a rainy day on my first week at **evo** just wouldn't have been right. Glorious sunshine, empty roads and an enthusiastic passenger in the shape of MHT salesman Nick Hill; as first Ferrari experiences go, this has got to be right up there.

Above: MHT salesman Nick Hill runs through the starting procedure for a paddle-shift Ferrari. Bovingdon's head is already at 7000rpm…

Above: it's always good to see a man who's happy in his work...
Bovingdon smiles the smile of someone who knows that life really
doesn't get much better. Driving any Ferrari for the first time is a
pretty major event, but a 355 Spider, top down, sun shining, is special

Nick is keen to demonstrate the 355's performance and cornering prowess – but for me that's secondary. I've driven much faster cars, grown used to mid-engined agility and high cornering Gs. I just want him to pull over, hand me the keys and let me acquaint myself with a legend. Which he does. Good man.

As he hands me the unremarkable looking key I can't hold back that same grin that cracked across my face when I'd see or hear a Ferrari as a kid. It's a little embarrassing, really, when you're standing with a guy who drives and sells these cars everyday. To make it worse, photographer Morgan – who is fresh back from the launch of the 575 Maranello and a veteran of plenty of Ferraris – is capturing my child-like delight on film. No chance of pretending I took it all in my stride back at the office, then.

I slide into the black leather seat, put the key in the ignition and then pause. This is something of a golden moment, a rite of passage for someone like me (or you). Then I fire it up, hear that quad-cam V8 whoop into life, select first with the paddle-shift, and coolly burble away on a light throttle opening. The next 30 minutes or so will live with me forever.

I'm determined not to put my road tester head on and instead immerse myself in the noise, the view and all the sensual pleasures of finally piloting a Ferrari. Fittingly the engine is the dominant ingredient and I quickly forget any notion of taking it easy for the sake of salesman Nick. Just as any of you would, I give the 355's engine its head – over and over rushing to the red line with a smile a mile wide, letting the screaming V8 take off speed on the approach to corners with the help of gratuitous downchanges.

The 355 feels scorchingly quick at the top end, its damping is fantastic and as I spear over some of the best roads that Gloucestershire has to offer I can't help feeling that life doesn't get much better than this. The 355's dynamics are just about spot on, save for the slightly slow steering,

but it's the screaming engine and the knowledge that you're driving the dream car of millions of petrolheads that really gets to you. Like I said, it's an emotional thing.

In fact it's pretty close to a religious experience and despite the fact that I've driven a number of incredibly exotic, expensive and desirable cars the excitement and sense of privilege are undiminished. It helps that the 355 is a fantastic driver's car but to be honest I can't imagine the

anticipation or thrill being any less if I was given the keys to a less dynamically accomplished Ferrari, or if the F1 team were still searching for that elusive world championship. In fact the only thing that didn't match up to my dreams as a young boy can be attributed specifically to Ferrari's motorsport programme. There was no open gate gearbox, no metal-on-metal clack-clack to accompany gearchanges. That's the problem with motorsport improving the breed... △

RED ROUTE

The Mille Miglia was the greatest road race and a key part of Ferrari's heritage. Richard Meaden recalls the final event, and drives part of the classic route in the fabulous 360 Spider

Pictures: Gus Gregory & Klemantaski Collection

Edward Eves

Above: Brescia, May 1957, just before the start of the final, fateful Mille Miglia, and the crowd in the Piazza Vittoria press in on the cars during scrutineering

There's never been

anything quite like the Mille Miglia. One thousand miles of flat-out racing through towns and open country, it was motorsport on a massive scale. Open to a vast array of machinery, from 750cc bubble-cars to hugely powerful V8 and V12 road-racers based on the Grand Prix cars of the day, the Mille Miglia brought drama, danger and heart-pounding spectacle to the doorsteps of five million Italians.

Starting from Brescia in the far north of Italy, the route twisted its way to the Adriatic coastline. From here it hammered down through Rimini and Ancona, then across the Appenine mountains to Rome, up along the backbone of Italy through Tuscany, over the Futa and Raticosa passes, before descending into Bologna, Modena and eventually back to Brescia. It was a race that consumed an entire country.

Last run as a competitive event in 1957, the Mille Miglia is still a source of fascination for many enthusiasts. Not only was it the scene of some of the most Herculean drives in motor racing history, but as the vast majority of the

route is still used as public road today, it is possible to follow in the tyre-tracks of Moss, Fangio and other heroes from a bygone age.

It's this promise that brings us to the Piazza Vittoria in the heart of Brescia, home of the Mille Miglia and the starting point for our story. We're privileged to be driving Ferrari's new 360 Spider; the ideal car for such a challenging drive as it shares technology and takes inspiration from today's F1 cars, just as the quickest Mille Miglia racers did in 1957.

Some of you might be of the opinion that a soft-top Ferrari is a soft option, the purer driver's car being the coupe. That has often been the case in the past, but the 360 was designed with a barchetta version in mind from the start, giving it the best possible chance of matching the dynamics of its berlinetta brother.

The result is, without any shadow of doubt, the world's most savage soft-top: all-aluminium construction, 400 searing horsepower, six-speed Formula 1-style paddleshift transmission, acceleration from 0-60mph in under 5sec, 100mph in a shade over 10sec, top speed of »

'400 searing horsepower, six-speed Formula 1-style paddleshift, 0-60mph in under 5sec, top speed of 185mph, and an engine note that makes your ears bleed'

MILLE MIGLIA
Km. 1564

Left: the route of the Mille Miglia (Thousand Miles). Actually it's 972 miles long, but what's 28 miles between friends? **Above:** the Piazza Vittoria on a quiet Sunday morning. **Right:** Collins and Klementaski roar out of Brescia and into the dawn. Closeness of crowds made the event special – and ultimately deadly

185mph and an engine note that makes your ears bleed. If this isn't in keeping with the spirit of the Mille Miglia, then I don't know what is.

On race day in 1957 the piazza would have been a seething mass of exuberant Brescian spectators, race officials, bustling mechanics and impatient drivers, but now, at 7am on a peaceful mid-summer Sunday morning, the town has sensibly elected to stay in bed.

It's a fittingly dramatic starting point for such an enormously gruelling race, with the imposing Post Office building towering above us, making us feel very small and insignificant as we fire off a few static shots of the Spider.

Hood down it's a wonderful sight, a combination of sharp, pointy 21st century edginess and classic Ferrari curvaceousness. It's the twin humps behind the head restraints that do it for me, harking back to its racing forebears that still haunt this historic civic square.

Fittingly, Ferrari were race favourites in '57, although previous winners Stirling Moss and

trusty co-driver (and journalist) Denis Jenkinson were much fancied in their fearsome 400bhp Maserati 4.5. The fastest cars started last, the final few leaving Brescia at around 5.30am, their exact start time being their race number.

Car number 534 was Ferrari's best hope of victory, driven by British ace Peter Collins, accompanied by Louis Klemantaski, the finest motoring photographer of his day, who would act as Collins's co-driver and document the race from the passenger seat of the 4.1-litre V12 Ferrari. It's mostly his amazing work that you can see in this feature, alongside that of **evo** photographer Gus Gregory, a man after Klemantaski's heart if ever there was one.

Static shots completed, we leave the town square and complete the short blast along cobbled backstreets to the start ramp at Via Rubuffone. The 360 Spider ambles across the uneven surface, its Pirelli tyres slapping a knobbly, staccato beat on the road, while its electronic dampers coolly isolate the washboard »

Left: the Ferrari of Wolfgang von Trips is pushed towards the starting ramp. The number signified the start time (5.32am). **Below:** Piero Taruffi accelerates away from the Rome Control. **Above:** a typically eye-popping stretch of road. **Opposite above:** the Collins/ Klementaski 335S moves in on two slower cars

bumps. Pedestrians and cyclists whistle and wave as we pass, their passion for fast, fabulous cars still wide awake even at this ungodly hour. The sun is low but warm, the atmosphere already sticky – a precursor to another scorching Italian summer's day.

From Brescia the route heads first for Verona. Running pretty much straight and flanked by elegant, proudly shuttered town houses and tall horse chestnut trees, the road out of Brescia is nothing short of a suburban drag strip. Almost immediately you're struck by the fierce challenge that lies ahead. Given the freedom (and courage) that Collins and Klemantaski had in 1957, we too could quite easily be topping 160mph within

Peter Coltrin

the first few miles; instead the 360 is chomping at the bit as we burble through traffic.

When gaps do appear, its razor-keen throttle response and flip-shift gearbox whip us to indecent velocities. But to avoid a night or two's stay at the pleasure of the local carabinieri, we reluctantly settle for enjoying the excellent low-speed ride quality, incredible tractability and short but fabulous stabs of engine noise bouncing off the buildings and trees.

After a quick cappuccino stop in Verona, it's clear that even a brand new, bright red Ferrari is going to struggle to cut through the dawdling ranks of Fiats and Alfas, so we decide to hit the autostrada to make up some time on our journey

to Ravenna on the Adriatic coast. The 360 Spider is a sublime companion. We've had the roof down from the start, the air-conditioning taking the sting out of the sun and the clever aerodynamics eradicating any buffeting, even when cruising at over 100mph.

From Ravenna the road is eerily straight, and it is nothing short of awe-inspiring to think that even if we could travel back some 43 years, to May 1957, our state-of-the-art 400bhp, all-aluminium, all-singing, all-dancing 360 Spider would struggle to keep pace with Ferrari's Mille Miglia racers. Imagine the Mulsanne straight running from Calais to Paris and you'll have some idea of what the coastal run is like.

It's hard to imagine the noise, heat and fierce concentration that would have filled the Collins/Klemantaski Ferrari as they hammered flat-out towards Ancona in excess of 170mph, peering into the shimmering heat-haze in an attempt to pick out fast approaching and potentially lethal S-bends. For a more graphic illustration of how fast they were travelling, take a look at a map of Italy and imagine driving from Brescia to Rome via Verona, Ferrara, Ravenna, Rimini and Ancona in just five hours, including pit stops and the tight mountain run inland. That's an average speed of 107mph, in case you were wondering. I almost feel embarrassed to be driving on the same piece of road.

'For the first time, the 360
feels like it's working hard, the
engine note hard and insistent'

It's the first week of the Italian holidays, and judging by the number of mopeds and cars on the road, all of Italy has decided to have a day at the seaside. By now it's clear that there's no way we'll be able to do the whole route and complete all the photography we need, so rather than slog all the way down the coast and then across the mountains to Rome, we high tail it west for an overnight stop in Tuscany. It's a wise decision, as tomorrow we'll be tackling the toughest section of the Mille Miglia, over the hills of Radicofani towards Siena, Florence and the switchback-laden Futa and Raticosa passes.

Fascinating though it was to experience the wide open coast roads, they didn't tell us much about the Spider, but the breathtakingly quick SS2 that slices through the wonderful Tuscan

scenery of the Val D'Orcia is a far sterner test. The climb to Radicofani is the most memorable, the road cresting and falling like a bitumen rollercoaster. For the first time, the 360 feels like it's working hard, the engine note remaining hard and insistent, the cornering and braking loads more severe. Increased engine and wind noise apart, there's no other indication that you're in a convertible. The steering and turn-in are as sharp and instantaneous as in the berlinetta, and the suspension is just as taut and tolerant of mid-corner bumps. It feels together, cohesive, tight as a drum. Without pushing beyond eight-tenths we're still chomping through this fabulous stretch of road, but the proximity of trees, not to mention walled bridges positioned on tight bends, means it is an unforgiving playground for

journalists, and a potentially lethal test for the race drivers of 1957.

With close to the same power as our 360, but with narrow tyres and no seat belts, let alone traction control or ABS, it is no wonder drivers described competing in the Mille Miglia as like walking a high wire without a safety net. Nevertheless it was a challenge the very best drivers relished, and a perfect backdrop on which to display their dazzling talent.

By this stage Collins and Klemantaski were romping away from the opposition. Not only were they ahead of all their Ferrari team-mates, but such was their pace that Moss and Jenkinson's 1955 record time was seriously under threat. One of the fastest drivers in the world at the time, Collins was looking forward to

Right: classic Klemantaski study of Collins' gloved hands on the 335S's wheel. With its 4-litre V12 producing around 400bhp, it was capable of over 180mph. Above left: 360 Spider retraces the Ferraris' tracks across the Futa Pass. Top right: Alfonso de Portago and co-driver Edmund Nelson leave their last stop. A tragic end to the race awaits

the tortuous mountain stages of Futa and Raticosa, just north of Florence. Despite having been driving solidly for more than seven hours, he was confident of stretching his lead even further. If only he knew what really lay ahead, for as Klemantaski described in his report for Motor magazine, it would be a far sterner test than they imagined.

'Every corner of note had a crowd on it, all waving us on excitedly, for they knew we were winning. This was second gear work all the time, with a drop down to first gear for the hairpins. The steering ratio was such that on the hairpins, using the wheel and the throttle, Peter could get around without having to take another bite at the wheel. As we reached the top, the sky to the north of us, towards Bologna, was black and soon

a physically welcome but morally distressing rain began to come down.

'Goggles misted up, faces were stung by the raindrops, and then, worst of all, we began having difficulty in getting around right-hand corners. Almost simultaneously a slight crunching noise was occasionally heard, coming from the region of the back axle, on left-hand bends, and I tried to think of a connection between the two. The rain stopped, leaving the roads terribly slippery, then it turned to sleet...'

Quite where Collins got his stamina from is beyond me. It really is an incredible run, the seemingly endless SS65 twisting and turning first over the Futa and then, almost immediately after, the Raticosa pass. From wide open sweeps and fresh air corners, the character of the road

can change in an instant as trees close in, casting deceptive shadows across the tarmac.

The prospect of man-handling Collins's fearsome car along this stretch on streaming tarmac sends a shiver down my spine, but now, just as you'd hope, the 360 is absolutely in its element. The feelsome power steering and darty front end carve into the tightest turns with utter confidence. You begin to push yourself harder and harder, relying more and more on the Spider's reserves of grip and poise.

Having the latest generation F1 shift is a massive help too, as it allows you to grab a lower gear as soon as you see the corner tightening. Seemingly no matter how late you flip down a gear the Spider remains planted to the road, and the shifts are absolutely flawless, with perfectly judged ❯❯

'Most corners are second-gear,
the fastest straights topping out in
the shrieking upper reaches of third'

heel-and-toe style blips every time. The upshifts are now smoother too, proving conclusively that the second generation F1 system is much more satisfying than it used to be. I've always been a bit of a Luddite when it comes to self-shifting transmissions, but now even I have to concede that it frees you to concentrate more on the road ahead. And you need to if you're to stay one step ahead of the SS65, for it seems to take great pleasure in reeling you in with its hypnotic, rhythmic sequences of second- and third-gear corners, only to pitch a savagely tightening switchback into your path.

Any mistake, no matter how small, punches your pounding heart into the back of your parched throat. To be a passenger here, as Klemantaski was in the leading car, must have been like being caught in the eye of a storm, pitched and tossed from corner to corner, his life held in Collins's whirling hands.

If the brain-out missile-run down the coast from Rimini to Ancona was an almost sadistic test of the driver's courage, and the true domain of those with the tallest final drive and the biggest balls, then the relentless tarmac bobsled run from Florence to Bologna was for the artists. Only those with sensitivity, exquisite car control and an almost telepathic ability to read the road ahead could balance their over-powered machines on a knife-edge for hours at a time.

The great masters of the Mille Miglia could cope with the monstrous demands of both sections, but for me this is by far the most exciting, largely because it is immeasurably less daunting. Most of the corners are second gear, with the fastest straights topping out in the shrieking upper reaches of third. There's less time to think here – you simply become immersed in your own world, concentrating on each and every bend, revelling in the acceleration, noise and fierce braking forces. For the drivers of 1957, making a mistake over the Futa or Raticosa was one of the few occasions where it would simply mean an exit from the motor race rather than the human race.

Above: one of the great motor racing photographs. The Collins/Klemantaski Ferrari leads the race as it charges through the mountains on the approach to Rome. The record time set by Moss and Jenkinson in 1955 appears to be under threat

It would still have hurt though. Wicked concrete fences line the valley side of the road, while equally unyielding rock, trees or stone walls run close to the left-hand side of the car. In the Mille Miglia heyday much of this would have also been lined with people, drunk on the spectacle, not to mention the odd swig of Chianti. Today we share the SS65 with a constant stream of noisy, hard-ridden Ducatis. Mixing it amongst them is fun, and gives us some idea of what it must have been like for Collins and the other Scuderia Ferrari drivers dicing amongst themselves and dispatching slower traffic.

The corners come at such a pace it is almost impossible to watch your mirrors and the road ahead, but the 360 has so much in reserve that it is laughably easy to empty our mirrors of distractions. None of the bikes can live with the combination of 400 prancing horses and the adhesive qualities of four Pirelli P Zero tyres. It takes no more than three corners to leave them in our venturi-tunnelled wake. On tight, tricky roads like this, the 360 rules supreme.

We've criticised the 360 Modena for washing into understeer prematurely, then snapping into oversteer when you inevitably back-off. On these hill-roads, the corners either seem to be tight unsighted second-gear bends or fast sequences that you can straightline with confidence hard in third or fourth. At high speeds, understeer isn't a problem, and you can feel the underbody aerodynamics start to draw the Ferrari closer to the tarmac. In the thick of the tight stuff, the fact that the front-end gives in before the rear conditions you to focus all your concentration on your braking points and turn-in speed. There simply isn't the scope for gathering up an excess 5 or 10mph's worth of scrabbly understeer, so you don't push into the last 10 per cent or so of the Spider's ultimate ability. With Armco, stone walls, trees or – worse still – a fresh-air drop waiting to embrace us, it just isn't worth it.

Besides, the 360 has another weakness. The brakes, though fade-free and feelsome, have a spookily unpredictable habit of what feels like prematurely triggering the ABS when really pressing on. They can be fantastic for five or six corners, then for no apparent reason the pedal hardens, pulses at a higher frequency than you'd get by triggering the ABS, and halves the

Left: the Ferrari team cars being prepared in the courtyard at Maranello, which is where, 43 years later, our man Meaden reluctantly hands back the keys to the 360 (far right). **Top right:** Collins/Klemantaski about to take the lead. Mechanical woes would end their race just 100 miles from the finish

effectiveness of the brakes for a heart-stopping moment. It's impossible to drive around, and can happen when the brakes are very hot or stone cold. Weird.

Collins and Klemantaski had more to worry about. After surviving the sleet-covered mountain roads, their ailing Ferrari deteriorated rapidly, the battered transmission finally failing just 100 miles from an historic victory.

As the knotted tarmac starts to untangle its way towards Modena, we decide to peel off the Mille Miglia route and head to some of our favourite roads in the hills above Maranello for one last blast before taking the car back and reluctantly handing over the keys.

We knew it already, but this last thrash just goes to underline the 360's magnificence and addictive spirit. Far from being the poor relation, the Spider feels more immediate and involving than the Berlinetta, if only because with the roof down you genuinely fear for your hearing every time the revs pass 6000. It's the sort of car for which you'd set your alarm for 4am to drive to Scotland and back just for the hell of it.

Collins and Klemantaski's misfortune opened the door for fellow Ferrari driver Piero Taruffi to win the Mille Miglia after failing to finish more than a dozen times. In fact Ferrari would fill the next two places as well, but celebrations were short-lived when news filtered through of a massive accident involving another Ferrari driver, the King of Spain's nephew, the Marquis de Portago. Witnesses reported his Ferrari careering off the road at well over 160mph having suffered a puncture or possibly a wheel or transmission failure. Completely out of control

the car was launched into the air by a granite mile marker and snapped a telegraph pole in half before spearing into the crowd with hideous consequences. The Marquis and his co-driver were killed instantly, along with nine spectators. Inevitably the Mille Miglia died with them. They were less than 30 miles from the finish.

The speed and power of the cars (the factory teams were talking of cars hitting 200mph in 1958), and the huge uncontrolled crowds lining the streets finally became too lethal a combination, leaving the Italian Authorities with

no option but to abandon any future events.

There's no doubt the Mille Miglia was a brutal race, an anachronism, but it was also an intrinsic part of Italian culture, and formed a major thread that runs through Ferrari's genetic code. The 360 Spider might be a million miles safer and more refined than the racers of 1957, but you only need drive it on the Mille Miglia route to discover that the same raw passion that powered them to victory in 1957 still burns inside every one of Maranello's red cars. Peter Collins would have approved.

S O L A R
P O W E R

We go chasing the sun with two of the most desirable
convertibles money can buy: Lamborghini's Gallardo
Spyder and Ferrari's F430 Spider

Words: Richard Meaden   Photography: Andy Morgan

Gallardo's wedgy shape loses none of its aggression in decapitated form, helped by a profile that, with the roof folded away, is uninterrupted by protrusions, from wing mirror to tail light

The Touareg driver

never saw it coming. Mesmerised by the receding sight and sound of the slate-grey Gallardo Spyder burbling through the bustling Highland town of Glen Coe, his eyes are glued to his rear-view mirror rather than the road ahead.

Watching incredulous from the Ferrari, it's clear that the Corsa innocently parked in his path doesn't stand a chance. Nailed by two and a half tons of wayward SUV with a grimace-inducing *crump-thump-skrrsssch*, the hapless Vauxhall hatchback buckles under the force of the collision, while the distracted Touareg driver wears the expression of a man who's just swallowed his own tongue, snapped from blissful daydream to waking nightmare in one sickening thud.

It's an unexpectedly dramatic end to a fabulous two days in which we've enjoyed these Modenese roadsters to the full amongst the towering peaks and tranquil lochs of the Scottish Highlands. It's also a timely reminder of just what a spectacle these cars make amongst ordinary traffic. They certainly made an impression on the Corsa...

Rewind 48 hours, and John Hayman and I have just emerged from the Gallardo after a five-hour haul from Northamptonshire to Livingston, on the outskirts of Edinburgh. We've not lowered the roof once, which feels a bit fraudulent, especially when the sun's out, but when you've got big miles to cover you stick to the motorways, at which point the appeal of open-top driving is torn to shreds in the conversation-killing slipstream. Better, we think, to keep our powder dry until tomorrow, when we're due to collect the Ferrari F430 Spider and make for the roads that lie between Fort William and Mallaig, on the west coast. Not only are they a fittingly epic stage on which to drive these two towering supercars, but the endless Highland days see the sun rise at just after 4am and darkness held at bay until almost 11pm. Short of driving to Scandinavia, nowhere packs more sunshine into a summer's day. Let's just hope Mother Nature doesn't rain on our parade.

We arrive bright and early at Rio Prestige (the supercar hire company) to collect the Ferrari which they have kindly made available to us for this test. It's finished in the classic combination of Rosso Corsa paint and Crema leather, and looks quite a sight. More of a surprise is that it's also fitted with an equally 'classic' manual gearbox and steel brakes, rather than the optional F1 paddle-shift transmission and carbon stoppers »

'The Lambo is more pleasingly proportioned than the Ferrari'

that the vast majority of F430 customers are reported to select. It's fortunate in a way, because the Gallardo has three pedals and a stick, too, so we'll be comparing old-school like with like.

For the most part, the drive up to Fort William isn't a memorable one, thanks largely to a satnav system that seems determined to take us through every unremarkable, traffic-choked town between Edinburgh and the Highlands. Things pick up once we get to Crianlarich, from which point the roads open, the traffic abates and Hayman decides to stretch the Lambo's legs.

It's quite something to follow, even when you're chasing it in a Ferrari. Emitting a ground-shaking soundtrack, the chiselled Gallardo, with its broad, square shoulders, looks just as cohesive as the coupe from which it's derived, and is more convincingly sculpted and pleasingly proportioned than the slightly awkward-looking Ferrari.

The reason becomes apparent when we decide to drop the roofs. The complexity on show in both is jaw-dropping, even if the assorted whirring, clunking and straining of electric motors is ultimately a bit of a palaver compared with the simplicity of, say, a BMW Z4. But while the entire engine deck of the Lambo tilts skywards to allow the tightly folded hood

to contort itself into the small rectangular compartment close to the rear scuttle, the Ferrari's mechanism is confined to the small humps that surround each roll-hoop, thereby preserving the beautiful 'display case' engine cover.

While it's wonderful to see the red crackle-finish of the Ferrari's 4.3-litre V8 on show, the roll-hoops, roof cover and humps interrupt the F430's sharp lines. The Lamborghini's design is tidier and less disruptive, even if it does deny you any glimpse of the equally impressive V10. The flat, vented deck runs in one unbroken line from cockpit to tail lights, creating a beautifully clean, lean profile. It also incorporates a brilliant glass anti-buffeting screen, which raises and lowers like an electric window from the bulkhead behind the seats. It's a very neat touch.

With our pace increasing and the road punctuated by some wicked crests, dips and smooth sequences of corners, both cars are finding a fast rhythm. The F430 has that distinctive, pointy-steering feel of the Berlinetta, with very keen front-end responses, and it's an easy, satisfying car to thread along these unfamiliar roads at a brisk pace.

I have to confess to inadvertently pulling at the indicator stalk a few times and wondering why the transmission wasn't delivering a punchy shift, before remembering, somewhat

GALLARDO SPYDER
SPECIFICATIONS

Engine
4961cc V10, dohc per bank, aluminium alloy head and block, dry sump

Power
513bhp @ 8000rpm

Torque
376lb ft @ 4500rpm

Transmission
Six-speed manual, four-wheel drive, rear lsd, ESP, ASR

Suspension
Front and rear: double wishbones, coil springs, dampers, anti-roll bar

Brakes
Ventilated discs, 365mm fr, 335mm rr, ABS, EDB

Weight
1570kg

Performance
0-62mph 4.1sec (claimed)
Top speed 195mph (claimed)

Basic price
£131,000

embarrassed, that I should be stirring that quaint alloy stick down by my left knee. It feels odd in a car I normally associate with fingertip immediacy, but the action of the clutch and lever are light and positive, and the evocative ball-topped stick is soon clacking between the fingers of the hallowed open gate in satisfying style.

We power through the humbling beauty of Glen Coe, two raucous wedges of aluminium darting through the holiday traffic, in pursuit of possibly the only car and driver combination capable of upstaging us: a Hertz rental Focus driven by photographer Andy Morgan. By the time we pass Fort William and find the roads we enjoyed so much back on eCoty 2003 (**evo** 063), it's well into the afternoon, and Morgan's shutter finger is clearly getting itchy.

While he and Hayman busy themselves with some shots of the Lambo, I make off with the Ferrari for a solo drive. It's a sharp, dashing blade, the F430. Quick-witted and hungry for revs, it thrives on the fast, flowing roads that characterise this remote region of Scotland. You need to work at it, though, for although tractable, the V8 really hits its stride, and finds its voice, above 5000rpm. Below this the engine emits an intrusive but not especially pleasant blare. Stay above it, though, and the Spider builds to a shrieking crescendo that ricochets off the craggy outcrops at the road's edge, filling the open cockpit with echoes of Fiorano.

There's tremendous feel to the brakes, and excellent stopping power too. In fact, for all but the most extreme road and track use they feel plenty strong enough, even if they do look a bit weedy behind the five-spoke alloys. It's delightful to brake hard into a corner, roll your ankle across to execute a heel-and-toe downshift and find the brake and throttle pedals perfectly placed.

Less satisfying is the scuttle-shake that shivers through the structure over major road imperfections. It's not catastrophic, but it is noticeable, and it does diminish the sense of precision you feel compared with the Berlinetta. Worse is the pronounced kick-back through the steering wheel when you hit a mid-corner drain-cover or pothole with the inside front wheel. It really does jar, especially when the flow of information is otherwise detailed and delicate. The impact wrong-foots the car for a moment or two. If you've experienced the rock-solid integrity of the Berlinetta, it comes as quite a shock.

Inherently, though, the F430 Spider's chassis balance remains exciting, exploitable and minutely adjustable. Entering one of the countless tightening corners a shade too fast, I'm forced to brake deeper than ideal, and wind-on another quarter-turn of lock. It's one of those moments that makes you catch your breath, but the Ferrari is with me all the way, tightening its line without complaint, the mildest

F430 SPIDER
SPECIFICATIONS

Engine
4308cc V8, dohc per bank, aluminium alloy head and block, dry sump

Power
483bhp @ 8500rpm

Torque
343lb ft @ 5250rpm

Transmission
Six-speed manual, rear-wheel drive, E-diff, CST

Suspension
Front and rear: double wishbones, coil springs, 'Skyhook' adaptive damping, anti-roll bar

Brakes
Ventilated and cross-drilled 330mm discs front and rear, ABS, EBD

Weight
1505kg

Performance
0-62mph 4.1sec (claimed)
Top speed 193mph+ (claimed)

Basic Price
£127,050

'The F430 is a sharp, dashing blade,
quick-witted and hungry for revs'

Quiet, open roads of the
Highlands provide the
perfect territory for
enjoying cars with this
level of performance. An
11pm sunset is an added
bonus. Gallardo's raucous
exhaust note emphasised
when you have the top
down (and a towering
rockface close by)

'The Gallardo is astonishingly sure-footed and surreally rapid'

hint of understeer the only outward sign of my misjudgement. For an agile, prickly mid-engined car, it's impressively forgiving.

By the time I return to Morgan's photographic base on the shores of Loch Shiel, he's done with the Gallardo. Having got really dialled-in to the F430's responses, the contrast between it and the Lamborghini is immediate and startling: where the Ferrari is all about lightness of touch, the Gallardo is a chunky heavyweight that demands a more muscular approach.

The clutch, gearbox and steering are all

significantly weightier than the Ferrari's. The engine brims with bombast from the moment you fire it up, and the chassis feels beefier, all four tyres planted squarely on their treadblocks where the Ferrari always feels light on its feet. It's a more physical, all-encompassing car. You drive it with your forearms rather than your wrists, and while you don't have to bully it, you do have to assert yourself before the Gallardo gels.

If there's one element that dominates the Gallardo experience, it's the engine. Moments when the Ferrari can be caught off the boil simply don't exist in the Gallardo, for the big-capacity V10 has grunt to spare. It pulls with conviction from nothing and even manages an inspiring second wind between 7000 and 8000rpm, it's note hardening, the sense of acceleration intensifying just when you think things are about to tail off. Full-revs with the roof down is a cataclysmic experience, the brutal, tortured howl surely ranking as the most visceral cry since Chewbacca did his flies up too quickly.

The gearshift isn't as quick as the Ferrari's, thanks to the extra effort required and also

because of a slight gristly feel as the lever passes the neutral plane of the gate. It's not obstructive, in fact if you like to get stuck in, the shift's meaty quality can be particularly satisfying. However, for sheer speed and purity, the Ferrari 'box is best, although I can't help thinking that the superb F1 system better suits the F430's character. Heresy I know, but...

Wearing Pirelli P Zero Corsas, the Gallardo is a gripfest on these smooth, well-surfaced roads, long swooping corners highlighting its high-g abilities to perfection. Coupled with weighty steering that increases in effort and feel as you pile on the speed and cornering force, it's astonishingly sure-footed and surreally rapid. The one fly (or should that be midge?) in the ointment is a pronounced self-centre effect that tries to pull the car straight when you relax your grip on the suede-rimmed wheel as you see a corner begin to open out. You can drive around the trait, but you're forced to steer the car straight rather than let the wheel flow through your hands, which compounds the physicality of hustling the Gallardo.

As ever with the Gallardo, the brakes come in for criticism. Not for their lack of staying power, as the roads here are fast and flowing rather than tight and twisty, but for the initial lack of feel and pedal travel, making smooth driving, not to mention effective heel and toeing, less than intuitive. Again, you do learn to compensate with time and familiarity, but it could be better.

It's been a memorable day's driving, but it's not over yet, for we have an appointment with a sunset on the shores of the Sound of Arisaig. Keen to get prepared in plenty of time, Andy leads us back to our hotel, the amusingly named Cnoc-na-Faire in the equally chucklesome Back of Keppoch. The plan is to check in, dump our bags and head back out, but as we assemble outside at just after 7pm the sun's still beating down as though it's mid-afternoon. As photographers are as fickle as farmers when it comes to the prevailing weather conditions, we go back indoors 'to let the light soften', whatever that means...

Three fine courses and two hours later, it's still broad daylight, but with Hayman twitching every time a resident orders a pint of lager, we decide to head back out, finally running out of light at 11pm. The nights really are short this far north.

Next morning we have a few more shots to do before heading back to Edinburgh. It's an opportunity to let thoughts and feelings crystallise, and hopefully find a way of picking a winner.

As we've established, faults are few and far between. The Ferrari's biggest failing is the mild but noticeable scuttle-shake and serious steering kick-back, while the Lambo suffers from clumsy brake feel and a lack of delicacy. Neither, it has to be said, are as pure or precise as their tin-roofed relatives, but hasn't that always been the case?

After many memorable miles, deciding between them is almost impossible. Both deliver a rare sense of occasion and connect you with the world you're driving through like few other

cars, their speed, sound and involvement all top-drawer. In all honesty, when two cars are this closely matched, aesthetics are as good an arbiter as any.

Forced with making a choice, we'd go for the Lamborghini. While annoying, with time you learn to drive around its ham-fisted brake response and the steering's over-keenness to self-centre, but the Ferrari's steering grates more. Perhaps the surgical precision of the Berlinetta means the F430 has more to lose in the transition to Spider. That to our eyes the Gallardo also gets the styling nod seals the win for Sant'Agata, but by the slimmest of margins.

If you fancy following in our tyre-tracks and recreating this test, Rio Prestige now has both a Gallardo Spyder and an F430 Spider. For more information on these and other cars in Rio's impressive fleet, visit www.rioprestige.com or call Edward Legge on 01506 466911.

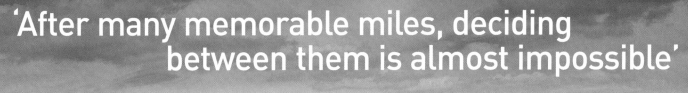

'After many memorable miles, deciding between them is almost impossible'

POWER TO THE PEOPLE

Capitalism meets communism as we drive a
Ferrari 612 through the People's Republic of
China. Driving adventures don't come any bigger

Words: Richard Meaden | Pictures: Andy Morgan

阜康收

服务

落实科学发展观，构建社会主

诚信服务奉献社会

CHINA
15 000 RED MILES

法拉利

PIRELLI

PIRELLI

CT 250ND

临时入境
00032

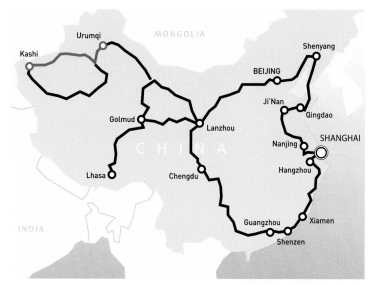

The sign says

'Urumqi', but it might as well say 'Centre of the Earth', for the gritty, grimy, smog-cloaked Chinese industrial city in which we've just arrived is, according to the Guinness Book of Records, further from the ocean than any other major city on the planet. So why are we here, some 1400 miles from the sea and, seemingly, a million miles from home? Why, to drive a Ferrari 612 Scaglietti of course! Surprised you had to ask.

We've been invited to take part in Ferrari's '15,000 Red Miles' tour of China, an incredibly ambitious stunt that must surely rank as the most significant Italian foray into the Far East since Marco Polo decided he'd pack-in his job manufacturing mints with holes and do a bit of travelling.

On August 29, a pair of Maranello's finest 2+2 supercars (one red with a silver nose, the other silver with a red nose) set off on a record-breaking journey around this vast country, from the vibrant city of Shanghai on the east coast to Shenzen in the south, then to the mystical Tibetan city of Lhasa, high in the Himalayas, and then to Urumqi in the far north, which is where we come in.

The mammoth tour has been split into 11 sections, with a fresh pairing of journalist and photographer put into each car at the beginning of every leg. Our portion of the journey promises to be a corker, requiring us to drive from the middle of nowhere, sorry, Urumqi, to Kashgar, westernmost outpost of the People's Republic of China and age-old cultural and commercial crossroads on the ancient Silk Road. All that stands between us and there are 850 miles of tarmac and gravel roads that will take us over mountains that make the Alps look like molehills, and through arid deserts that stretch as far as the eye can see. Drive stories don't come much bigger.

Opposite: toll booth on road out of Urumqi (we saw lots of booths but rarely anyone collecting money). **Top left:** route of '15,000 Red Miles', with our leg in red. **Top:** lots of carts but very few cars in Urumqi. **Above left:** first fuel stop (petrol is around 30p a litre). **Above:** everywhere you go there are men in uniforms; this one's at the entrance to a national park

While Ferrari wanted to keep the Scagliettis as close to standard as possible, certain essential modifications have been made to protect them from the rigours of China and its rugged terrain. First and most obvious is the increased ride height, upped by an inch or two to stand a chance of coping on loose, uneven surfaces, and a set of Pirelli SottoZero winter tyres to find some grip and resist punctures. A pair of funky mesh grilles cover the headlights, while sturdy underbody protection plates guard the sump and other vulnerable components from rocks. The boot space is occupied largely by an auxiliary fuel tank, which boosts the 612's capacity to a whopping 150 litres for a dawn-till-dusk driving range. With their flamboyant liveries, they »

look like refugees from the Paris-Dakar Rally Raid. Essentially, though, each Scaglietti's core hardware remains, from the 540bhp dry-sumped V12 and its assorted management systems to the six-speed H-pattern gearbox (silver car) and F1 paddle-shift transmission (red car).

Only a fool would embark on such a trip without back-up, and in support of the two Ferraris are two Fiat Palio estate cars, two Iveco minibuses carrying luggage and spares, and a very cool camouflaged military-spec Iveco 4x4 for what eventuality we're not quite sure but, to be honest, we hope we don't find out. There are nine full-time expedition members – three Italian technicians from Maranello, led by Gigi Barp, an official photographer, a video crew and a friendly gaggle of Chinese interpreters and fixers. Together the convoy makes quite a sight.

A surprise late addition to the group is Ferrari's esteemed and charismatic head of PR, Antonio Ghini. That he has chosen to participate in our section of the drive is the best hint yet that of the 11 legs we could have landed, Urumqi to Kashgar promises to be particularly special. Naturally, Ghini is as excited and fascinated as we

are at the prospect of exploring the breathtaking terrain and experiencing the ancient cultures of this far-flung corner of China, but he's also keen to explain the purpose of the '15,000 Red Miles' expedition, and Ferrari's aims for the emerging Chinese market.

'We didn't want simply to import our cars to China, build showrooms and offer them for sale,' he says. 'We know it's a complicated market and that it's not going to be easy to sell Ferrari in China. Driving for pleasure is firmly established in the West, but over here you only drive to get from A to B. Driving just for the sake of it is an alien concept. People aspire not to drive themselves but to be driven, in a large saloon or SUV. This is a sign of status for wealthy, successful Chinese. As for two-seater sports cars, well, the feeling is often, "Why would I want one of those? What am I going to do with that?"

'Of course, the first Chinese GP was a big step towards introducing the Western passion for

cars. We had a great race that year, too, so our red cars made a big impression, but it is important to us that we show to China that there is more to Ferrari than racing. This 15,000-mile adventure is our opportunity to do that, and by driving around China we aim to show that we've taken the time and made the effort to get to know the country and its people, to explore its culture and experience the spectacular scenery. You could say we've come to pay our respects to China.'

After an eventful night in Urumqi, where your intrepid journo and snapper manage to sidestep Chinese culinary delicacies such as Ox penis and Turtle's Rim (whatever that is), not to

'Through the chaotic traffic we adopt the local technique of hooting first, asking questions later'

These policemen strolled up and took turns to have their photos taken with the Scaglietti. Speeding isn't really an issue in China, but the official limit is 80kph on the highway, 40kph in towns. Though most people we met had no idea what a Ferrari was, they recognised that it was something special. **Opposite top:** early-morning street scene in Urumqi – vast junctions like this are typical and, when they're heaving with traffic, crossing them is an adventure in itself. **Below left:** farmer's truck had sheep on upper deck, cows underneath. **Bottom left:** nomadic shepherd had found a riverside pitch for his tent. **Bottom right:** boulders block our path

mention escaping the over-friendly attentions of numerous 'professional' women stalking the hotel's Romance Bar – I know, the clue's in the name, but we were very jet-lagged – we're pleased and relieved to be leaving next morning.

By night, Urumqi is a sprawling, neon-splashed melting pot of large Western-style hotels, vast, shadowy industrial areas and shambolic, decaying slums. By day the city is robbed of the neon's rose-tint, leaving your eyes to cast across a grubby skyline torn asunder by fast-growing ultra-modern skyscrapers, fume-belching brick chimneys reminiscent of our own industrial city-scapes of the 1800s, and, as though making a last stand against the march of Westernisation, traditional Chinese temples perched on distant hilltops. This strange scene

is crowned by a thick blanket of smog, and the air is heavy with the sooty tang of coal smoke. Welcome to China.

We take no prisoners as we break free of Urumqi, tucking the nose of our 612 into the wake of the Chinese-driven Iveco van, cutting through the chaotic traffic as though protected by some unseen forcefield and adopting the local technique of hooting first and asking questions later. Braking or any kind of steering-based avoidance manoeuvre is regarded strictly as a last resort, but by some miracle the traffic not only flows freely but with good humour.

It's already clear that while the average Urumqian on the street doesn't fully grasp what the Ferraris are, let alone what they are

doing cutting and thrusting through the Xinjang province's capital city, they know that they are something special, particularly when a gap in the traffic allows us to unleash a healthy lunge of second gear. However, it's also obvious that while the Scagliettis have immense curiosity value, the 5m-long supercars are but chocolate fireguards to many of the down-to-earth Chinese, who appear to reserve genuinely lustful looks for the more practical charms of the Iveco vans and rugged off-roader.

Once clear of the tumultuous city centre, Urumqi's high-rise zone soon sinks to low-rise slums that hug the muddy fringes of the road. Cars and buses are scarce, their number replaced by lorries, tractors and donkey-carts. The people are dirt-poor but industrious, and while they all have clothes on their backs and food in their bellies, it surely won't be long before they begin to wonder when China's burgeoning economy will benefit them. One thing's for sure: the gulf between the outskirts of Urumqi and the manicured, high-gloss image of China that's beamed into our living rooms from F1's Shanghai finale extends beyond simple geography. Even our Chinese guides refer to what we're seeing as 'the real China', and I for one believe them.

We stop to brim the convoy, not the work of a moment with two cavernous Scaglietti fuel tanks to fill, but with a bootful of PetroChina's finest we climb back into our silver 612S and watch as Urumqi shrinks in our mirrors. Despite the modifications, and the gruelling 6000 miles or so that have already passed beneath the Ferrari's wheels, our Scaglietti feels remarkably together. The ride is softer and the initial steering response has been dulled, thanks to the lateral give and squirm of the chunkier tyres' open treadblocks, but the 612 retains much of its commanding, imperious manner and makes effortless progress as we head into the open countryside. Bumps in the road trigger assorted rattles from the suspension but there's nothing

to suggest it's anything to worry about, and we soon settle into a steady, satisfying rhythm, rural China gliding past our windows.

In fact, although the signs say we're in China, the scenery's more like northern France, with long avenues of plane trees lining the road and broad pastoral countryside rolling away on each side. Only the growing spikes of the distant mountain ranges hint at what's to come. We've been climbing almost since leaving Urumqi, imperceptibly at first, but now, as we begin to look down on, rather than across, the fields of crops it's clear we're driving into the foothills of the Tian Shan range.

The sky is increasingly overcast and the edges of the road are closing in, jagged banks of rock

getting closer to the side window and casting a shadow over the car. The impression of being funnelled into a confined space is profound as we enter a deep and dizzying gorge that cuts its way through a series of peaks known as the Flaming Mountains. With a sheer drop into the river on our left, sheer rock face climbing to unseen heights on our right, and nothing but a series of red and white painted posts standing between us and oblivion, this road certainly focuses the mind.

The gorge winds on for miles, each corner revealing ever-more-spectacular views. In what will become a recurring game during our journey, the changing scenery prompts Morgan and me to think of where it reminds us of, and we decide that the gorge, complete with tumbling river, abundant pine trees and humbling scale is like the wilds of British Columbia or Yosemite National Park. The sense of solitude is marked as our incongruous string of red dots winds its way through this giant landscape, with only the occasional encounter with sheep-herders or impatient drivers of coal-laden trucks to break the sense of isolation.

As if to remind us of our vulnerability, the road appears blocked by a landslide. Rocks the

Above: compacted snow, sometimes with a glossy coating of ice, and a sheer drop on one side – the journey suddenly gets more interesting. Highest point is 4280 metres up. **Opposite page:** lorry has been stuck on this hillside for a couple of days; cement factory pumps dust into air already polluted by coal-fired power stations. **Opposite below:** the Iveco back-up vehicle, nicknamed Shaggy, and some shaggy locals

size of small cars litter our path and we're forced to take to a diversion onto a makeshift road built of scree and boulders. The red Ferrari is ahead of us, straddling the deepest ruts with aplomb, but then one wheel slips off the high ground and with a graunch the car is beached. We can hear the grinding and scraping on the undertray from our distant vantage point, but with some gentle fore-and-aft shunting the Ferrari frees itself and continues unharmed.   **»**

'You have to concentrate intently on

You could be forgiven for thinking that such remote, tranquil and beautiful mountains would be out of China's dirty, industrial reach, but no. Tucked away in this bleak, isolated place is a coal-fired power station. Smoke stacks pump clouds of fumes into the innocent mountain air, and all that's unfortunate enough to find itself downwind (including the grimmest town you've ever seen, and a school playground teeming with kids) is shrouded in a noxious fug of God-knows what. A few miles further on, a dust-caked cement works adds to the filth. I take some solace from the fact that we're doing our bit to improve the local environment, for thanks to its pollutant-scrubbing catalytic converters, the gasses coming out of the Ferrari's exhausts are surely cleaner and less harmful than the air which

entered its combustion chambers.

Whether it's due to the epic pollution or, as is more likely, the increasing altitude and rapidly decreasing temperature, the pine trees have long gone and the road now cuts through rocky snowfields, its surface a glistening, slushy grey-black emulsion of mud and stones. Ahead of us is a towering wall of white, topped with menacing crags. We can't seriously be driving up there, can we? Yes is the short answer, for as we get closer to the impossibly sheer face, a thin, zig-zagging road can be seen clinging to the mountainside by its fingernails. Look harder and it's possible to see lorries clawing their way towards the summit, inch by perilous inch. And we're next.

Though levels of tension have risen appreciably inside the **evo** Ferrari, the car itself is untroubled

by the situation, Pirelli tyres finding reliable, consistent grip, V12 lugging heartily despite the gruel-thin air, traction control system blissfully inactive, even when the sludgy gravel cedes to packed snow and then patchy ice. And so it's with buttocks clenched tight that we press on, rounding hairpin after treacherous hairpin, slowly making progress as the outside temperature gauge sheds degrees C. Then, just as the wind whips up and the temperature hits zero, our convoy stops. We all climb out, clinging to our cars for stability, and crane our necks to the heavens. Three tiers up we spot the problem: two, no, three lorries, stationary in the snow. Great.

From what our interpreters can gather, there was a heavy snowfall a couple of days ago and the trucks have been stuck ever since. Stuck? For

the road, avoiding the bigger rocks'

a couple of days! What the hell are we going to do now? Keep driving of course. So we climb slowly towards the stranded lorries, then teeter around them on the edge of the abyss before finally, triumphantly cresting the 4280m summit. It might be small beer compared with the 5200m the team reached on their run to Lhasa, but for Morgan and I this is our own personal Everest and we savour the moment.

What goes up must come down, and if we thought the icy ascent was a bit hairy, the view that greets us as we begin our descent makes our mouths go dry. Despite the sunshine and blue skies the downward run is just as snowy. In fact, thanks to the combination of sun and a cold wind, the surface has melted then frozen, turning the road into a 1-in-3 ice rink. It's a

challenge none of us is really all that keen on facing, but short of reversing back down from whence we came, radioing in a rescue helicopter or adopting the foetal position and crying for our mothers, there's nothing for it but taking a deep breath and pointing the Scagliettis down the mountain.

The trick, apart from making sure that each vehicle is separated by a healthy margin, is to build minimal momentum: just enough to keep going but not enough to have to rely too heavily on braking, for you get the feeling that should the car begin to run away with you, things would get very ugly very quickly. Amazingly the Scaglietti manages to find some front-end grip, which means we could steer away from the drop and into the rockface if all else fails, but apart

from a few faint zizzes of ABS and the occasional slither, the steepest section of ice passes without incident. And r-e-l-a-x.

After the initially scalp-prickling icy descent, the gravelly section that follows, though still steep, is more like fun. We get up some speed, and by quietly dropping back, away from Barp's eagle-eyed gaze, manage a few tentative slides on the loose surface. As the snow fades, bleak, fractured rock faces are revealed, and as the view opens out a little, barren boulder-fields stretch out before us. It's stark but less oppressive than the gorge, with a real sense of ever-expanding space and optimism. Eventually the rocky tundra is replaced by smoother, more habitable terrain, the highlight of which is a breathtakingly beautiful plain, lush with swaying, corn-coloured 》 grass and fenced by majestic, snow-dusted peaks. A freight train hoves into view, seemingly from nowhere, and runs parallel to us for a time before arcing gracefully in front of us as we approach a level crossing. Our surroundings look more like Mongolia – no surprise as we're relatively close to the border – and just as we think the scene couldn't get any better we catch sight of a herdsman on horseback with his flock of sheep, silhouetted against the velvety hillsides. It's a magic moment and a welcome distraction from the ragged gravel track on which we're attempting to make progress.

Pounded by the infrequent passage of overloaded coal lorries, it's a constantly shifting bed of crushed stone and semi-submerged boulders. The surface has two distinct lanes, the centreline and fringes marked by ridges of loose material that clatters and scrapes along the Scaglietti's belly every time I steer around parked lorries or herds of sheep. It's energy-sapping driving, for you have to concentrate intently on the road surface, avoiding the biggest rocks, straddling ruts and slowing for dips and hollows

that threaten to smack the Scaglietti's precious alloy nose. Dust from the lead car is choking and thick enough to mask oncoming trucks. Only a barked alert over the walkie-talkie prevents a sickening head-on impact.

Trucks aren't the only hazard, nor indeed are they the worst. That honour goes to the sinister motorcades of blacked-out Land Cruisers that overtake us, showering the Ferraris with stones and gravel as they pass. Police? Government officials? We never find out who they are, but if he spots them in time, Barp implores us to pull over and let them pass. It's a largely vain effort to protect the vulnerable bodywork and avoid a broken windscreen; by and large, even such evasive driving fails to save the Ferraris from a pebble-dashing.

Our progress is excruciatingly slow. At one point I make the mistake of looking at my watch and cross-referencing it with the odometer. Half an hour later I look again: we've done five miles. Another 30 minutes pass and I groan as the odometer confirms we've managed another 10 miles, bringing our tally to little more than

150-miles in just over seven hours. Right now I'm beginning to wonder if we'll ever get to our overnight halt at Korla.

And then, like a geological full-stop, the mountains and grassy, snow-dusted pastures cease without warning, the lush Alpine surroundings brutally butt-jointed to a vast, arid plain of near-lunar nothingness. It's as though God simply ran out of rock and inspiration. Squinting into the void, it becomes clear that the dustbowl is bisected by an arrow-straight strip of tarmac that pricks the shimmering, far-flung horizon. After a gruelling non-stop day-long slog that's seen us wind through wooded valleys, ascend perilous icy switchbacks and crest the snowy peaks of the Tian Shan mountain range, the parched, sandy fringes of the Taklamakan Desert are a new and menacing challenge. Our journey, it seems, has only just begun. △

Opposite, top right: you can travel through mile after mile of deserted landscape and then come across a town heaving with people. **Middle left:** Meaden at the wheel. **Middle right:** tarmac roads occasionally peter-out and you have to work out which side of an approaching truck to pass. **Bottom right:** big, Western-style hotels are among first signs of a changing culture

'Sinister motorcades of blacked-out Land Cruises overtake us...'

HORSE POWER

We figure the Ferrari 612 to find out if it meets its maker's claims
Words: John Barker Pictures: Kenny P

Top left: 612 disguises its size well from behind the wheel; it feels like a sports car, it goes like a sports car, but it also accommodates four adults in fine style

There have been

2+2 Ferraris for decades, some handsome and dynamic, such as the 1990s 456GT, some more accommodating but less agile and desirable, such as the 1970s 365 GT4 2+2 and its 400-series successors. The 612 Scaglietti sets out to be both dynamic and spacious, but handsome? At almost five metres long it's certainly imposing, but its proportions are – how shall we put it? – aesthetically challenging.

The engineering purist will see beauty, though, because function has dictated form. In pursuit of the best dynamics, Ferrari has configured the front-engined 612 to have the weight distribution of a mid-engined supercar, with 46 per cent of the mass over the front wheels and 54 per cent over the rears. To this end, the 5.7-litre V12 is mounted mid-front, aft of the front

axle line, giving the 612 its unusually long nose. Meanwhile, the cockpit is much more spacious than that of its predecessor, the 456M, with proper, adult-sized rear seats. As a consequence, it's generously proportioned.

The Scaglietti is a big car with a big price tag – £170,500 'basic', £7000 more with the F1A gearbox, and over £180K if, like this car, it's equipped with a few options. This 612 is ours for a week to do with what we will, so as well as driving it as far as possible (natch), we're going to performance test it at Millbrook Proving Ground, set a lap time around the West Circuit at the Bedford Autodrome, power test it on the dyno and weigh it with corner-weight scales. On hearing this, Ferrari asked if they could observe our test procedures, and sent a development engineer, Simone Caselli, from Italy to be present

when we obtained our data. We didn't object.

The long doors swing open easily, a reminder that the whole structure of the car is made from aluminium. The cockpit styling is more sports car than luxury saloon, busy with vents, dials and switches like an F430, and when you drop into the driver's seat you find yourself firmly supported and set low. Directly ahead there's a large rev-counter redlined at 7400rpm. The message seems clear: this is a sports car that just happens to have four seats.

Four good seats, too. Access to the rear is better than in most coupes, the front seats whirring forward to allow graceful entry to the sculpted rear buckets which feel superb for those of average build and height. For short runs they're more than acceptable for six-footers too, and despite the rising waistline, the ambience

'It devours the mile straight in a determined yet curiously relaxed lunge'

is far from claustrophobic, with a good view through the large windscreen.

The 5.7-litre V12 fires up quietly and idles demurely, only a deep rumble that seems to emanate from the bowels of the V hinting at its potential. Pull back on the right paddle for first gear, press the throttle gently and the automatic clutch juggles the bite deftly, keeping the revs steady as you pull away.

Both the shift speed and the 'Skyhook' adaptive dampers can be sharpened with a press of the Sport button, yet in regular mode the ride quality is firmer than you might expect. Transverse ridges and cats-eyes in particular can be clearly felt and heard. Press the throttle a bit harder to get the 612 shifting and it's as if it hits its stride, the supple yet keenly controlled primary ride disguising the pace of travel almost as well as the

remarkably linear delivery of the V12 disguises the rate of acceleration. When you glance at the speedo you're often travelling 20 or 30mph faster than you imagined...

The front end feels alert and incisive, much keener than you expect given the 612's scale, and there's so much poise, so much grip, that you soon

find yourself tackling corners with real spirit. Understeer simply isn't a factor on dry roads, and the traction that the 612 finds is exceptional. You have to be trying pretty hard to activate the stability control system. In Sport mode it loosens its grip slightly, the Scaglietti feeling beautifully composed with a smidgen of slip at the rear. It's »

the strangest thing to then glance in the mirror and see two people riding along behind you; it's so easy to forget they're there.

The shift speed of the F1A gearbox doesn't feel as fast as in the F430, even in Sport mode, but this suits the nature of the car, and it's smooth and responsive to both up- and down-shift requests. To be honest, you don't need to use the paddles as much as you do, because the naturally aspirated V12 has such a massive reach. Snap the throttle open at any revs in the first few gears and the 612 surges forward instantly with neck-straining urge. A bit more aural enthusiasm from the engine wouldn't go amiss, though. Climbing up the rev-range it passes through a hammery stage between 2000 and 3000rpm, but otherwise the cultured roar is pretty much as linear as the delivery.

We'd like to try the 612 with the sports exhaust that comes as part of the HGTC package. This costs a cool £16K but also provides revised gearbox software for shorter shift times and, more pertinently, carbon-ceramic brakes. It's a minor gripe, but the standard steel brakes could be improved. They're strong, progressive and full of feel when you're using them firmly, but there's a fraction of dead travel at the top of the pedal that shouldn't be there.

The conditions at Millbrook weren't ideal when we figured the Scaglietti. It was dry and there wasn't a breath of wind, but the temperature hovered between zero and -1 deg C. The Scaglietti's gearbox has a 'launch control' mode, but it's not like others we've tried. In the Lamborghini Gallardo, BMW M5 and Ferrari's own F430 you can build revs in first gear without the clutch engaging. You go through a similar enabling sequence to access launch control in the 612 – select Sport, disengage traction/stability control, flick the left paddle – but when you press the throttle with your foot hard on the brake you find that the clutch is still engaged.

Unsure that this was correct, and unwilling to risk the clutch plate, we tried a few tentative runs before asking Caselli to demonstrate. 'The system in the F430 is brutal; despite the clutch slip this is better for the car,' he said, before lining the 612 up. Working the throttle against the clutch, rather like stalling the torque converter on a conventional automatic, Caselli quickly got the revs to just under 3000rpm and jumped off the brake. The trick is not to hang around.

Despite the freezing tarmac, the Scaglietti took off exceptionally sharply, without a hint of wheelspin, and devoured the mile straight in a determined yet curiously relaxed lunge. Interrogation of the VBOX showed that our best »

Scaglietti is a natural for power oversteer, but the car dishes up more than enough dynamic thrills to keep you engaged and entertained even when not on the absolute limit

+ ROAD TEST DATA +

SPECIFICATION

FERRARI 612 SCAGLIETTI

Engine	65-degree V12
Location	Front-mid, longitudinal
Displacement	5748cc
Bore x stroke	89mm x 77mm
Cylinder block	Aluminium alloy
Cylinder head	Aluminium alloy, dohc per bank, four valves per cylinder
Fuel and ignition	Bosch Motronic ME7 electronic engine management, multipoint sequential injection
Max power	533bhp @ 7250rpm (test car 547bhp)
Max torque	434lb ft @ 5250rpm (test car 440lb ft)
Transmission	Six-speed manual gearbox with F1A paddle-shift, transaxle, rear-wheel drive, lsd, CST traction and stability system
Front suspension	Wishbones, coil springs, adaptive damping, anti-roll bar
Rear suspension	Wishbones, coil springs, adaptive damping, anti-roll bar
Steering	Rack and pinion, power-assisted
Brakes	Drilled and ventilated discs, 345mm front, 330mm rear, ABS
Wheels	8 x 18in front, 10 x 19in rear, aluminium alloy
Tyres	245/45 ZR18 front, 285/40 ZR19 rear, Pirelli P Zero Rosso
Kerb weight	1860kg (test car 1914kg)
Power-to-weight	291bhp per ton (test car 290bhp per ton)
Basic price	£177,500 (F1A model)
Price as tested	£183,680
Extras fitted include	Daytona-style seats (£1985), Ferrari wing shields (£1045), sat-nav (£1565), silver brake callipers (£585), heated front seats (£540), yellow-faced rev counter (£460)
Insurance group	20
On sale	Now

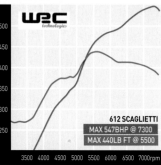

612 SCAGLIETTI
MAX 547BHP @ 7300
MAX 440LB FT @ 5500

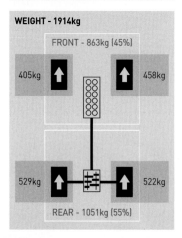

WEIGHT - 1914kg

FRONT - 863kg (45%)

405kg — 458kg

529kg — 522kg

REAR - 1051kg (55%)

FERRARI 612 SCAGLIETTI

PERFORMANCE

ACCELERATION TIMES

0-30	1.9
0-40	2.5
0-50	3.5
0-60	4.3
0-70	5.6
0-80	6.8
0-90	8.3
0-100	9.8
0-110	11.5
0-120	13.9
0-130	16.3
0-140	18.9
0-150	23.1

1/4 MILE

secs	12.7
speed	116

IN-GEAR TIMES

	2nd	3rd	4th	5th	6th
20-40	1.8	2.8	3.4		
30-50	1.5	2.4	3.4	4.5	7.0
40-60	1.6	2.2	3.3	4.4	5.8
50-70	2.0	2.1	3.0	4.3	5.7
60-80		2.2	2.8	4.3	5.8
70-90		2.4	2.8	4.0	6.0
80-100			2.9	3.9	5.9
90-110			3.3	3.9	5.8
100-120			3.6	4.1	5.7
110-130				4.6	5.9
120-140				5.3	6.2
130-150				5.8	

BRAKING

100-0	4.41
dist. ft	326

TOP SPEED

Peak	177 (see text)

0-100-0

612 SCAGLIETTI — 14.2sec

0 1 2 3 4 5 6 7 8 9 10 11 12 13 14 15 16 17 18

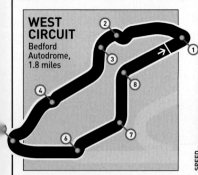

WEST CIRCUIT
Bedford Autodrome, 1.8 miles

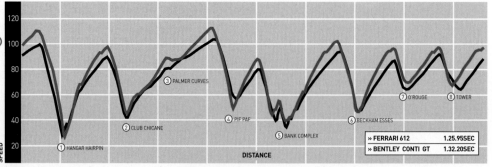

① HANGAR HAIRPIN
② CLUB CHICANE
③ PALMER CURVES
④ PIF PAF
⑤ BANK COMPLEX
⑥ BECKHAM ESSES
⑦ O'ROUGE
⑧ TOWER

» FERRARI 612	1.25.95SEC
» BENTLEY CONTI GT	1.32.20SEC

Bentley's 4wd Conti GT is an exceptional car in many respects, but on track the 612 leaves it for dead. The Scaglietti is no lightweight but is 400kg less than the Conti and hits much greater peak speeds. The four-seat Ferrari's rear-biased weight distribution and responsive, composed handling make a big difference through the complex and the final two corners

run had yielded a 0-60 of 4.51sec, just three tenths shy of the factory claim of 4.2sec (recorded one- rather than two-up). Scanning further down the data, Caselli's slightly more aggressive starts had sliced a couple of tenths off for a remarkable two-way, two-up average of 4.3sec, with 0-30 dispatched in under 2sec – four-wheel-drive territory – and 100mph in 9.8sec. The in-gear times make equally impressive reading, the V12 demonstrating its consistent, massive strength from tickover to the limiter.

In all honesty, we didn't expect to be able to verify the Scaglietti's claimed top speed of 199mph. The hands-off speed on Millbrook's two-mile bowl is 100mph, so there'd be some serious cornering going on if we got to near double that. And then, shortly before our run, there was a radio message for all track users announcing that there was a gritter on the high-speed circuit. Oh how we laughed, dep ed Bovingdon and I, before pulling on our crash helmets.

We settled initially at an easy 150mph canter. All seemed well so we tried 160. For some reason 150mph is a threshold on the bowl and above this lapping suddenly becomes more demanding. At 170mph you're really hanging on, fighting the lateral g, concentrating hard and feeling the big bumps report through the car. At an indicated 180+ (an actual 177mph), with a half inch of throttle travel left, the car felt somehow lighter, like that tipping point when a car is on the verge of sliding... We decided to call it a day.

There didn't seem any doubt that this Scaglietti was producing anything less than the full complement of brake horsepower – a claimed 533 – and it confirmed as much in just three runs on the dyno rollers. On the first run the thin power line streaked up the real-time graph like a bonfire rocket and moments later the readout blinked 546.6bhp. The next run read 546.1bhp, the third a smidgen less, and it was job done, the first pair having been within 1bhp.

At the 612's launch, Ferrari claimed a kerb weight of 1840kg, but since then an extra 20kg of sound deadening has been added. Sat on our four-pad electronic scales, this 612 recorded 1914kg, distributed 45 per cent front, 55 per cent rear. That's about 50kg over, which can't be accounted for entirely by the options fitted.

Tail-biased it may be, but the clever distribution of masses means that when the rear breaks loose, it doesn't keep going as it does in, say, a Murciélago. On track, the 612 can be provoked and then held in a massive broadside for the length of a gear – in this case, third – and recovery is clean and progressive. It's exceptional for what, with a couple of testers aboard, amounts to more than two tons. However, the best speed around the West Circuit at the Bedford Autodrome is gained with a much neater approach. Our first couple of laps were in Sport mode with CST engaged, and while the stability system kept the 612 on a tidy line, it was a little slow to reinstate power. Given how benign the Scaglietti is, it doesn't feel brave switching CST off, especially as the gutsy V12 is instantly responsive and sensitive to the throttle.

As on the road, the 612's front end is obedient and incisive, with no hint of slip even into the fastest corners. Despite the huge power being fed to the rear, the tail is only as unsettled as you choose to make it. Get on the gas too early or too hard and the rear will drift wide, but you have options. Play the throttle and you can stabilise the slide before it escalates, or you can ease back to get the rear tyres hooked up for maximum drive. Be patient getting on the power in a corner, squeeze the throttle progressively, and the weight transfer will increase traction to the point where, at times, the 612 fires out of turns almost as if it's four-wheel drive.

The best lap we put together yielded a time of 1:25.95, which is superb, especially as the brakes felt a bit cooked after four laps and this time was recorded on the fifth. To their credit, the Brembos recovered their full performance after a short breather. For such a big, weighty four-seater, the 612 is incredibly lithe. It makes a Continental GT feel like a very blunt instrument and offers the sort of responsiveness and balance that you'd hope a DB9 (1:28.90) would have but doesn't. A BMW M6, which we lapped straight after the 612, was a little over a second slower (1:27.05). Still impressive, but the BMW was very loose and ragged in comparison.

It's a very clever car, the 612. Its proportions disguise its full four-seat capacity, while the unusual weight distribution gives superb handling. There's enough mass over the nose to give responsive steering and keen bite, while the heavier tail pins the rear tyres to the road for superb traction. I can't think of another production car that better demonstrates the benefits of the front-mid-engine/transaxle-rear layout. It's a massive achievement.

With familiarity the Scaglietti gets easier on the eye, if no more beautiful. However, in terms of meeting its design objectives, the 612 is every bit as impressive as the F430. The question isn't 'Why would you want a four-seat Ferrari?' so much as 'Why wouldn't you?' △

'The 612 can be held in a massive broadside for the length of a gear'

60 FACTS ABOUT FERRARI AT 60

What is the least expensive part you can buy for a new Ferrari? What do all those model numbers actually mean? Octane brings you 60 Ferrari facts, one for each year of the company's history

Words: Giles Chapman

Clockwise from facing page: 'Sharknose' replica built for Chris Rea's '97 film La Passione; Dino – never badged as a Ferrari; 1940s Ferrari 125 barchetta

1 Enzo Ferrari was born on February 18, 1898, outside Modena. His grandpa was a food wholesaler, his dad Alfredo a metal-basher in the local railway workshops.

2 Enzo saw his first race aged 10, and could drive at 13. He was invalided out of the army during WW2; neither his father nor brother survived it.

3 In 1920, Alfa Romeo employed him as a team driver, and he came second in that year's Targa Florio. In 1929, he switched from driving to admin, undertaking management of Alfa's racing team.

4 One of Ferrari's stranger Alfa projects was the Bimotore, a single-seater with engines at both ends. It was fast but temperamental.

5 When he wasn't living and breathing sports and racing cars, Enzo relaxed by riding his beloved – and British – Rudge motorcycle.

6 By 1940, Enzo's private company, Auto Avio Costruzioni, had built a Fiat-based sports car. Alberto Ascari drove it in the 1940 Mille Miglia. It led its class until blowing up. Enzo blamed the Fiat bits...

7 The first Ferrari car proper appeared in 1947, the Tipo 125. Its V12 engine was designed by Giaochino Colombo, and it was made at Maranello, a factory outside Modena backed partly by Mussolini so Ferrari could make tools for his war machine.

8 Ferrari had only one son – officially – Alfredino, or 'Dino', born in 1932. He died of muscular dystrophy in 1956.

9 Enzo had, however, more than one woman. He divided his time between wife Laura and mistress Lina Lardi – with whom he had another son, Piero. When Laura died in 1978, Ferrari's second family moved into his vast, sombre villa.

10 The first Ferrari race victory was in a minor event at Rome's Caracalla circuit in 1947. The driver was Franco Cortese.

11 The first Grand Prix a Ferrari won was the 1949 Swiss GP, where Alberto Ascari drove a supercharged 125.

12 Also in 1949, a Ferrari took the first of nine Le Mans victories for the marque, including six in a row over 1960-65.

13 Cultivating his own enigmatic image, Enzo took to wearing sunglasses in public during the 1950s and did so until he died – even when interviewed indoors!

14 Ferrari's 'prancing horse' logo was given to Enzo by Countess Baracca, whose late WW1 flying ace son Francesco had used it as his emblem. Ferrari changed its background colour from white to yellow, and created an icon.

15 Mr Ferrari's nickname, Il Commendatore (The Commander), is thought to originate from an honour bestowed upon him by Italy's fascist king Victor Emmanuel III.

16 Enzo's mum Adalgisa and wife Laura hated each other, but that didn't stop Enzo from buying a large villa in Modena and giving them half each to live in. Adalgisa Ferrari died in 1965 after, apparently, choking on a boiled egg.

17 One of the ugliest Ferrari road cars was also the only one bodied in Britain. A 166 was given ungainly Abbott coachwork in 1954.

18 For all his brilliance, Enzo Ferrari was volatile and prickly. Mauro Forghieri, his long-time chief designer and engineer, once said: 'As a businessman he is excellent, as a human being he is a zero.'

19 Ferrari driver Mike Hawthorn was the first Brit to win a Championship GP when he beat Fangio's Mercedes in 1953 at the French GP.

20 Hawthorn was devastated when Ferrari team-mate Peter Collins was killed at the Nürburgring in 1958. World Champion Hawthorn decided to retire, but died in a road accident just months later.

21 The Testa Rossa name, Italian for red head, was given first to the 3-litre V12 engine in 1958 because its camshaft covers were painted red. It was revived in 1984 for a mid-engined supercar.

22 Ford tried to buy Ferrari for $18m in 1963, but the deal collapsed when the Americans refused to cede Enzo total control over the racing programme. Ford responded by producing the GT40.

23 Phil Hill's Dino 246 won the 1960 Italian GP – the last major victory for a front-engined GP car.

24 Colonel Ronnie Hoare became Britain's Ferrari importer in 1960, when he established Maranello Concessionaires at St Swithin's Lane, London. In 1967 he moved the company to Egham.

25 Tractor tycoon Ferruccio Lamborghini only decided to make a supercar of his own after complaints about the quality of his Ferrari were met with frosty indifference by Enzo.

26 The ASA was a pint-size Testa Rossa designed by Ferrari engineer Giotto Bizzarrini in 1958. It had a 1000cc, all-alloy, four-cylinder engine giving 91bhp. It could do 113mph. However, the prohibitive price meant that in three years just 52 were sold.

27 The 1968 365GTB/4 (the Daytona) disappointed some because it was front-engined when the vogue was for mid-mounted engines. At 174mph, it was still the world's fastest car.

28 Nowhere on the Dino 246GT did the word Ferrari appear. Supposed to be the affordable 'junior' marque, the £6500 Dino was three times costlier than a Jaguar XJ6 in 1969.

29 Fiat bought Ferrari in 1968, taking a 40% stake that eventually increased to 90%. This still left Enzo in charge of the racing side while Fiat controlled road car production.

30 Almost all road-going Ferraris since the mid-'50s have been styled by Pininfarina. At one time, Sergio Pininfarina also held 1% of the company. The 1973 308GT4 is the only one designed by Bertone.

31 Early 308GTBs came with glassfibre bodywork, but Ferrari soon switched to steel due to the high cost of manufacturing in GRP.

32 The 1976 400GT was the first Ferrari to be made with an automatic gearbox.

33 Ferrari considered making a four-door car in 1980. Pininfarina's 'Pinin' concept saloon won critical acclaim but Enzo vetoed it.

34 The most expensive Ferrari ever is a 250GTO which reputedly changed hands privately for £7.2m. A similar car was sold at auction in 1990 by Sotheby's for £6.35m.

35 When the Ferrari F40 was launched in 1987 to celebrate the marque's first four decades, it was, at £193,299, the most expensive car on sale in Britain.

36 In the early hours of August 14, 1988, Enzo Ferrari passed away peacefully in his sleep. He was 90.

37 The Tipo 640 of 1989 pioneered semi-automatic transmission in F1, adding wheel-mounted 'paddles' for up and down. Nigel Mansell won the Brazilian GP on its first outing.

38 Ferrari was the first team to notch up 100 GP wins when Alain Prost won the 1990 French GP. At Belgium two years later, Ferrari entered its 500th Championship race.

Above from top:
Fiat Dino, named
after Enzo's late son;
Mansell won 1989
Brazilian GP in F640;
a surprising 1284
Daytonas were built

Below:
From the earliest –
1947 Ferrari 125S
had a 1497cc V12
producing 118bhp...

Below:
...to the latest –
2007 599GTB has
a V12 of 5999cc and
delivers over 600bhp

39 The best-selling Ferrari model ever is the 2000-05 360 Modena/Spider, with 17,500 sold.

40 The factory today offers 16 standard colours but can provide any paint used on a previous model. A 10-colour 'historic' range is now offered for the 612 Scaglietti.

41 Although perceived as exclusive, some Ferraris are surprisingly numerous; 1315 F40s were made between 1987 and 1992, while 1284 Ferrari Daytonas were built between 1968 and 1973.

42 In 1985 a Ferrari 250LM brochure fetched an astounding £1070 at a Christie's auction in Monaco. They now go for even more!

43 Ferrari engines have been used in other cars. The Lancia Stratos, Lancia Thema 8.32 and Fiat Dino all have Maranello power, while Cooper, Minardi and Scuderia Italia have used the company's F1 engines, as did the Lancia D50 single-seater.

44 Enzo Ferrari hated Britain's Grand Prix 'industry', so the Brits chuckled when, in 1988, the Ferrari F1 chassis design HQ moved to Guildford to accommodate the wishes of John Barnard.

45 Ferrari's president today, Luca di Montezemolo, is part of the Fiat-owning Agnelli family. From 1973 (aged 26) to '77 he was Enzo Ferrari's personal assistant, effectively running the F1 team and masterminding Niki Lauda's Championship quest.

46 The F50 was Ferrari's half-century celebration, and just 349 were made – at a retail price of £340,000 each. It could do 202mph and hit 60mph in 3.7sec.

47 Blues guitarist Chris Rea was so fascinated by German Count Wolfgang von Trips and the 'sharknose' Ferrari in which he died in 1961, he financed a movie about them, La Passione (1997).

48 Can't afford to buy a Ferrari? Don't worry – you can hire one. Bespokes (+44 (0)20 7833 8000) offers a 430 Spider for £1195 a day, or a Dino 246GTS for £475.

49 Cheesiest Ferrari role: Tony Curtis driving a 246GT in TV's The Persuaders; naffest Ferrari appearance in a pop song: Big Red GTO by Sinitta; every Ferrari owner's nightmare: Lord Brocket armed with a penknife.

50 There are more books on Ferrari than any other marque except Porsche, according to London bookshop Motorbooks. It stocks over 100 new titles, ranging from £4.95 for the glossy Cavallino journal to £35.99 for Dino: The V6 Ferrari by Brian Long.

51 Between 1997 and 2005, Maserati was managed by Ferrari, but Fiat has since transferred it to the same division as Alfa Romeo.

52 Ferrari's model naming system was traditionally rooted in logic: the first official model, the 125, was so-called because 125 was the cubic-centimetre capacity of one cylinder. Starting with the 246 Dino, though, the company's smaller cars went their own way: '24' stood for a 2.4-litre engine, while '6' was the number of cylinders. This continued through the 308 and 328 models until the 348 (3.4-litre, eight-cylinder), but the F355 meant 3.5-litre and five-valves-per-cylinder.

53 In the mid-1950s, racing cars took a different route: 'Tipo 158' stood for '1.5-litre, 8-cylinder' and '1512' meant '1.5-litre, 12-cylinder'. The late-'80s 640 and 641 F1 cars were named simply from their drawing office project numbers.

54 The cheapest replacement component Ferrari GB stocks costs 5p – it's a washer to attach an undertray. The most expensive is a 599GTB Fiorano replacement engine: £32,486.99. But that includes VAT.

55 Sotheby's knocked down a driveable 1964 330GT for just £10,000 in 1985 – the cheapest example it's ever sold, around half its estimate, and the cost of a new Ford Granada then.

56 There have been 13 British Ferrari team drivers: Cliff Allison, Derek Bell, Tony Brooks, Peter Collins, Mike Hawthorn, Eddie Irvine, Nigel Mansell, Mike Parkes, Reg Parnell, Roy Salvadori, John Surtees, Peter Whitehead and Jonathan Williams.

57 Ferrari has seen peerless success in Formula 1, boasting the most Constructors' Championships, Drivers' Championships, pole positions and outright wins. In 2004, Ferrari finally bested Ford's Cosworth as top engine maker, its 182 wins trouncing Ford's 176.

58 The worst F1 season for Ferrari was 1980, when it scored eight constructor points; 2004 was the high-point, when it grabbed 262 points.

59 The most powerful road-going Ferrari ever is the 660bhp Enzo, but today's 612bhp 599GTB Fiorano is the 11th most powerful production road car of all time, just behind the 10th-placed 617bhp Mercedes-Benz SLR McLaren.

60 In 2006, Ferrari sold 5671 cars – 635 of them in the UK. One V12-engined car is sold for every three V8s.

THE ULTIMATE TEST

Words: Mark Hales
Photography: Charlie McGee

The F40 has been the ultimate pin-sharp, aggressive
supercar since 1987. Can the Enzo match it? Until now,
no-one has been able to compare the two directly

There is an argument

that says supercars are a profligate irrelevance whose extra capability can't be researched on today's roads. That their layout is unforgiving, gives a driver no clue as to where the limit lies, denying them the confidence to press on. That ownership is a quick way to lose large sums of money along with your licence...

There's more, and it would be a skilled lawyer who could mount a genuine defence to any of it, but given the number of different examples popping up all over the world there are obviously plenty of people with the necessary means who are willing to take the risks. The two Ferraris in the pictures here are both numbers in limited production runs, all of which were sold before manufacture, and both are owned by the same man – amiable property investor and accomplished racer Grahame Bryant. Cars built as ultimates whether relevant or not.

The idea was to see if and how the breed has evolved in the last two decades, and for me there is no better starting point than the Ferrari F40. I've driven a fair few miles in the early example owned by Nick Mason and, on a dry road, it was always massively, hugely exciting, a raw and brutally visceral experience, intoxicating for its sheer energy and the more so because it remained unpredictable. It became a huge favourite

as much for its capacity to thrill as the fact that it never pretended to be anything it wasn't.

The Enzo – the new millennium's F40 – I knew little about. Grahame's was the first example I had seen in the flesh and there is no denying it's a striking sight. The red paint, which saturates the schnozzle-heavy shape, has a kind of chromed allure that richens the hue and only adds to the controversy over the styling – those who like the blend of space-age insect front and chunky kit car back and those who don't already seem to inhabit equal sized camps. Both cars, though, have angular lines, each a composite carapace apparently hewn from blocks of ice rather than a skin pulled tight over smooth sinew. For the F40, folded paper was simply the style of the mid-1980s; the Enzo, you get the impression, is that way for a more specific purpose – the square edges defining channels to direct the passage of air over and through its body.

It also features an engine twice the size of the F40's – six litres – with half as many cylinders again (12 in a vee) and a claimed output of 650bhp at 7800rpm. It's a big lump of metal and, together with the computer-controlled semi-automatic six-speed gearbox, fills half the Enzo's dimensions, pushing the cockpit space forwards because there's no other choice. The F40's more conventional five-speed transaxle and compact 2.9-litre V8 are smaller in every respect and the claimed

Below: mid-corner, pushing hard, and the turbos cut in. Suddenly the F40's rear is pushing sideways. It's not as friendly as an Enzo...

'The muted hum turns to a harsh buzzing, the whoosh becomes a bellowing roar. The car rocks from one rear corner to the other as the tyres scrabble'

'The F40 is a more stripped-down, sweaty and intimate experience and, whether you like it or not, you are always involved with a chassis that is beautifully balanced'

478bhp at 7000rpm is mainly thanks to a pair of Japanese turbochargers. These, we will sample first.

The F40's door is ample but it's still a scramble across a wide sill latticed with signature carbon-fibre weave. Sink into the thinly padded bucket seat and survey the dash ahead, trimmed by afterthought in grey suede cloth and speckled with dials and switches borrowed from the Fiat parts bin. Push the button and there comes not the offbeat rattle of a traditional V8 but a muted wheezy hum, more like a low-revving four than a fire-breathing eight. The footwell seems too crowded for a pair of size 12s and the clutch is heavy. Pull the round black knob and glinting wand of a gearlever (which pokes up from the traditional slotted gate) towards you and back, into the first slot. The engine seems benign and you drive off as you would in any volume model.

Bruntingthorpe's concrete road sends a rumble and boom through the bare plastic, mixed with such a clatter from the stones pinging off the wheelarches that, had Grahame not already mentioned it, you'd fear for the structure. Meanwhile the car jiggles over the ruts but rides rather than reacts to the bumps, a sense of control which immediately feels good, while all the time the wheel writhes gently in your hands.

This, I remember, was one of the car's defining features. A wonderfully sensitive instrument which feels out the road surface and sends the report back to your fingertips – take your hands off and watch the rim gently shuffling this way and that while the nose of the car gently follows suit. I remember too that it's a means of feeling out puddles and changes in grip

Above: the F40's ahead, with turbos spinning hard, but there's no chance for it – the Enzo will be able to overtake

»

things that can never quite find their way past the numbing of power assistance and a tactile asset unknown to so many drivers of modern cars.

As the revs rise, the gentle hum takes a harder edge overlaid by a breathy whoosh as the turbos start to spin up, accompanied by a gentle but insistent push in the back. Thus far I don't let it run much beyond 4000rpm, which leaves time to deal with the Ferrari gearshift, a device whose details and foibles could almost fill a chapter on their own. The synchros are tough and instead of a nice metallic snick they feel oddly rubbery; you push against them and they give a little, apparently trying to spit your effort out, then they give in and let the lever clack against the gate.

This and the heavy clutch make a smooth and elegant shift something to be savoured – especially when changing down. Trying to match the revs seems to make little difference to the feel of things and inevitably your efforts to align an engine that spins up at the touch of the accelerator with a gearshift that seems to need both guidance through the gate and a wait for the synchros means a learner's jerk every time. Timing rather than force is the way forward and although it does get easier, it's hard to say why. You just find yourself grinning and saying to yourself, 'that was a good one...'

Time, then, to up the effort. Leave the long straight road and turn off to the right, lift the revs and push the lever

against the slot for second, wait what seems an age for it to slip home, then instead of tickling the accelerator, give it a proper push. The result is like flicking a switch halfway through the turn. At first there's nothing but a gentle surge, but suddenly, like a feline alerted from slumber, the lazy loaf morphs into a predatory ball of energy. The muted hum turns to a harsh buzzing, the whoosh becomes a bellowing roar. The car rocks from one rear corner to the other as the tyres scrabble, and instinctively you must catch the tail slinging off to the left with a quarter turn of reverse lock. The body corkscrews as the car responds and weight shifts between tyres already struggling for grip, then as you straighten up, the rump squats, digs in and launches you down the following straight. Seven thousand-five comes up in an instant. The tug for third seems easier. Another savage fist in the back lasts only an instant longer than the last. It's time for fourth.

Folklore says that the 478bhp claim is rather modest and the real figure is much more. It certainly feels like it because there's but a moment to contemplate the long sweep to the left which is fast-forwarding at an unfeasible rate. Ease the car in, use the feel of the wheel, take note of the gentle tugging that says there's grip to point the nose, then follow it through with the power. About the mid-point, the tail gently but firmly steps to the right as the revs rise. The tyres have lost the battle again despite the higher gear and you still couldn't

Below: could there be two more distinctive body shapes? The F40 is pure mid-1980s, while the Enzo's cab-forward style is dicated by the massive engine and semi-auto transmission

'I'd heard how Schumacher had the rear tyres permanently on
fire and how even his freakish talent couldn't make the
car quicker than it was with traction control switched on'

feel it coming. The reaction still has to be instinctive. It's not so much the amount of acceleration – although 500bhp in 1100kg is always likely to be exciting – it's the suddenness of it all.

You notice too that your ears are ringing and that the brakes are not remotely up to the performance. They grumble and judder, the car slows rather than stops, and there's no reassuring bite. Maybe it was the technology of the time but it still seems a surprising oversight given the rest and it makes you realise more than ever that this style of performance really can't be fully unleashed on the public road. In which case, what of the Enzo, which promises to be faster still?

Hook the fingers under the sunken door catch and click it open, let the massive structure swing up, propelled by hissing gas struts and supported on a huge, forged central crank. Notice the similar lack of trim in the cabin, the weave of carbon fibre, the rubber mats fixed to the floor. Spot that the seats, which look more substantial than the older car's, tilt forward to reveal a small hammock where you can stow your toothbrush and spare underpants. See that there are only two pedals, brake and accelerator, and there's no gearlever – shifting is by two paddles, right/up, left/down, each a fingertip's distance from the computer-game steering wheel. You begin to realise more and more how the layout has influenced, if not defined, the styling.

Sliding in is easy with half the sill missing, then haul the door down and feel the solid clunk as it closes. The simple

Above:
this is much more difficult to induce. With traction control on, it just won't happen, and even with it off the front initially pushes out. But if you try hard enough, eventually the rear loses its grip…

circular crank handle at the front turns out to be the window winder, and you see why the glass is smaller than you might like – there has to be room for the side pocket below it, which in turn creates room for the left elbow. The driving position, though, is perfect. Deep, grippy seat, good view through the bowl of a screen, sensibly sized wing mirrors, wheel straight ahead and well clear of the legs, feet straight ahead, big footrest for the left one, padded shin rest for the right leg... The designers have thought about this.

Now survey the rows of buttons and strings of lights. The only ones we need today are those marked 'R' for reverse, 'ASR' to turn off the traction control, and 'RACE', which hands back most of the gearshifting decisions that the normal mode assumes for you, or as Grahame put it, 'will let you get the wrong one and make an arse of it...' Pull back on both paddles to bring up 'N' for neutral on the screen next to the red and white speedo and tacho, and press the starter. A proper V12 rasp comes swiftly from behind, hook the right paddle for first, lift up and release the handbrake and press the right pedal. The car eases forward and, without any more effort than it takes to tell, you are soon trundling down the straight wondering how much louder the road roar drumming at the fibre and the thump and bang as the 35-section tyres slap the gaps in the concrete can get.

Meanwhile, it's hard to resist the schoolboy delight of hooking the right paddle just to see whether it will produce the same result every time... And every time the engine holds ➤➤

its rpm while the note changes from a rasp to a metallic clatter before the electronics thump the clutch back in. Not exactly quick and not as smooth as a conventional auto but impressive in the way it revises the process to suit the power you use and the speed you go. Hook the left paddle to go down and the system blips up the big, rasping engine to match the road speed. This is even more fun, especially if you are coming down from an illegal rate, because the blips are bigger.

It's very seductive all this control at your fingertips, but it does take its time – it has to because the gaps between the six gears in a 200mph-plus car are necessarily wide, so you can't zip through them like you can in a Touring Car. Within a mile, though, you realise that anyone could drive an Enzo, and do so with three digits. A finger and thumb to hold the power-assisted wheel and one more to hook the paddles. No-one need ever fluff a shift or stall the engine.

Which also releases you to look at the road. You realise how much concentration is involved dealing with basics like getting the F40's gears selected smoothly and in time, and how tense it makes you. You also notice things like the Enzo's ride, which is stiffer over the bumps, massively taut but not uncomfortable, and how the car tracks dead straight towards the first corner, wheel inert in your hands. Nothing like the living thing in the F40, and composure which only makes the way the nose points as you ease the wheel to the right even more surprising.

You get used to a bit of lag while a car's body takes up an attitude and the wheel settles at whatever slip angle the tyres

FERRARI F40

dictate, and you also know the alternative is often a sudden lunge, which upsets everything. Here it's more a feeling of authority that never makes itself felt until summoned. The possibility it might do the same at high speed is then an exciting prospect normally exclusive to race cars equipped with downforce...

Head towards the long sweepers and aim the nose to find out. It points in as expected but... then there's a hint of push from the front, which if you try and balance with the power only summons the traction control. By that time you are going mighty fast and although, unlike the F40, the car remains completely composed, somehow it wasn't what you expected. Only afterwards in a reflective moment, when you crouch down and look at the car's side view, does it make sense. The gap under the car necessary to make it usable over speed bumps and cambers cannot help but allow air underneath, and keeping this out is the first law of formula car aerodynamics. The flow over the top and through the channels does make some difference, but air below is what lifts the car at speed, so the Enzo's initially pointy front must come more from a stiff chassis and clever dampers. Not a disappointment exactly, just a reminder that this is, after all, a road car.

The Enzo skips and jitters, rocks from one corner to the other in traditional mid-engined style through the bumpy loop that heads back to the straight, where, without the slightest effort, 140mph comes up on the screen. You really would have to be very, very careful in this car... Idly, I prod the pedal further and, just for devilment, hook the

'Sink into the thinly padded bucket seat and survey the dash ahead, trimmed by afterthought in grey suede cloth and speckled with dials and switches borrowed from the Fiat parts bin'

'The driving position is perfect: deep, grippy seat, good view through the bowl of a screen, wheel straight ahead and clear of the legs, feet straight ahead… the designers thought about this'

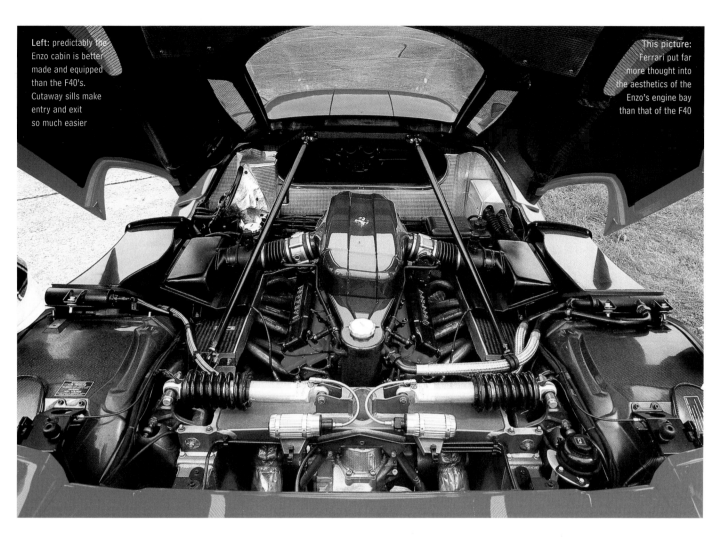

Left: predictably the Enzo cabin is better made and equipped than the F40's. Cutaway sills make entry and exit so much easier

This picture: Ferrari put far more thought into the aesthetics of the Enzo's engine bay than that of the F40

left paddle. The car hesitates while the gear slips in then, as the massive engine comes back, the Enzo doesn't suddenly explode like the F40, instead it surges forward with massive, seamless ease. Leave the foot hard down, let the needle climb round the rev counter, anticipate the limiter, and tweak the right paddle with a forefinger. The shift is quicker now and the thump as the clutch goes home sends young Ollie Bryant's head rocking back. Halfway along the long straight and 180 is already showing. The book says 217.5mph, and, maybe because 180-and-counting was so easy, you believe it.

When the time comes to shed all this energy, the response to a gentle push on the left pedal is truly astonishing and, like the initially pointy nose, it's the kind you'd expect from a formula car. The bite from the four enormous 13.5in carbon-ceramic discs is massive and consummate without being sharp and jagged, and the car just stops without dipping its nose or weaving. Back up to speed again, just to lean on them harder, but they just bite harder back. The Enzo, it seems, takes care of everything for you; the shifting, the braking, the steering, everything, even the potential to sling the tail like the F40. There are no turbos, the power delivery is much, much more progressive and there's more grip from the 345-section rears, but the Enzo's 650bhp is still a mighty lot of power and you can feel the traction control cutting it again and again. It's very subtle.

Pressing the button to turn it off could therefore have been the eventual chink in the Enzo's so far seamless armour. The kind of electronic cut that renders an F16 unflyable, or the difference between the Enzo's composure and the F40's barely

FERRARI ENZO

SPECIFICATIONS

Engine
5998cc V12, double overhead cams, four valves per cylinder, Bosch Motronic engine management and fuel injection

Power
650bhp @ 7800rpm

Torque
585lb ft @ 5500rpm

Transmission
Six-speed sequential paddle-shift gearbox, rear-wheel drive, limited-slip differential, traction and stability control

Suspension
Double wishbones, pushrods and horizontal coil spring/damper units

Brakes
Ventilated 380mm diameter carbon-ceramic discs front and rear, ABS

Weight
1365kg

Performance
0-60mph 3.5sec (claimed)
Top speed 217.5mph (claimed)

Value
£450,000

containable exuberance. I'd heard how Michael Schumacher had the rear tyres permanently on fire at Fiorano and how even his freakish talent couldn't make the car quicker round the lap than it was with the ASR switched on... Maybe so, but there was no hideous transformation to trap mere mortals. On the slow corners and in second gear, at first the extra power just picked up the front and made the car push on, then as you tried harder, it gently broke the traction and swayed the tail, then promptly hit the rev limiter, which acted as a form of traction control.

Third gear took a little more time to push the tail out of line but once there it drove obligingly through the corner like some vintage two-wheel-drive rally car. The power steering weighted up at odd moments – as it does over the sharper bumps round the top loop – but apart from the fact my thumbs kept hitting the horn buttons it was so very much easier to manage while out of shape than the F40, and almost entirely because there was no wheelspin spiking out of control the moment the turbos got a sniff of freedom.

So is the Enzo the perfect supercar, and is it light years ahead of the F40? Well, that depends. It is extraordinarily impressive. Ferrari has done a wonderful job packing and balancing all the basic ingredients, and at last has found a set of brakes to equal their engine. They have used electronics to manage the more challenging tasks, but let them take the strain only where they felt it was necessary. The result is a carefully integrated whole, not so much sanitised but sensible and, as far as anything like that can be, safe. Turn off the only bit you can and the Enzo behaves like any other powerful, well-sorted car. Push it hard **»**

'The Enzo, it seems, takes care of everything for you; the shifting, the braking, the steering, everything, even the potential to sling the tail like the F40'

enough and it will push its nose into the corner then, when you light up the rears, slew the tail on the way out. This is how it should be, but the stiff platform, big tyres and what aerodynamics they could contrive means the threshold has been shifted way above the norm. Few will find an opportunity to experience it.

The F40 is a much more stripped-down, sweaty and intimate experience, and whether you like it or not, you are always involved with a chassis which is beautifully balanced in its own right – not least because it has a relatively small engine sited close to the middle. The means by which Ferrari persuaded that engine to develop supercar power, though, dominates the car and the driving experience, and although the turbos make it so very exciting, it will never be easy or predictable. In that respect, the Enzo is definitely progress, because it provides more of everything without the drama. Whether that makes it everyday usable or not, is another matter entirely... ◬

HORSE TRADING

No trip to Maranello would be complete without a visit to the official Ferrari shop.
Harry Metcalfe took his Amex along for a workout
Pictures: Andy Morgan & Harry Metcalfe

It's one of those shops that really ought to carry a wealth warning to car enthusiasts the world over. I'm afraid you're not going to escape from here without seriously damaging your bank balance. Imagine Ferrari meets Bond Street meets Prada and it'll give you a clue as to just what's going on at the Ferrari Store right in the heart of Maranello, perfectly positioned directly opposite the hallowed factory gates and next door to the famous Cavallino restaurant. It doesn't stop here either, because the success of this store since it opened in 2003 has lead to an ever-growing chain of Ferrari shops in locations as far flung as Las Vegas, Venice, Shanghai and Beijing. And they all sell the most fabulous Ferrari goodies, the like of which you've never seen before.

Of course there has always been Ferrari memorabilia, but never quite like this. In the past the company gave its official blessing to outside concerns to make and sell goods on its behalf, netting Ferrari a tidy £11.2m a year in royalties from those happy to pay for the privilege. But the opening of the Maranello store marked the start of this business being brought under Ferrari control. After all, Ferrari is one of the top ten most recognised names in the world, and company president Luca di Montezemolo sees taking full control of this other side of the business as a neat way of maximising the brand

whilst still limiting the number of cars they produce, so preserving the marque's mystique. Even a natural marketing man like Montezemolo is wary of stretching the number of cars that Ferrari builds each year too far, so the new shops are a clever way of increasing profits without damaging the core product.

While the rest of the **evo** team are storming round Fiorano in a 575M, I slip back to Maranello to check out the shop. As the glass doors glide open you're faced with Schumacher's 2001 Championship-winning car (not for sale), complete with the perfectly reproduced roar of an F1 car under full power, cannoning from Bose speakers elegantly suspended from the ceiling. In front of you is a bank of beautifully displayed models depicting everything from a Hot Wheels miniature of a 360 to a superb, large-scale replica of last years' championship-winning F1 car – yours for around £2000. Yet delve deeper and you soon realise that this is far from the most expensive article on sale in the shop. Elsewhere there are utterly beautiful Girard-Perrigaux watches with prices ranging up to £17,000, and actual parts from F1 Ferraris, beautifully displayed on their own carbonfibre stands. It's these that really catch my eye – and wallet – and separate the Ferrari Store from anything I've ever seen before.

»

WHAT DO ALL THOSE BUTTONS DO?

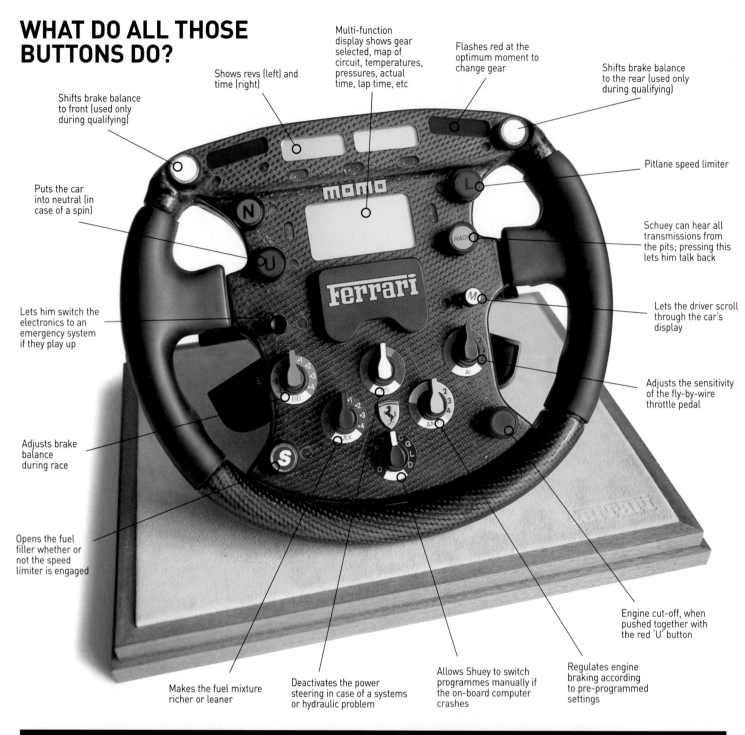

Shifts brake balance to front (used only during qualifying)

Shows revs (left) and time (right)

Multi-function display shows gear selected, map of circuit, temperatures, pressures, actual time, lap time, etc

Flashes red at the optimum moment to change gear

Shifts brake balance to the rear (used only during qualifying)

Puts the car into neutral (in case of a spin)

Pitlane speed limiter

Schuey can hear all transmissions from the pits; pressing this lets him talk back

Lets him switch the electronics to an emergency system if they play up

Lets the driver scroll through the car's display

Adjusts the sensitivity of the fly-by-wire throttle pedal

Adjusts brake balance during race

Opens the fuel filler whether or not the speed limiter is engaged

Engine cut-off, when pushed together with the red 'U' button

Makes the fuel mixture richer or leaner

Deactivates the power steering in case of a systems or hydraulic problem

Allows Shuey to switch programmes manually if the on-board computer crashes

Regulates engine braking according to pre-programmed settings

SCHUEY'S STEERING WHEEL

How the ex-world champion reinvented Ferrari wheel design

There's nothing new in mounting gearshift paddles and clutch levers on an F1 car's steering wheel, but for the 1997 season Michael Schumacher asked Ferrari to put all his car's dials and buttons on the wheel. By the time this example was crafted in 2000, it had developed into a £30,000 masterpiece that let the German control every facet of the car's computer without moving his hands from the wheel.

Made from carbon composite, the wheel has to sustain the equivalent of 40kg of force through it as the driver turns into fast corners. This, along with the delicate nature of the electronic contacts, means Schuey will use anywhere between 12 and 15 examples in a season.

James Foxall

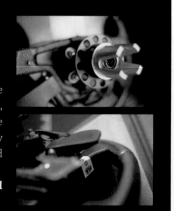

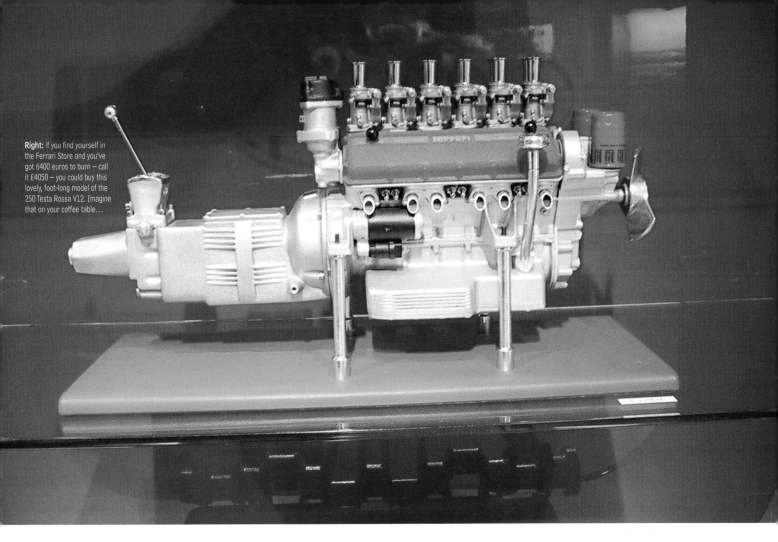

Right: if you find yourself in the Ferrari Store and you've got 6400 euros to burn – call it £4050 – you could buy this lovely, foot-long model of the 250 Testa Rossa V12. Imagine that on your coffee table...

Prices start at around £600 in this most exclusive of motor racing autojumbles. That's enough to buy you a roll-hoop cover from a 2000-year car, or perhaps a carbon fuel intake surround for the same price. Move the budget up to near £1000 and you can have a '95 F1 titanium conrod mounted on its own stand, or perhaps two carbonfibre brake scoops from a '97 car.

Amongst this extraordinary collection of car-related bits-and-pieces are beautifully crafted leather desk ornaments, like a gearlever and alloy gate from a 456GT on a leather plinth. Or perhaps you'd prefer the ex-F1 engine air intake trumpet, on a leather coaster, pretending to be a pen holder. Around the corner are proper works Ferrari jackets, as modelled by Jean Todt et al for a not inconsiderable £527, while the shirt to match would cost you another £186.

There are posters, bags, dubious driving shoes and plenty of T-shirts on offer as well, but it's the range of F1 parts that continually stops you in your tracks. Air intake snorkels from the top of engines are on sale for £1200, or a carbon sump from a '97 car can be yours for the same price.

Just as I begin contemplating the merits of owning a crankshaft from a '93 season F1 engine (3000 euros), I spot something that suddenly seems like a conspicuous bargain in these surroundings. There, on a leather plinth, under

a plastic cover, is a genuine Schumacher steering wheel from the 2000 campaign for a mere 2946 euros, or £1800.

You've got to love a shop that gives you such dilemmas. Crankshaft or steering wheel is not one I've come across before, but I reckon the wheel has more universal appeal, and lots of

buttons to impress friends with. Plus it's newer and a useful £34 cheaper than the crank, leaving enough to buy my wife some flowers, which should hopefully ease the tricky justification process once I get it home.

And I've just had a brilliant thought: I wonder if it could be made to fit my Lotus 340R...

Harry fell for ex-Schumacher wheel (top left), but you could buy a signed helmet (above left) or a genuine F1 conrod (above right) if you fancied

Spirito di
Enzo

With a 611bhp version of the Enzo's V12, the Ferrari 599
promises to take GT-supercar performance to a new level.
We drive it back-to-back with a 550 Maranello to find out

Words: Richard Meaden | Pictures: Gus Gregory

Driving the 550 down to Italy to meet the 599. Cockpit, with no garish satnav screen, has the feel of a modern classic

The literal journey

from Maranello to Fiorano is a short one. Out through the famous factory gates, past the celebrated Cavallino restaurant, and on, through a warren of side-streets packed with workshops, engineering companies and souvenir shops, until you reach the guarded entrance to the hallowed test track itself.

The metaphorical journey takes rather longer – a decade to be precise. It's hard to believe ten years have passed since the introduction of the 550 Maranello. Back then, supercars were wide, unwieldy mid-engined monsters, just as they had been since the '70s. When Ferrari decided to replace the flamboyant, side-straked F512M with the useable, comparatively understated front-engined 550, it was almost considered sacrilege.

Time, of course, has proved the ultimate arbiter, the burgeoning vogue for front-mid-engined designs vindicating Ferrari's move to a front-engined GT supercar. It's this fact, coupled with the measured process of evolution from 550 to 575M, that has made the Maranello one of those rare cars that has stayed on top of its game.

When in 2004 we rated the ten greatest cars of the previous ten years, the 550 was our champ.

Harry Metcalfe, **evo**'s editorial director, even bought one. His blood-red 550 was built a couple of years after the model's '96 debut, but thanks to its standard, option-free spec, it's totally representative of the earliest cars, providing a perfect snapshot of what the 550 Maranello was like at launch.

When we received our invitation to try the new 599 GTB Fiorano, both on the Modenese roads we know and love, and on the test track with which it shares its name, driving Harry's 550 out to Italy to meet it was too good an opportunity to miss. It is undoubtedly the best yardstick by which to measure the 599.

Even if you're not in the fortunate position of having an all-time-great Italian supercar at your disposal, the 1000-mile journey from the UK to Modena remains one of the classic European road trips. Admittedly, the vigilant British and French police have denied us much of the flat-to-the-boards drama so redolent of supercar drive stories of the '70s, but there's still a tremendous »

Above: despite its advancing years, 550 is still an impressive supercar and a wonderful long-distance partner. The 599 (right) has its work cut out to move the game on significantly

sense of freedom and anticipation as you emerge from the Eurotunnel and head out onto the wide, open French autoroutes.

The 550 is a magnificent partner, loping through France at an effortless, unobtrusive 100mph, its turbine-like V12 providing endless urge and emphatic sixth-gear response. Displacing some 5.5 litres and developing 485bhp and 415lb ft of torque, the Maranello's stats remain compelling. Short-shifting away from the péage barriers, slotting sixth and gently squeezing the throttle to its stop becomes something of a 550 party piece, for feeling the elastic, velvet-smooth surge of its big-capacity V12 hauling hard from low revs is highly addictive. The subdued but softly simmering soundtrack fits the sensation to a tee.

Aside from its epic engine and tremendous

reach, what makes the 550 such a terrific long-distance machine is its fuel range. A tank capacity of 115 litres means you can take great chunks out of your journey between fuel stops, magnifying the sense of relentless progress. It's also extremely comfortable, the 'Daytona' seats offering plenty of support, enabling three- or four-hour stints at the wheel without fatigue or discomfort. Only the constant rustle of wind-noise around the mirrors and door seals, along with a weak stereo, hint at the Maranello's advancing years.

Luggage space is more than acceptable, but the boot aperture was clearly designed around the legendary 'squashy bag', for it's restrictive and forces us to stow Gus's rigid Pelican case on

the useful rear luggage shelf. The lack of interior stowage space is more irksome, especially for small, slippery items like mobile phones. I lose count of the times I have to fish my Motorola out from under the seat after bursts of spirited acceleration.

An unusually generous schedule means we don't have to drive through the night to compensate for our afternoon departure from the UK, but nevertheless it's still dark by the time we approach our overnight halt in Strasbourg. The Maranello's interior takes on a new and even more soothing ambience by night, the pleasing array of round, analogue instruments illuminated with a soft, green-tinged glow. The absence of a satnav screen and other ugly technology completes the 550's modern-classic feel.

We start early the next morning, crossing the Rhine into Germany. As is increasingly the case, the autobahnen are choked with traffic and roadworks, but given a fleeting glimpse of open carriageway, the Maranello still breezes to 130mph with the ease that normal cars hit 90.

Crossing the frontier into Switzerland always feels a bit James Bond to me. Perhaps it's the uniformed border guards, brandishing side-arms and a licence to bill. Whatever, 40 euros lighter and windscreen wearing a Swiss road-tax sticker, we head through the grim, industrial city of Basel before picking up signs for St Gotthard and the Italian border beyond.

It's great to feel the mountains close in around you: snow-capped peaks flaring against an azure sky, the 550's scarlet profile spearing through the scenery like a dart. Peeling off the lorry-beaten track, away from the St Gotthard tunnel and up into the web of the Susten, Furka, Oberalp and Gotthard passes is a truly liberating experience, for it offers you so much more than basic expedience.

Empty roads, a smooth surface and some fantastic sequences of hairpins are too good to miss, as they provide our first opportunity to taste the Maranello's dynamics. The steering is heavier than I remember, but direct enough to cope with the switchbacks, and we're soon finding a rhythm, each up- and down-shift accompanied by a delicious *schlick-schlick* as the ball-topped gearlever slides weightily between the open gate's alloy fingers. The clutch shares the steering's ❱❱

'It's hard to
believe that ten years
have passed
since the introduction
of the 550'

'On a challenging, twisty road
it's an absolute riot, the car up on tiptoes
through quick direction changes'

'The Enzo-derived engine has lost none of its aural ferocity'

meaty weight, and there's great satisfaction when you time a downshift perfectly, with engine speed, road speed and gears meshing with sweet precision. It doesn't happen every time, but often enough to keep you absorbed in the process of consistently finding that sweet spot.

By the time we crest the climb and power out onto the fast, open sweeps and straights across the Gotthard's snowy plateau, there's no doubt that the Maranello has abiding appeal, not just through its sheer breadth of ability but also in the unshakable confidence of its delivery. Seemingly, however fast you want to go, it always feels like there's something in reserve.

Once in Italy we're increasingly swept along, not just by the fast-moving traffic and our proximity to Modena, but also by blind faith in the carabinieri taking a charitable view of a red Ferrari making rapid progress down the autostrada, just as Enzo intended. Naïve or not, it's a nice thought, so we keep the beautiful cast-alloy throttle pedal pinned to its stop for a little longer, until we're regularly nudging 160mph. It's a final rousing demonstration of the 550's supercar credentials

before we head into downtown Maranello, peel off the Via Abetone, drive through the factory gates, and park beneath the hallowed entrance to the old factory courtyard. Stationary at last, the 550's sleek snout is spattered with bugs and road grime, the hallmarks of a classic **evo** commute to Modena. What a great car.

NEXT MORNING, OUR FIRST sight of the 599 GTB Fiorano is, appropriately, in the test track's courtyard. We've bagged a red car with a black interior, just like Harry's 550. It's also fitted with the optional Brembo carbon-ceramic brakes and 'Challenge' alloy wheels (20in front and rear, as opposed to the standard 20in rears and 19in fronts). From experience with the 575 HGTC, Ferrari is confident that more than half of all 599 customers will tick these boxes.

More than 90 per cent are expected to opt for the F1 transmission, as fitted to this car, with only a tiny minority of customers – possibly fewer than 50 per year – choosing the traditional H-pattern manual. It hardly seems worth the effort of offering a stick-shift, until you realise that the

overwhelmingly popular F1 'box remains a £10K option. Multiplied by the 500 or so Fioranos that will be built every year, that equates to around £5million additional revenue per annum...

The 599's interior is spacious, the boot more useable (swallowing the dreaded 'Peli' with ease) and the detailing immaculately executed. Carbonfibre is used extensively, while aluminium is also employed to create a sporting, high-quality feel. The instruments are very like those in the Enzo, combining a big rev-counter with a complex LCD panel. This panel now works in conjunction with the manettino to display clearly which dynamic setting you've selected. In Race and CST-off modes you also get a lap timing facility, triggered by a button on the back of the steering wheel.

The seats are excellent multi-adjustable items developed by Recaro and come with additional, adjustable support around your hips and ribs thanks to pneumatic bladders that squeeze you tight for high-speed road or circuit driving. It's a more effective and less disconcerting solution than the aggressive 'active' seats fitted to the BMW M5 and M6, and certain AMG Mercedes.

Twist the key, step on the brake and press the big red 'Engine Start' button on the steering wheel, and the 6-litre V12 wakes with a boom. Bypass valves take the edge off the decibel level soon after, but a blip of the throttle confirms the Enzo-derived engine has lost none of its aural ferocity, sounding every inch the 611bhp, 448lb ft hyper-GT.

From start-up the transmission defaults into automatic mode. Normally I'd immediately engage »

New 'F1-Trac' stability and traction control system enables 599 to lap Fiorano test track 1.5sec quicker than with just traditional ASR

FERRARI 550

SPECIFICATIONS

Engine
V12

Location
Front, longitudinal

Displacement
5474cc

Bore x stroke
88 x 75mm

Cylinder block
Aluminium alloy

Cylinder head
Aluminium alloy, dohc per
bank, four valves per cylinder

Fuel and ignition
Electronic engine
management, multi-point fuel
injection

Max power
485bhp @ 7000rpm

Max torque
415lb ft @ 5000rpm

Transmission
Six-speed manual, rear-wheel
drive, traction control

Front suspension
Double wishbones, coil
springs, adjustable dampers,
anti-roll bar

Rear suspension
Double wishbones, coil
springs, adjustable dampers,
anti-roll bar

Brakes
Vented and cross-drilled
discs, 330mm front, 310mm
rear, ABS

Weight (kerb)
1716kg

Power-to-weight
287bhp/ton

0-62mph
4.4sec (claimed)

Max speed
199mph (claimed)

Basic price
£143,685 (1997)

Above: shift-lights mounted in the top edge of the steering wheel; rev-counter takes centre stage in binnacle, supported by an LCD 'multidisplay' (bottom left) which shows different info depending on which mode is selected on the manettino

modulate power delivery for optimal acceleration, and the result (according to Ferrari's comparative test data) is a 20 per cent increase in longitudinal acceleration out of a corner, which translates to a 1.5sec reduction in lap time at Fiorano compared with a car relying on conventional ASR.

Central to this system is the now-familiar manettino, located on the steering wheel. First seen in the F430, this tactile little switch is the key to unlocking the 599's potential and revealing each layer of its personality, from open-handed friendship to clenched-fist aggression. It's an uncanny system, its five stages – ranging from low grip to brain out – each accompanied by damper settings, throttle mapping and F1-Trac sensitivity tailored to suit the conditions or your mood. I say mood because although the first two stages are Ice and Low Grip, I can imagine, after a long drive or a hard day, that the added security and compliance of the Low Grip setting would make perfect sense, especially if you also opted to let the 599 handle the gearchanges in its much-improved auto mode.

On warm, dry Italian asphalt, Sport (the third of the five settings) is really your base setting, for traction isn't an issue through fast, smooth corners, and the Fiorano finds plenty of drive out of tight hairpins. If you do manage to wake the stability systems, you soon appreciate that they are only as intrusive as you are clumsy. Turn in too sharply, attempt to carry too much speed, or get greedy with the throttle, and you get that treacly feeling as the car momentarily bogs down. It's quick to react, though, and as you begin to wind off the lock, the steering sensors talk to the throttle and engine management systems and the V12's taps are opened, feeding as much torque as your steering angle permits.

This is also true in Race mode, but because the thresholds have been upped, the 599 is allowed to dance that bit closer to the limit, even letting its rear wheels spin a little and its tail slide ❯❯

the manual setting, as F1 transmissions are generally hopeless when it comes to self-shifting. Not so in the 599, which makes an impressive fist of it, neither short-shifting excessively nor stubbornly hanging on to a low gear. It also manages clean starts, and with a button rather than a fiddly T-bar to engage reverse, low-speed manoeuvring isn't the trauma it once was.

Early impressions are of light steering, quick responses and a very rigid structure. The ride is hard but not unyielding, and you're immediately aware of the magnetorheological dampers' minimal reaction time and uniquely clipped action. Shunning gas or oil-filled dampers with electronically altered valving, the new Delphi-developed items are filled with a special fluid

which alters in viscosity when subjected to an electronically controlled magnetic field. The result is a damper that reacts four times faster than previous designs, can be infinitely adjusted, and yet contains fewer moving parts.

The suspension is just the start of the Fiorano's groundbreaking technological content. F1-Trac is Ferrari's latest take on controlling stability and traction, and it employs ideas and software developed for the Scuderia's Formula 1 cars. Using a vehicle dynamics model stored in the 599's control systems, F1-Trac is a predictive system that estimates optimal grip by continually monitoring the speed of both front and rear wheels. By comparing this real-time data with that stored in the model, F1-Trac is able to

'Driven as fast as you dare, it devours the road and corrupts your soul'

under power. On a challenging, twisty road it's an absolute riot, the car up on tiptoes through quick direction changes, sliding enough to need correction but not enough to slow your progress or give you too much of a scare. It's like those special days when you know you're driving out of your skin: very fast, but smooth, precise and controlled. The wonderful (or sobering) thing is that often you don't know where your talent ends and the Fiorano's electronic magic begins.

Until you try the CST-off mode. Now you realise that the manettino is also an honesty switch. The Race setting's latitude means you've already had to think carefully about your abilities before engaging it on the road, but another twist to the right means you're exploring wild and uncharted territory. No traction or stability control can come and save you here; you're on your own.

Initially you're more circumspect with the throttle, waiting longer before you explore the second half of its travel on the exit of a corner,

but after the first twitch of oversteer you know that the 599 is with you all the way. The speed-sensitive steering is perfectly weighted and geared for quick corrections, and the engine so strong and responsive, even from low revs, that you have plenty of control. It's also clear that the 599 doesn't wag its tail readily, even with the stability and traction systems deactivated. Some provocation is needed to get it out of shape, but once you have there's more than enough poke to keep the rear Pirellis spinning. So long as you're dialled-in to the zero-inertia responses of the chassis and the quick-witted reactions of the steering, the Fiorano responds to analogue inputs just as sweetly and readily as it accepts computer control. However, you do need to have your wits about you.

Whether you choose to fly by wire or by the seat of your pants, the time comes when you feel sufficiently buoyed to take a deep breath and truly unleash the Fiorano's full force. When you do, and the shift-lights across the top of the

steering wheel begin to illuminate, your whole world streams into fast-forward. Flat-out in the 599 is an all-encompassing experience, each gear delivering a more intense hit than the last: first-*bang*-second-*bang*-third-*bang*... By the time you pull fourth everything seems hotter, brighter, more vivid, all your senses heightened by the frenzied ferocity of the acceleration and the guttural, malevolent engine-note that penetrates your very core.

The Veyron may post fiercer figures, but it surely can't match the Fiorano's naturally aspirated immediacy on give-and-take roads. You could shave with this car's throttle and chassis responses, while the F1-SuperFast transmission punches upshifts like a fully sequential racing car, with barely an interruption in acceleration. Downshifts are equally emphatic, a three-gear downchange from fifth to second executed in an instant, exhausts emitting a rolling barrage of thunderous pops and bangs. Driven as fast as you dare, it devours the road and corrupts your soul.

Hands and legs quivering with adrenalin, swapping back into the 550 for a drive along the same stretch of road is an education. It feels soft, with plenty of pitch under acceleration and dive under braking. Hard cornering generates noticeable body-roll, and you can feel the Maranello hunkering down on its outside corner. Steeply cambered hairpins, where the apex falls away from the inside wheel, set the unloaded wheel chirruping, and you begin to feel the 550 working hard. Ultimately, you're often waiting for the car to settle, its conventional dampers slow to recover from the last bump or crest. Of course, 'slow' is a relative concept, but once you've driven the road at Fiorano pace, the Maranello's best efforts are clearly from a bygone era.

Proof of this can be found when changing gear. Indeed, charging into one hairpin I catch myself frustratedly pulling back on the wiper stalk and wondering why I'm not getting any downshifts...

Working the clutch and stick is tremendously tactile, and the 550's gearbox is a good one, but it only feels appropriate because of its V12's mellow delivery. Specifying a 599 with a manual gearbox makes as much sense as Wayne Rooney playing football with his bootlaces tied together.

The Maranello's steering feels heavy after the delicately assisted Fiorano, especially if you need to apply some corrective lock, but it's still easy to appreciate the fluidity with which the 550 tackles a road. Its limits are lower, and it breaks away nice and progressively, but where the 599 slides, reacts to your inputs and comes neatly back into line without hesitation, the 550 is slightly lazy in its responses. Predictably, the brakes are a weak point, the initially firm pedal softening a little as the drilled and vented cast-iron discs begin to lose their bite. Towards the end of a spirited charge up our hill route they are grumbling for mercy, and it's also noticeable that the engine's oil and water temperature gauges have registered the effort required to keep pace with its younger, fitter sibling.

Don't misunderstand me, the 550 has shown its class, but ultimately the fight was even more one-sided than we imagined. Roomier, more comfortable and better equipped to isolate you from the rigours of urban and long distance driving, the 599 is the consummate GT. And yet, when you tap into its latent ability, it delivers spectacular performance coupled with unprecedented exploitability, while exploring its prodigious limits unaided presents as fierce and absorbing a challenge as you could wish for. It is, quite simply, the most enthralling, concentrated, mind-altering supercar I've ever driven. △

After a stint in the 599, the still-impressive 550 starts to show its age. New car's optional carbon brakes (top) particularly impressive

HORSE
TRIALS

The 599 GTB Fiorano gets wrung-out on the dyno, at the circuit and up and down the mile straight as we bring you the UK's only official test of Ferrari's most potent GT

Words: John Barker | Pictures: Kenny P

Ferrari F40. We see an

icon; Ferrari sees a benchmark for the 599 GTB
Fiorano. It sounds almost fanciful to set the
performance of a genuine, mid-engined supercar
as the target for a front-engined Grand Tourer.
The F40 may be almost 20 years old, but even by
today's standards the stripped-out, 1100kg, twin-
turbo road-racer is stupendously quick. *Fast Lane*
magazine stuck its test gear to one in the late '80s
and recorded 0 to 60mph in 3.9sec, 0-100 in 7.8
and 0-140 in 14 dead. Other independent tests
reckoned it was a couple of tenths quicker to 60
and 100mph. Whatever, that's a mighty challenge
for a leather-trimmed, V12-engined GT weighing
in at over 1700kg – that's 55 per cent more.

Of course, it helps that the V12 nestled well
back in the long nose of the 599 is derived from
that of Ferrari's most recent supercar, the Enzo.
The naturally aspirated 6-litre unit delivers a
claimed 611bhp (we'll get the exact figure later
on the dyno) and 448lb ft, which should test
the traction of the rear tyres, though their task

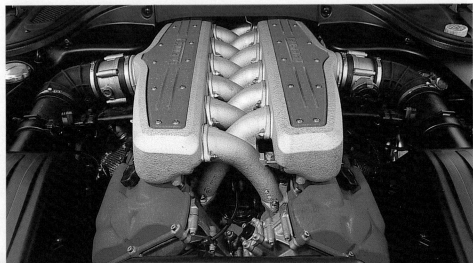

Above right: 599's 6-litre, 65deg
V12 is based on the Enzo unit,
albeit with 39bhp less and in a car
weighing 323kg more – according
to Ferrari's figures

'Subjectively, the 599 works superbly, but
can it really nail F40-matching figures?'

is assisted by the fact that the car's masses are configured to give a rearward weight bias.

This philosophy is key to the success of Ferrari's latest front-engined cars. A weight distribution approaching that of a mid-engined car gives enhanced traction, while having the engine set back behind the front wheels and the bulk of the car's other heavy components between the axles promotes an easy, natural handling balance. It works on both the 612 and 599, though Ferrari's engineers have had to put a lot more effort into making the sportier, shorter-wheelbase 599 capable of deploying its 600bhp-plus with ease.

The 599's fundamentals, based around the aluminium chassis technology shared by other current Ferraris, have been subject to an exquisite attention to detail (see box on page 207), and the car also introduces such features as hyper-responsive 'magnetorheological' semi-active adaptive dampers, a bespoke 'F1-Trac' dynamic stability system and the quickest-shifting version of the F1 auto-clutch manual yet, appropriately dubbed F1-SuperFast. The result is a car that's emphatically more advanced than the 550/575M Maranello it replaces.

Subjectively, it all works superbly, but can it really nail F40-matching figures? We'll find out soon, because our latest encounter with Ferrari's most potent production car ever (the Enzo is deemed a special series) starts at Millbrook. This particular 599 comes with the optional CCM (Carbon Ceramic Material) brake discs, the

box for which has so far been ticked by all UK customers, and the F1-S gearbox – the traditional open-gate manual is expected to account for less than 10 per cent of sales worldwide.

When we put the 612 through our test programme (see pages 158 to 165) a couple of Ferrari staff from Italy were in attendance. It's perhaps a measure of how important to Ferrari is the performance of the sportier Fiorano that staff writer Catchpole and myself are greeted at Millbrook by a phalanx of Ferrari personnel, six of them from Italy, clad in luminous red jackets. They're here to ensure that the 599 is in fine fettle and to offer tips on getting the best out of it, which, as we shall see, prove rather useful.

We make camp on the southern loop of the mile straight and set to installing our VBOX test gear, only to find ourselves fitting it alongside Ferrari's own. There's a moment of VBOX envy when we realise that theirs is more up-to-date than ours, but this is quickly forgotten when we see that their dash-top display gives an instant readout of 0-100kph (62mph). This will save us having to download all our data there and then to check which is the best start technique – and there is some considerable technique involved, as test driver Michele Coughi Costantini demonstrates. »

Top: Barker checks the results from the VBOX. Left: this 599 came with its own pit crew to ensure it was in tip-top condition for each of our tests

SLOW 40 MPH MAX · 1 MILE END · SLOW 40 MPH MAX

'The 599 lunges off the line, weight transfer further loading the rear tyres'

I belt myself into the passenger seat and Michele thumbs the big red start button. The starter motor whirrs at double speed before the huge V12 catches and booms into life. I smile. Yup, the resonant, deep-chested gargle of 12 cylinders sounds familiar; despite its squatter intake assembly and less freely curved exhaust manifolds, there's no question that this engine is closely related to that in the Enzo.

We make a few steady 100mph runs to bring the 599's vitals up to temperature. These involve tyre-warming zigzags that would impress Alonso, each steering input so obediently and immediately translated into a direction change that I'm slammed into alternate bolsters on my seat. Satisfied that all is primed, we line up with the simple perspective of the mile straight in front of us and Michele talks me through the start procedure.

This does not involve the button marked LC. Launch control is designed to save the clutch and transmission by spinning the rear tyres, which is spectacular but not fast. Instead the process is this: set the wheel-mounted 'manettino' switch to 'race' mode and then, with your left foot on the brake, select first with the 'up' paddle, then pull back and hold the 'down' paddle for a couple of seconds. There's a beep, which is the signal to mash the throttle. The revs build quickly but not as if the gearbox is in neutral, and as the tacho needle gets to 4000rpm you jump off the brake.

I make a hash of my first attempt, releasing the brake too slowly without full throttle, which adds a tang of clutch lining to the cockpit ambience, but a few tries later I make what feels satisfyingly like an optimum start. The 599 lunges off the line, weight transfer further loading the rear

tyres so that they're fully hooked up and driving all the V12's furious, bellowing energy into the surface. Shoved hard into the backrest, all I need do now is summon the wit to pull on the upshift paddle for second gear just as the howling V12 swings close to 8000rpm, but without snagging the limiter. That done, I can enjoy the noise and seemingly undiminished urge that drives us through 100mph, and marvel at the speed and precision of the upshifts – they're virtually seamless. We make an easy 160mph within the mile and top it with 170mph on the return run.

Interrogating our imperial-units VBOX, I find that the 599 is every bit as quick as it felt: 30mph comes up in a remarkable 1.5sec, 60 takes just 3.5sec and 100 is despatched in an equally awe-inspiring 7.4sec. Sure, at 14.3sec to 140mph the 599 is three-tenths adrift of the F40, but if they were lined up either side of the Christmas tree at Santa Pod, I wouldn't know which to back. Not only that, checking back I discover that the 599 is as fast as the Enzo to 60mph and only four tenths behind at 100mph – heroic times given that it weighs hundreds of kilos more and has 40bhp less.

Other stand-out figures include an 11.6sec quarter-mile (at 128mph) and a set of third-gear times which show every 20mph increment from 40-60mph to 80-100mph takes no more than 2.0sec. On UK roads, it's the overtaking gear of choice. Equally devastating is the 11.9sec 0-100-0 time, those massive carbon discs hauling the 599 down from 100mph to a standstill in less than 300ft and generating an average of 1.1g in the process.

There's no question that the F1-SuperFast gearbox is a factor in the staggering acceleration times. Its fastest shift speed – a mere 100 milliseconds – compares with 150ms for the Enzo and 250ms for the 575. This time is measured from when the clutch begins to disengage to when it has fully re-engaged, and is what Ferrari calls the 'acceleration gap'. It has been reduced to 100ms by slightly overlapping the disengagement and re-engagement of the clutch with the actual gear change (which takes a mere 40ms), the software anticipating the approaching parity in rotational speeds of the relevant shafts and gears. Imagine the peachiest, near-synchro-beating manual shift you've ever made and you're close. The lower-inertia twin-plate clutch helps, as do new gear-selector forks of pressed steel rather than cast iron, which again help to reduce inertia.

F1-SuperFast isn't all about making the quickest shifts, though. The overall shift time varies according to engine load and throttle opening, which is a welcome development of this type of gearbox and why, on the road, it goes about its business more unobtrusively than most. Compare this with, say, BMW's SMG system on »

Above: Barker talks technique with the Ferrari team. Top: Catchpole takes notes as the scales reveal the 599's corner weights. Above: fitting new brake pads

the M6, where the driver selects the shift speed; in its fastest setting the SMG gearchange is nowhere near as smooth or rapid as F1-S, and you're constantly changing it to suit your mood (or you simply plump for the middle setting). F1-S judges your mood from the way you're using the throttle. The only odd thing about it is that from start-up it defaults to auto mode.

There's little doubt the 599 is developing the quoted horsepower, but our next stop is the Dyno Dynamics rolling road at WRC Technologies, Silverstone. Lashed down, warmed up and driving hard in fourth gear, the Fiorano sounds terrifying and looks ready to leap off the rollers. All is not right, though. The first run peaks at no more than 570bhp and the next few are no better. Engine calibration engineer Giorgio

Francomarco plugs in his laptop as the 599 roars on the dyno and confirms that nothing is amiss at the pointy end.

The little black crumbs peppering Kenny P, rather bravely installed at the rear of the test cell with his camera, suggest another reason. The rear P Zeros are getting so hot that they're throwing off morsels of rubber and may actually be sticking to the rollers, increasing rolling resistance. A fresh, cool set is bolted on, and on the first run the graph shows peak power of 621bhp. Ferrari quotes 620 PS (611bhp) so that's better than expected, but only by 1.6 per cent. Torque is up by a full 10 per cent on the quoted figure, though, peaking at 493lb ft rather than 448.

The softness of the tyres is interesting. Ferrari wouldn't be the first company to get extra grip by specifying a soft compound. I ran a long-term Honda NSX back in the early '90s that was lucky to see 5000 miles from a pair of rears, while the original-equipment semi-slicks on recent Mitsubishi Evos are similarly short-lived.

On the road, the 599 is infused with a satisfying tautness. It starts with the seat, which is deeply sculpted, firmly padded and perfectly aligned with the pedals and fat-rimmed steering wheel. The transmission controls the clutch more

positively in manoeuvring than other F1 types, but just as smoothly; the throttle and brake have good weight and feel; the low-speed ride is firm but not crashy.

Right from the off, the V12 sounds glorious, and the ebb and flow of its complex, thunder-laden note when you press the throttle deeply in a high gear is epic. There's a distinct pick-up in the delivery at 3000rpm and another at 5500, by which time you're fast approaching three-figure speeds in fourth. The 599 merely feels like it's getting into its stride, the ride having settled, wind and road noise subdued. Floor the throttle and it snaps forward instantly with a force that stuns passengers.

The work of the magnetorheological dampers goes largely unnoticed, which is as it should be. By applying a magnetic field, the viscosity of the fluid within them can be increased, firming them up in about a quarter of the time it takes for an adjustable-valve damper to react. Roll, pitch and squat are tempered by the system, yet the 599 feels quite natural through a series of curves. Through the seat of your pants it feels pretty much as heavy as the scales will later show it to be, yet it is a terrifically agile car. Push hard through a sequence of corners and it changes

Left: the 599 struggled on its first run on the dyno, falling some 40bhp short of Ferrari's quoted power figure. Fresh rubber on the driven wheels would soon see it recording significantly bigger numbers, however

'Floor the throttle and it snaps forward with a force that stuns passengers'

tack more eagerly than, say, the mid-engined Lamborghini LP640, though personally I'd like a bit more weight at the wheel. Understeer can build if you're a bit ambitious with your entry speed (it's quite easy to arrive at a corner more quickly than you expect...) and this might be better telegraphed with a more distinct sensation of the steering shedding weight.

That said, the manettino's default 'sport' setting feels perfectly judged for keen driving on dry roads. You can feel the back end hunker down under power mid-corner and the rear tyres edge towards slip at the exit, but the situation will escalate no further. The F1-Trac system subtly modulates the power, based on the inputs of various sensors, including some measuring

front- and rear-wheel speed, which are fed into a dynamics model stored in the control system. For less favourable conditions there are the 'ice' and 'low grip' (read: wet road) settings, which make the dampers softer, while regular ASR takes over from F1-Trac, allowing less slip and activating individual brakes if necessary to maintain stability.

»

DOWN UNDER

THE INTRODUCTION OF the 599 completes an all-aluminium range of Ferraris, the superstructure of the new model using the now familiar combination of extrusions,

pressed sheet and sand castings. MIG welded, with structural rivets at key points to prevent heat distortion, the bare 599 chassis is said to be lighter and much more torsionally rigid than the 575's, despite its longer wheelbase. The fuel tank has been moved forward of the rear

axle so that some 85 per cent of the car's mass is concentrated between the axles (compared with 70 per cent for the 575), while the more rearward cabin contributes to a claimed 47/53 front/rear distribution.

In addition, the centre of gravity of the 599 is 20mm lower than the 575's. This is partly as a result of mounting the drivetrain lower, made possible by a new, more efficient scavenge pump which allows a much shallower engine sump, and, at the other end, a twin-plate clutch in place of a larger diameter single-plate type.

599 GTB's weight is concentrated between the axles, with a bias towards the rear

+ROADTESTDATA+

SPECIFICATION

FERRARI 599 GTB

Engine	65-degree V12
Location	Front-mid, longitudinal
Displacement	5999cc
Bore x stroke	92.0 x 75.2mm
Cylinder block	Aluminium alloy
Cylinder head	Aluminium alloy, dohc per bank, four valves per cylinder, variable valve timing
Fuel and ignition	Bosch Motronic ME7 engine management, multipoint sequential injection
Max power	611bhp @ 7600rpm (test car 621bhp)
Max torque	448lb ft @ 5600rpm (test car 493lb ft)
Transmission	Six-speed manual gearbox with F1-SuperFast paddleshift, transaxle, rear-wheel drive, lsd, ASR, CST, F1-Trac
Front suspension	Double wishbones, coil springs, SCM adaptive dampers, anti-roll bar
Rear suspension	Double wishbones, coil springs, SCM adaptive dampers, anti-roll bar
Steering	Rack and pinion, power-assisted
Brakes	Vented and drilled cast iron discs, 355mm front, 330mm rear (test car optional CCM discs, 398mm fr, 360mm rr), ABS, EBD
Wheels	8 x 19in front, 11 x 20in rear, aluminium alloy
Tyres	245/40 ZR19 front, 305/35 ZR20 rear, Pirelli P Zero
Kerb weight	1688kg (test car 1733kg)
Power-to-weight	368bhp/ton (test car 364bhp/ton)
Basic price	£171,825
Price as tested	£198,670
Extras fitted include	F1-SuperFast gearbox (£5500), CCM brakes (£11,495), carbon trim for interior (£6555), leather headliner (£265), Bose hi-fi (£1985), Scuderia Ferrari Shields (£1045)
On sale	Now

FERRARI 599 GTB FIORANO

PERFORMANCE

ACCELERATION TIMES

0-30	1.5
0-40	2.1
0-50	2.6
0-60	3.5
0-70	4.2
0-80	5.3
0-90	6.3
0-100	7.4
0-110	8.9
0-120	10.3
0-130	11.9
0-140	14.3
0-150	16.6
0-160	19.3

1/4 MILE

sec	11.6
speed	128.1

IN-GEAR TIMES

	2nd	3rd	4th	5th	6th
20-40	1.6	2.4	-	-	-
30-50	1.4	2.1	3.2	-	-
40-60	1.3	2.0	2.9	4.3	5.8
50-70	1.4	1.9	2.8	3.9	5.8
60-80	-	1.8	2.7	3.8	5.6
70-90	-	1.9	2.6	3.8	5.4
80-100	-	2.0	2.6	3.6	5.4
90-110	-	-	2.6	3.6	5.6
100-120	-	-	2.7	3.7	5.5
110-130	-	-	3.0	3.8	5.5
120-140	-	-	-	4.4	6.0
130-150	-	-	-	4.4	-
140-160	-	-	-	5.1	-

BRAKING

100-0	4.03sec
dist. ft	290

MAX SPEED

205mph (claimed)

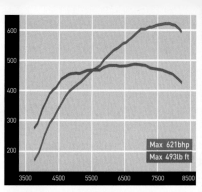

Max 621bhp
Max 493lb ft

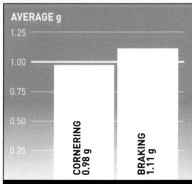

AVERAGE g

CORNERING 0.98 g
BRAKING 1.11 g

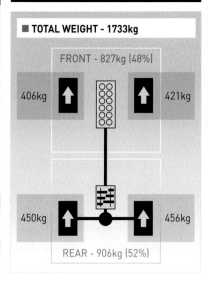

■ TOTAL WEIGHT - 1733kg

FRONT - 827kg (48%)

406kg | 421kg

450kg | 456kg

REAR - 906kg (52%)

0-100-0

599 GTB FIORANO	11.9sec

0 1 2 3 4 5 6 7 8 9 10 11 12 13 14 15

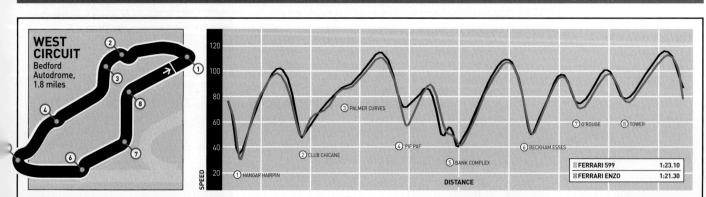

WEST CIRCUIT
Bedford Autodrome, 1.8 miles

① HANGAR HAIRPIN
② CLUB CHICANE
③ PALMER CURVES
④ PIF PAF
⑤ BANK COMPLEX
⑥ BECKHAM ESSES
⑦ O'ROUGE
⑧ TOWER

SPEED
DISTANCE

| ☒ FERRARI 599 | 1:23.10 |
| ☒ FERRARI ENZO | 1:21.30 |

☒ As at Ferrari's Fiorano test track, around Bedford the 599 is slower than the Enzo, but not by much. Lighter Enzo accelerates a bit harder, brakes a bit later and carries more speed through the last two corners. Lots of time is gained at the Pif-Paf chicane too, though overall the front-engine/rear-drive 599 stacks up remarkably well against the mid-engined supercar

One notch above 'sport' is 'race', which is deemed suitable for track use only. It offers maximum shift speed and backs-off the stability and traction controls to permit larger degrees of slip, though in extremis there is still some tailoring of the trajectory based on the F1-Trac dynamics model. Reckon you can do better and a final twist of the manettino cuts out all stability and traction controls entirely, leaving you with only anti-lock brakes. Helpfully, a coloured bar at the top edge of the electronic screen to the left of the rev-counter indicates at a glance which mode is selected.

At the Bedford Autodrome we slip the Ferrari onto the scales. Ferrari quotes a kerb weight of 1688kg for a manual gearbox model. This car, with its F1 gearbox and optional carbon brakes (which save 13kg) settles at 1733kg, split 48/52 front/rear.

For the laps, I start with the race setting. I've got my own target time: 1:24.45, set by the fastest front-engine/rear-drive car we've yet tried, the 505bhp, 1400kg Corvette Z06. Many powerful cars feel strangely slow out on the wide, flat West Circuit, but not the Fiorano. Glimpsing the odd moment of 8000rpm acceleration on the road is a huge thrill to be savoured. Keening the V12 to within an ace of the limiter for three laps is veering towards sensory overload.

Race mode certainly allows you some freedom of expression when cornering, yet once acclimatised to the phenomenal pace of the 599 it becomes apparent that there is a definite style

to be adopted for the quickest lap. As on the mile straight, the aim has to be to keep the rear tyres hooked up so that you're using all of the engine's power to drive forward rather than daub the track with black lines. This is fine through the simple, medium-speed corners, but through the scary-fast second part of the Palmer Curves, understeer dominates, and wrestling the car into oversteer doesn't feel (or prove) any faster. Also, at the exit of the fast corners at the end of the lap, the Fiorano is poised under power until the very last, and then swings further, as if its tyres have just got too hot. Happily, in race mode F1-Trac intervenes whenever there is excess like this, stopping it going any further, but without slowing the car as ASR tends to.

Exactly what F1-Trac is doing across the lap becomes apparent when I twist the manettino and take full control, and responsibility, for the last couple of laps. It's mighty difficult to be as hard on the power quite so early in the corners without the rear tyres then spinning up towards the exit. On the plus side, it's huge fun to balance the 599 in a heroic oversteer slide, calmly winding the lock on and off. On the downside, you know that you're wasting time, and the VBOX shows it – around a second is lost to the best time in 'race'.

We're under the Z06's time, but I reckon there's more to come, because the carbon brakes don't have the bite they did on the mile straight. Normally we'd make the best of what we've been given, but with six Ferrari staff on hand, we can

get close to a perfect car. So we grab a coffee while a new set of pads is fitted, along with a pair of the optional 20in rims for the front to see if they give less understeer through the Palmer Curves.

'The fastest drivers go slightly quicker with all the systems turned off,' says vehicle engineer Martino Cavanna, mildly. I don't think it's going to work for me, and with a few clean laps in the refreshed car (with only a very slight reduction in the understeer), I consider we've given the Fiorano a good shot. I'm happy with the best lap of 1:23.10 – that puts it ahead of the Z06, F430, 911 GT3 RS and Ascari KZ1. However, it transpires that the Ferrari boys had their own target and they're disappointed that I haven't been able to beat the time of the four-wheel-drive Lamborghini Gallardo (1:22.80).

I don't think that really matters. The 599 GTB is an extraordinarily accomplished car: five hours at the wheel, from Maranello to Castellane for our 2006 Car of the Year contest, proved its GT credentials, and here it has shown that its all-out performance is a match for the F40. That's amazing given how much heavier it is, but then it does have one of the best engines in the world... that just happens to be paired with the most impressive paddle-shift manual we've ever tried.

Simply put, there isn't another GT that comes close to matching the exceptional breadth of the 599's ability, nor the richness of the experience. It will be some machine that topples it from its position as the world's greatest GT. ⚠

The quickest lap times (if you're not a Ferrari test driver) are achieved with the manettino in 'race' mode and F1-Trac keeping things tidy. The 599 is great fun with the stability systems off, though...

This page:
Maurice Trintignant's
Ferrari 625 wins the
1955 Monaco GP"

Ferrari's F1
GLORY YEARS

By fair means or foul, Ferrari has had great periods – unrivalled in
motor sport – of success in Formula 1. Here's how they did it

Words: Doug Nye | Photography: The GP Library

Enzo FERRARI

He overcame a hard upbringing to create the greatest car marque the world
has ever known, ruling it in the uniquely tough, manipulative, emotional
and unpredictable manner for which he became famous

Enzo Ferrari was a hard-nosed wheeler dealer. He was also a master manipulator of multi-talented people. His long-time chief engineer of the 1960s through to the 1980s, Mauro Forghieri, furrowed his brow when I once asked him what The Old Man's greatest strengths had been. He responded, with a thin and decidedly rueful smile: 'Mr Ferrari had a great understanding... of human weakness.'

'Oscar' Tavoni, Ferrari's team manager of the late '50s/early '60s, told me that Enzo never lost his fascination with manipulating the great and wealthy. 'He liked to see them dancing to his tune,' said Tavoni, 'yet once a wealthy customer offered enough money, he would sell them anything. He loved always to make the big score. The wealthy might have got what they wanted, and gone away smirking, but first they had left their money with him – Ferrari.'

It was in part this merchant, some say peasant, ability which founded Ferrari's greatness – and the world's most charismatic motoring brand. For decades *Il Drake* or *Il Grande Vecchio*, as he became known around Modena, had an almost unerring eye for an engineer who would contribute to building the legend. And before one engineer's potential had been squeezed dry another would have been groomed and prepared to take his place. Once ultimately cast aside, that man's greatest potential would be behind him, trapped in Ferrari's pitiless filter.

Born on February 18, 1898, Enzo Ferrari was introduced to motor racing by his father, Alfredo, who ran a modest Modenese metal fabricating business. The boy was ten when Papa took him to Bologna to watch the Coppa Florio motor race. Felice Nazzaro of Fiat won, and Enzo was hooked. Brief World War I service in the Italian Army ended when he fell victim to the flu epidemic of 1918; both his father and elder brother had died the previous year. Alone in the world, the recovered Enzo found a job in the Turin motor trade and developed friends who took him to CMN, for whom he drove in the 1920 Parma-Poggio di Berceto hillclimb. Now he was a racing driver...

His CMN friend Ugo Sivocci moved to Alfa Romeo and fixed Ferrari a job there. He became right-hand man to Giorgio Rimini, Nicola Romeo's closest aide, and drove Alfa Romeos in the Targa Florio, at Mugello and in other races. In 1924 he joined the works team for the French Grand Prix, but his nerve broke – the P2 GP car was beyond him, and he non-started. He recovered back in Modena, building his successful Alfa Romeo agency, and resumed racing in minor-league events in 1927. His agency attracted numerous wealthy clients, and at the end of 1929 he persuaded three of them – the Caniato brothers and Mario Tadini – to finance the establishment of the Scuderia Ferrari. This new team was to prepare, enter and run Alfa Romeo cars for such wealthy owners, so all they had to do was report to the right venue, on the right day, to find their cars present and race-ready, entries and accommodation arranged.

When Alfa's in-house works team was closed on cost grounds in 1932, Mr Ferrari manoeuvred his Scuderia into assuming quasi-works team duties. From mid-1933 until 1937 the Modena-based Scuderia was 'Alfa Sport'. From 1934 Alfa's GP cars could not match the emergent German factory teams in men, money and material, so in 1937 Mr Ferrari recommended building 1.5-litre Vetturetta class ('GP2') cars instead. He had them designed for him at Modena by a team under Gioachino Colombo and they emerged as the Alfa Romeo 158 'Alfetta'. But the Scuderia did not live to race them.

Instead new Alfa President Gobbato took Alfa racing back in house for 1938. The Scuderia Ferrari was wound-up and Ferrari returned to Milan to manage the new Alfa Corse factory team. He hated this loss of independence and walked out later the same year. One clause of his severance agreement was that he would neither build nor race cars under his own name for four years.

Instead he founded a precision machining business, Auto-Avio Costruzioni, in his old Scuderia HQ. Around Christmas 1939 he was visited by local aristo *Marchese* Lotario Rangoni and young Alberto Ascari – son of Alfa's long-lost great Champion driver, Antonio – who wanted Ferrari to build them Fiat-based sports cars for the 1940 Mille Miglia. AAC produced two otherwise anonymous '815' cars to suit, with Fiat-derived straight-eight 1500cc engines. At Brescia they ran quite well, but then Italy entered World War II, during which Ferrari moved his company to Maranello in the Apenine foothills to escape allied bombing. He manufactured copies of top-grade German machine tools, finessed his way around the fall of fascism and advance of Italian communism, and even before peace returned in 1945 he was laying the foundation for post-war car production... and the launch of his own Ferrari marque. △

Right: Alberto Ascari in 1940 in the AAC 815 built for him by Enzo for the Mille Miglia

'He loved to make the big score. The wealthy might have got what they wanted, and gone away smirking, but they had left their money with him'

The Front-Engined Era 1947-1962

From tiny beginnings, Ferrari began a reign of giant-killing before turning into a giant itself – with all its attendant problems

Ex-Alfa Romeo, ex-Scuderia Ferrari engineer Gioachino Colombo was out of work in 1945, suspended and shunned by a highly politicised Alfa Romeo for too-enthusiast support of Mussolini. Such loyalty to a dictator was just fine by Mr Ferrari, Colombo was the man for him, and he was commissioned to produce a new breed of high-performance machine – in both sports and single-seater form – powered by a 1500cc supercharged V12 engine.

Through 1946 Mr Ferrari's tiny team developed its first V12s, then began racing them in primitive sports-bodied chassis in 1947. They entered the Grand Prix arena in 1948, fielding three new *Tipo* 125 *Monoposti* in the Turin GP – driven by Farina, Sommer and 'B. Bira'. They failed. Next time out at Lake Garda... Farina won.

Meanwhile Alfa Corse had taken a stranglehold on GP racing with its Ferrari-inspired cars in updated form. But post-war finance was always tight, and for 1949 Alfa took a sabbatical from competition – and the supercharged Colombo Ferrari V12s of Alberto Ascari – yes, him again – and Gigi Villoresi began winning GP races.

Having used up the butterfly-brained Colombo's original genius, and that of development engineer Busso to make these designs raceworthy, Ferrari massaged a perhaps greater engineer – Aurelio Lampredi – to take his company forward. A

Above, from left: Gonzales wins 1951 Pescara GP; Ferrari management at 1959 Dutch GP; winning the last Mille Miglia in 1957

tough-minded and ambitious man, Lampredi did brilliantly by Ferrari. He shelved the highly strung supercharged 1500cc V12s in favour of new unsupercharged 4.5-litre units, and launched an unsupercharged 2-litre four-cylinder for Formula 2, in which 2-litre V12s had been campaigned, sans supercharging.

In the 1951 British GP at Silverstone, works cadet driver Jose Froilan Gonzalez drove Ferrari's 4.5-litre V12 *muletto* to defeat the returned Alfa Corse team, for the first time. 'I feel I have killed my own mother,' wrote The Old Man, self-consciously theatrical as ever.

Lampredi's unblown 2-litre four-cylinder Ferraris then carried Ascari to history's first back-to-back Drivers' World Championship titles in 1952 and '53. On their shirt tails rode sales of Ferrari sports and production cars, still built in what were really penny numbers, but generating revenue to feed Enzo's passion: racing. With headline-grabbing consecutive victories in the Mille Miglia from 1948 to 1953, at Le Mans in 1949 and in myriad high-grade sports car, Formula 1 and Formula 2 races worldwide, *La Ferrari* was on an amazing roll, the company's creator bestriding the motor racing world like a colossus.

It took men of equal stature and hardness to cut him down. One such was Tony Vandervell, who made the Thinwall shell bearings that had cured the Ferrari V12's greatest frailty.

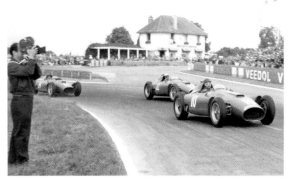

'Horsepower was God, chassis mere brackets that retained the wheels. Ferraris of the 1950s were seldom "easy" cars'

Between him and Mr Ferrari it was a pure case of diamond cut diamond. Lampredi was another hard nut. Yet when he failed to deliver the goods in 1955 against Mercedes-Benz and Maserati, he was overboard (to Fiat). By a stroke of good fortune Lancia went bust and both its Formula 1 hardware and its great ex-Alfa engineer Vittorio Jano landed instead in Ferrari's lap.

Enzo had already separated production from racing, in conjunction with yet another hard man – Battista 'Pinin' Farina – to build and sell GT cars. The dominant Ferrari characteristic was 'unburstability' – engines and drive lines that were bullet proof, gearchanges that loved being used 'like the bolt on a rifle'. Horsepower was God, chassis mere brackets that retained the wheels. Ferraris of the 1950s were seldom 'easy' racing cars. Many drivers died in them, most doing something they adored. When works drivers like Luigi Musso and the Marquis de Portago were killed, Ferrari was pilloried. He grieved, but he went on racing. Since 1920 he had seen it all before.

The empire grew, and grew. His son Dino died from muscular dystrophy in 1956, aged just 24. The Old Man publicly agonised over his creation's destiny. Into the mid-1960s the public grievings fell away, and Piero Lardi, son of Enzo's mistress, Lina, was working at Maranello.

In 1956 the Pinin Farina-styled 3-litre V12-engined two-seat Ferrari *Berlinetta* took root, de Portago winning the

Clockwise from top left: Rosier (left) in '53; Ferraris at Thillois (1956 French GP); Ascari in 1953 British GP; Fangio in 1956 Monaco GP

Tour de France to give the new model its popular nickname. As a road/race 'supercar' the Ferrari 250GT would develop through the famously successful short-wheelbase variant in 1960-61 to the now immortal 250GTO of 1962-64 – the most iconic road-useable Ferrari of them all.

The bad times for Ferrari were seldom far away. But the Lancia windfall plus Fiat financial backing – *por la Patria* ('for the Fatherland') – sustained Formula 1 fortunes in '56 and '57, with Fangio winning another title for Ferrari in the former year, before Jano master-minded the four-cam Dino V6 engine that would bring Mike Hawthorn the drivers' title in 1958. Ferrari's own conservatism came home to roost in '59-'60, when his faith in front-mounted engines, drum brakes and wire wheels proved near fatal in the face of British racing developments – rear engines, disc brakes and lightweight cast wheels.

Still, as team driver Phil Hill recalled: 'Mr Ferrari was always busily stoking the fire under the boiling cauldron into which every racing driver worthy of the name would willingly leap...' The great Manipulator of Maranello would declare, 'My number one driver is he who won last Sunday' – like an automotive version of the Fat Controller he toyed with both staff and works drivers like chessmen on a board. Increasingly, in a developing age of big-money sport and major-league motor racing, Ferrari's in-house politics would do much more harm than good... △

The classic
REAR-ENGINED
Era 1961-1974

When the front-engined cars began to be overwhelmed, a new era of 'Motore Posteriore' Ferraris took over – and began to dominate once more…

The demonstrable superiority of the
new wave of rear-engined Grand Prix cars from Cooper, BRM and Lotus (1959-60) simply overwhelmed the front-engined Ferraris that confronted them. Mr Ferrari had always had a unique power to influence the governing body, the FIA, in its decisions concerning the future of International racing. When 1.5-litre Formula 2 racing was launched in 1957 his Jano-conceived Dino V6 had begun to shine. It burned pump petrol instead of the exotic alcohol fuel brews standard in Formula 1, and when AVGas aviation spirit was specified by the FIA for Formula 1 (1958-60), hey presto, Ferrari had just the ticket, ready developed to burn the stuff.

Dino development had devolved upon Ferrari's new chief engineer, Carlo Chiti, who came from an aeronautical background and who persuaded The Old Man to sanction major modernisation at Maranello. A wind tunnel was built, real progress was made and, early in 1960, the first rear-engined Ferrari emerged – the 2.4-litre Dino V6-powered 246MP – 'Motore Posteriore'. American test driver Richie Ginther drove it in the 1960 Monaco GP before it was fitted with a 1.5-litre V6 for Formula 2 racing. Team-mate 'Taffy' von Trips promptly won the F2 Solitude GP with it, defeating the Coventry Climax four-cylinder-engined Brits. For 1961, 1500cc Formula 2 was effectively upgraded to Formula 1 status, and again Ferrari was poised and ready, and Chiti's distinctive rear-engined 'Sharknose' 156s destroyed all opposition, Phil Hill emerging as World Champion after Trips' ghastly death – together with 14 hapless spectators – in the Italian GP.

Legal action against Ferrari for the de Portago 1957 Mille Miglia crash – which also claimed 12 other lives – had only just evaporated with the conclusion that road-centreline cat's eyes had slashed the sports Ferrari's tyres. Now legal action resumed against Ferrari – and others – for the 1961 Monza disaster. When pilloried by press and even the Vatican, Ferrari would pull up the drawbridge and adopt a stance of wounded persecution… while always planning, manipulating, researching, developing his next manoeuvre.

By 1962-63 he was definitely feeling the chill once more. Formula 1 fortunes had dived, then recovered thanks to the shrewd signing of frontier-technology British engineer/drivers John Surtees and Michael Parkes. Sports and GT success had continued – against patchy opposition – and rear-engined Dino 246 sports-prototypes of 1961-62 had spawned the 3-litre V12 rear-engined Ferrari 250P legends of 1963.

Enter Ford Detroit. To promote its wares before the new moneyed youth market of the 1960s, Ford lusted after Ferrari's ready-made glamour and capabilities. Ferrari proved a terrible old tease. He used America's advances to wind up Fiat, secured additional backing from Turin, and dismissed the Motown men. They swore revenge and – eventually – smashed Ferrari in the GT Championship of 1965, and at Le Mans in '66… and '67-8-9! The Old Man had always regarded Le Mans as the great promotional prize upon which he sold his road

cars. After winning it in 1949, 1954 and 1960-65 inclusive, he was stung. Worse, the ploy of roofing-in the 250P V12 sports-prototype as a GT car to create the 250LM as replacement for the GTO line was rejected by the FIA homologation committee. Perplexed and enraged by such 'betrayal' The Old Man reacted to this sudden loss of manipulative success by handing-in his entrant's licence… for a while.

Surtees and a new V8 Ferrari Formula 1 car had edged Maranello the 1964 World Championship titles, but into 1966 and a new 3-litre Formula 1 era The Old Man was struggling to make ends meet. His rearguard action against Ford in endurance racing was draining his coffers and the new Formula 1 V12 was a 380bhp cobble-up from sports car parts already on the storehouse shelf. Still John won the Belgian GP before being faced with an impossible situation engineered by *Direttore Sportivo* Eugenio Dragoni. John left the team in mid-'66 and Ferrari waved goodbye to another World title.

For 1967 The Old Man famously sank his dwindling funding into the 330P4 sports-prototype project, inflicting a 1-2-3 defeat upon Ford in the Daytona 24-Hours to avenge Le Mans '66, only to go down fighting back at the Sarthe that June. But not before the launch pad had been established for Ferrari's latest production *Gran Turismo* – the 365GTB/4 Daytona.

Clockwise from top left: Bandini inspects the engine of the 1512; Chris Amon in the 1969 French GP; 1967 Daytona-winning P4s

But by 1969 everything was going wrong. Ferrari built too few production cars to maintain adequate profitability. Formula 1 fortunes were slithering down the tubes. The flat-12 engine to replace the F1 V12s was teething badly. Ferrari swallowed his pride and approached Gianni Agnelli at Fiat. As an old friend the younger magnate agreed to buy. The deal was done under the Italian legal form of *in vitalizio*. Fiat bought half Ferrari's stock for a fixed annual sum to be paid as long as *Il Drake* might live. Had he died in 1970 Fiat would have secured Ferrari very cheaply. As it was Fiat would pay for nearly 20 long years – which in general numbered some of Ferrari's finest, thanks largely to Fiat money and – where the production division was concerned – to Fiat management and investment in manufacturing machinery.

In F1 the flat-12 engine came good halfway through the 1970 season, and reigned dominant until halfway through that of 1971. Had those two half-seasons been just one, Jacky Ickx and Ferrari would have been World Champions. But Fiat funding was haemorrhaging into the sports car programme to confront the Porsche 917s. They failed. However, a 3-litre flat-12 'enveloping-bodied Formula 1 car' – the 312PB – emerged in 1971 and with a fine team they put all opposition to the sword through 1972 and won yet another title. In 1973 Matra fought back as Ferrari's F1 fortunes collapsed in disarray. Fiat winced at sports-prototype costs and for 1974, the sports car programme was dropped – total concentration focused upon F1, and Niki Lauda and Clay Regazzoni came within a whisker of success. Just one more push was needed…

For many years of Ferrari's history from 1969, financial backer Fiat fought shy of being seen to meddle – too publicly – with *La Ferrari*. Its input and control of the *Reparto Industriale* production operation was perceived as being both effective and benign. Its studious non-interference with the *Reparto Corsa* racing department was due as much to well-founded fear of the merciless Italian sporting paparazzi as respect for *Il Grande Vecchio* – 'The Great Old One' – Enzo Ferrari himself.

During 1974 Niki Lauda (right) had yet to become a fully fledged Formula 1 star, while his veteran team-mate Clay Regazzoni – in his second stint with Ferrari – provided invaluable support. Chief engineer Mauro Forghieri had been pushed aside in 1973, Sandro Colombo taking his place before Forghieri was hastily recalled! After thorough development of a new 312B3 model through 1974, Forghieri's group produced the 312T in which Lauda and Regga dominated the 1975 World Championship, securing Maranello both titles for the first time in 11 years. They repeated the Constructors' title in 1976 and after Lauda's German GP fire Mr Ferrari doubted his ability to bounce back, engaging Carlos Reutemann as potential replacement. Instead it was Regazzoni who took the bullet – partly because he dared market ladies' jeans with Ferrari's Prancing Horse badge on the hip pocket – 'He put our soul on a bird's bum!' is a fair presentation of The Old Man's detonation.

Lauda gelled with neither new DSs Daniele Audetto and Roberto Nosetto nor – most decidedly – with Reutemann, yet he and Ferrari repeated their World titles – Ferrari scoring the first hat-trick of Constructors' Championships, 1975-6-7. Lotus's revolutionary ground-effects cars re-wrote the form book in 1978, but Ferrari flat-12 horsepower told in startlingly ugly 312T4s driven by Scheckter and Villeneuve in 1979 – Champions again. A strategic decision was then taken to invest in new 1.5-litre turbocharged technology, so 1980's naturally-aspirated flat-12 312T5s proved a low-budget flop.

Turbo V6 technology with Gilles Villeneuve and Didier Pironi

MODERN MARANELLO
1975-2007

And so Ferrari's Formula 1 effort really took off, admittedly in fits and starts – first with Lauda, then Villeneuve and Prost and, finally, Schumacher. So, what happens next?

'Would the old man have resorted to a judiciary had he found someone "spying"? I suspect not'

driving then saw the French-Canadian triumphant at Monaco and Jarama. The 1982 turbo Ferraris were real challengers, and after Villeneuve's death and Pironi's career-ending crash, Patrick Tambay and Mario Andretti shepherded Ferrari to yet another Constructors' title.

Dr Harvey Postlethwaite brought composite construction technology to Ferrari at *Il Grande Vecchio*'s invitation, but in The Old Man's dotage – while he could still drink Harvey under the table – Ferrari became a house divided against itself. The old guard retired, leaving Fiat and family elements manoeuvring for Enzo's legacy. The increasingly eccentric Forghieri was ousted at the end of 1984, Postlethwaite prevailing as chief designer with Ildo Renzetti engine head. Into 1986 Jean-Jacques His – ex-Renault – took over engine development and The Old Man hired John Barnard from McLaren. Factional in-fighting tore the team apart before Gerhard Berger won the last two GPs of 1987. Harvey, latest DS Marco Piccinini and Piero Lardi Ferrari wanted to continue with 1.5-litre turbo engines. Barnard wanted 'atmo' V12s. Mr Ferrari backed him. Fiat's Pier-Giorgio Capelli was installed to run the racing team, Piccinini sidelined, Harvey left to join Tyrrell. And in August, 1988, Enzo Ferrari died, aged 90.

Fiat took full control. From 1989-91 Cesare Fiorio became DS and Barnard's latest Ferrari 641 V12 emerged for drivers Mansell and Berger. Maranello required revolving doors as engineers and execs came and went. Pierguido Castelli, Enrique Scalabroni, Henri Durand, Steve Nichols and Paolo Massai each had their time in the sun. Alain Prost shone for the team in 1990 but was fired ending 1991 by Fiat's latest *capo* Claudio Lombardi, for publicly criticising the car.

Fiat reappointed Luca di Montezemolo to head Ferrari overall, and Postlethwaite was re-hired, but in July 1993 – with Ferrari still unsuccessful – Jean Todt was recruited ex-Peugeot to run the *Reparto Corse*. Chassis were entrusted to Gustav Brunner and John Barnard, engines to Paolo Martinelli. Moderate improvement attracted Michael Schumacher from Benetton for 1996. Late that year, at his recommendation, Ross Brawn and Rory Byrne joined from Benetton, Barnard left, and from 1998 Formula 1 Ferraris were designed by South African-born Byrne, and run by Brawn. In 1999 Ferrari won its first Formula 1 Constructors' title since 1983.

The Schumacher Ferrari era had dawned – in 2000 Michael becoming Ferrari's first World Champion Driver since Scheckter in 1979. In the Byrne/Brawn cars Schumacher and Rubens Barrichello brought Ferrari the Constructors' titles of 2000, 2001, 2002 plus 2003 (when Byrne eased off) and 2004. Michael won five consecutive Drivers' titles. Ferrari was well-beaten in 2005-06 by Renault and, with Schumacher's retirement, Ross Brawn and Paolo Martinelli also opted for a quieter life. And today, with Kimi Raikkonen and Felipe Massa confronting McLaren's finest, Ferrari has a heavily-tainted 2007 Constructors' Championship title – its 15th – to its name.

Would The Old Man have resorted to a judiciary had he found someone 'spying'? I suspect not. He had his own ways of manipulating vengeance, and few ever dared test him. Perhaps the House of Ferrari he had so painstakingly built was too conspicuously well-glazed for him to risk throwing stones. Part victory march, part tragi-comedy – what a record, what a legend, what a brand.

TOY STORY

The 1.5million-euro Ferrari FXX is the ultimate track car. We join an owner as he drives his for the very first time

Words: Richard Meaden | Pictures: Gus Gregory

Even when you've

seen it you can't quite believe it. No, not the Ferrari FXX – although now that you've asked, yes, it's every inch the sensational, heart-pounding projectile you'd hope – but the pantomime that surrounds it.

We're at Fiorano for a behind-the-scenes glimpse of what it's like when an FXX owner sees and drives their car for the first time. There are two FXXs being handed over today, but only one of the customers is happy to deal with the media. In the moments before he arrives, it's pandemonium. Like an A-list celebrity encircled by flunkies, minders, managers and assorted hangers-on, the FXX is swamped by Ferrari personnel, an island of calm surrounded by a choppy sea of scarlet that fusses and fettles and fiddles with anything that looks like it needs fussing, fettling or fiddling with.

Right now there must be more than 40 people crammed into the plush but hardly spacious confines of Fiorano's famous pit garage. Half are FXX programme technicians, the other half an assorted gaggle of edgy managers and PR bods,

The beginning of one of the best days of his life: FXX owner unveils his new trackday toy in a Fiorano pit garage. He'll soon be lapping the famous test circuit as a 'Client Test Driver'

furtive journalists, scurrying photographers and, lest we forget, the bloke who, bluntly, has paid for this bunfight: the FXX's new owner. Small, fit, tanned and surprisingly unassuming, our man is a middle-aged Italian American. Friendly, but preferring anonymity, we'll call him Mr X, or better still, Mr FXX.

The crowd gathers closely around his car, which was swathed in a scarlet cover moments before he entered the pit garage. Giuseppe Petrotta, the FXX project manager, makes a short speech

then beckons our man to pull back the cover. The silken sheet slips away, revealing the red, bestriped machine, and there's a moment's awed silence before spontaneous applause spreads around the pit. Suffice to say, Mr FXX looks chuffed, if a little nervous. But then so would you given the surroundings, the circumstances and the scale of the challenge (and invoice) that awaits him.

It's a scene that could only happen at Ferrari. But then the FXX is a car that only Ferrari could

make, and perhaps a car only Ferrari could sell. There's genius at work here, but not all of it has been channelled into the engineering. How else do you explain the audacious concept of 'inviting' 29 hand-picked clients to shell out a cool one and a half million euros – plus local taxes, naturally – on a car they can only drive on a race track, but can't actually race?

The core of the FXX's appeal, at least to those in a sufficiently privileged position to be approached by Ferrari in the first place, isn't its extreme performance or even its rarity, rather it's the fantasy being sold along with it: the dream of becoming part of Ferrari's test team.

According to Giuseppe Petrotta, these 'Client Test Drivers' will be a valuable source of

'The FXX is every inch the sensational, heart-pounding projectile that you'd hope'

information. 'How much is too much?' he asks rhetorically. 'Can we continue to offer more and more performance in our ultimate cars? And if the answer is yes, where do we define the limit? How do we make them exploitable and accessible to our customers? These are the kinds of questions we believe the FXX programme will enable us to understand.'

It's a reasonable enough quest given the rapidly escalating performance of series production supercars like the 599 GTB. But an 800bhp, 1155kg super-Enzo? That's quite some starting point. For those at the less able end of the 29-person spectrum, you can't help but fear that the FXX dream could rapidly turn into a carbonfibre-splintering nightmare with one ill-timed flex of their right foot.

Of course, that's something Ferrari desperately wants to avoid, which is why every FXX customer

towards silencing the screaming motor.

As a result, power is up from 650 to 800bhp – a specific output of some 128bhp per litre, arriving at a cataclysmic-sounding 8500rpm – while an impressively muscular 506lb ft of torque makes its presence felt at 5750rpm, up 250rpm and 21lb ft over the Enzo. Crucially, the FXX is 100kg lighter, tipping the scales at 1155kg (dry). In fact, it would be lighter still were it not for the added weight of a roll-cage, fire extinguisher system and other equipment that befits the FXX's role as a track-based development car.

Brembo and Bridgestone, two of Ferrari's closest technical partners in Formula 1, have worked hard to provide the FXX with the very best brakes and rubber. Ceramic composite discs, measuring 398x36mm up front and 380x34mm at the rear, are clamped by six-piston callipers and supported by ABS and ASR systems recalibrated to work with the grip levels provided by the bespoke slick tyres. While that translates into awesome dry performance and security, it also means that the FXX will be a far more malevolent beast for novice hands to control in the wet, which perhaps accounts for the FXX crew's nervous skyward glances towards the threatening, steel-grey clouds.

As you'd expect, Ferrari has also reduced the shift speed of the F1 paddle-shift transmission for the FXX. It now takes just 80 milliseconds to swap cogs – amazing, but still more than twice as long-winded as the F1 car.

But perhaps the most impressive aspect of the FXX is its revolutionary aerodynamics. Along with under-floor aero and a three-stage in-car-adjustable wing, it also employs something called 'base bleed' aerodynamics. It's a concept that stems from aerodynamic techniques applied to artillery shells, where it was discovered that reducing the area of low pressure behind the base of a shell results in a reduction in drag.

The same principle has been applied to the FXX, using a speed-related system that can cunningly redirect the air that ordinarily flows through the front air intakes, to the radiators and back out via the venturi tunnels that lead to the tail. When required, those hungry front intakes can be automatically blanked off via a series of electro-mechanical flaps. This redirects the airflow along the car's flanks into the side intakes, where the air then passes through carbonfibre ducts that run through the engine compartment and emerge as pancaked pipes in the rear bodywork.

Ferrari has established that the engine can do without this cooling airflow for 40 seconds without harm – long enough to dispatch most »

goes through a full day's intensive familiarisation and training – both in their new toy and a 360 Challenge race car – around the technical twists and turns of Fiorano. One-to-one tuition with a professional test and race driver is the best way to negotiate such a steep learning curve, and it's all backed-up with a detailed classroom session tackling the specific demands of Fiorano as well as providing a refresher of basic trackcraft.

Mr FXX has changed out of his civvies and into his Client Test Driver uniform: a shimmering red race suit with FXX emblazoned across the shoulders. There's no doubt he looks the part. In a quiet moment I ask him if he managed to get any sleep last night, adding that if I knew I was driving my own FXX for the first time, and at Ferrari's holiest of holies, Fiorano, I'd have been bouncing off the walls.

Mr FXX smiles. 'Well, of course it's a very big day for me, but I only flew in from the States last night, so to be honest I was feeling pretty jetlagged. The last thing I wanted to do was spend all night staring at the ceiling, so I had a glass of wine and a sleeping pill! Now I'm fine.'

Each FXX takes to the track alternately, so that each customer has the circuit to themselves and, presumably, to avoid any potentially embarrassing tangles. Helmet on and harness pulled down

tight, Mr FXX is ready to go. A shrill whirr from the starter prepares us for the explosion to come, and as the 12 cylinders catch, the assembled crowd flinches in unison as the FXX roars into life, filling the pit garage with a soundtrack straight from the Targa Florio, accompanied by a rich, eye-watering haze of exhaust fumes.

As it heads off down to Fiorano's distant Turn 1, the FXX looks like a Le Mans racer, bobbling stiffly on its suspension, coughing and crackling with impatience as its driver short-shifts through the gearbox on the first lap while checking all the systems are functioning.

When you appreciate what Ferrari has done to create the FXX, it's no wonder that it makes the Enzo on which it is (loosely) based seem tame. At its heart is a thoroughly re-engineered 6262cc version of the Enzo's 6-litre V12. The cylinder heads, pistons, cams, crankcase and combustion chambers have all been reworked and redesigned, while the exhaust system has lower back-pressure, doubtless thanks to the fact that it makes only the smallest of token gestures

'The FXX is devastatingly quick around Fiorano, lapping six seconds faster than the Enzo'

Taking to Fiorano's hallowed
tarmac. Revised aerodynamics
mean FXX has 40 per cent more
downforce than Enzo – and less
drag at high speed.
Far left: Meaden straps in for a
passenger ride to remember

'The explosive rush is momentarily sense-scrambling,
redefining in an instant what constitutes top-end power'

Below: as befits a dedicated track car, the FXX is fitted with a full roll-cage and a fire extinguisher system. **Bottom:** Enzo V12 has been reworked to give 800bhp

straights on most circuits around the world. Beyond 40 seconds, the frontal intakes are opened once more to resume flow through the radiators. It's a beautifully executed idea that's just one of a number of aerodynamic revisions for the FXX which result in a 40 per cent increase in downforce over the Enzo.

The combination of more power, less weight, vastly increased grip and race-car levels of downforce means the FXX is devastatingly quick around Fiorano, lapping a whole six seconds faster than the Enzo. In fact the only thing quicker on this hallowed loop is the Scuderia's Grand Prix car. The FXX is a monstrous machine for the customers to even begin to get their heads around, but it's to the instructors and Mr FXX's eternal credit that every session passes without incident, the red and white car's pace building appreciably with every lap, the driver's right foot remaining planted for longer down the straight and being applied earlier on the exit of each corner. Mr FXX is looking confident

Note the absence of rear-view mirrors – instead the pod on the roof contains a rear-facing camera that relays action from behind the FXX to a TFT display on the dash

The eBay FXX

FERRARI FXX
SPECIFICATIONS

Engine	65deg V12
Location	Mid, longitudinal
Displacement	6262cc
Cylinder block	Aluminium alloy
Cylinder head	Aluminium alloy, dohc per bank, four valves per cylinder
Max power	800bhp @ 8500rpm
Max torque	506lb ft @ 5750rpm
Transmission	Six-speed sequential manual gearbox, rear drive, ASR
Suspension	Front and rear: double wishbones, pushrod links, coil springs, gas dampers
Tyres	245/35 ZR19 front, 345/35 ZR19 rear
Weight (kerb)	1265kg
Power-to-weight	642bhp per ton
0-62mph	sub-3sec (estimated)
Top speed	217mph+ (estimated)

NOT ONE OF THE 29 ELITE customers selected by Ferrari? Well don't despair, just keep an eye on eBay.

Shortly after the ultra-exclusive, invitation-only FXX was launched, Exotic Motorcars of Boynton Beach, Florida, offered one for sale on the ubiquitous internet company's US auction website.

Some 46 bids were received before the car was eventually sold for a cool $3,000,100. However, there's some doubt as to whether the buyer was genuine or just some spotty kid having a laugh, as the successful bidder's eBay log reveals no other purchases anywhere near as significant.

Urban myth or awesome truth, the eBay FXX has registered on Ferrari's radar. When I mention it to an insider, he's quick to say that whoever has bought the auctioned FXX will have no involvement in the Client Test Driver programme, nor be invited to the international FXX driving events or receive technical support from the factory.

I think it's also safe to assume that the vendor himself is no longer on Messrs Montezemolo and Todt's Christmas card list.

but considered, obviously keen to explore the otherworldly performance, but mindful to keep his aspirations firmly in check.

Which is all terrific news as far as I'm concerned, for while the original schedule for the day states that I'll be treated to a passenger ride in Mr FXX's FXX alongside Ferrari test driver Dario Benuzzi, we've been informed that Mr FXX is having so much fun that he's decided to be our taxi driver himself. Fair enough, but as regular readers will know, the last time I sat next to a Ferrari owner on a test track, the ride ended somewhat abruptly in an F50-shattering crash that did irreparable damage to my faith in Ferrari owners and, it has to be said, my underwear.

This time, though, it's different. Mr FXX is completely dialled-in, and from the moment we drive out of the garage I know I'm in safe hands. He's building speed gradually, working temperature into the tyres, brakes and fluids, girding himself for another three laps in what must rank as the world's ultimate trackday car.

Our first flyer is like opening a window on another world. The power is all-encompassing, pushing and pulling and squeezing me in ways accelerative g hasn't managed since I rode in the back of an Arrows F1 car. My neck's stinging with the effort of keeping my chin down, and as we plunge into the braking area for Turn 1, those hard-worked muscles burn once more as my chin smacks into my breastbone. The brakes are like a brick wall, but you can feel and hear the ABS working its subtle magic, waiting until the onset of lock-up and a whispered chirrup from the Bridgestone slicks before bleeding the faintest amount of pressure from the most lightly loaded front wheel.

My favourite sensation comes at a section of the lap where Mr FXX holds fourth gear, slowly and smoothly increasing the throttle opening through the early phase of a long right-hander. The combined result of downforce and slick grip pulls hard on my neck, then he spots the exit and cracks through the remaining throttle travel

while straightening the steering wheel. It's this explosive rush, from 7000 to 8500rpm, that is momentarily sense-scrambling, redefining in an instant what constitutes throttle response and top-end power. Those FXX customers who also own Enzos will never look upon their road cars with quite the same awe again.

On our cool-down lap, I ask Mr FXX if the car is everything he hoped it would be. I get a predictable but reassuringly adrenalin-soaked answer. 'Honestly, it has completely exceeded even my wildest expectations. I've got an F430 at the moment, and it's an incredible car, so much better than the 360 in every respect. But this, this is incredible. The power is amazing, the braking totally beyond anything I've ever experienced. And yet it's so tractable, so friendly to drive. Of course, it takes great concentration to drive it, but that's the speed rather than the car itself, if you know what I mean. Apart from the birth of my children, I'd have to say that today has been the best day of my life.'

www.ferrari.co.uk

FIORANO | Ferrari

Club
Sport

The Ferrari brand is stronger than ever, but is it special enough? A new club,
Fiorano Ferrari, gives owners the chance to visit the factory, drive at track
days and take part in VIP events. We sampled what they'll experience
Words: David Lillywhite

It was the short drive from the Maranello factory to the Fiorano test track that summed it up. As we were whisked through the circuit gates towards the helicopters waiting to fly us to the next stage of this Ferrari adventure, a young couple in a parked Nissan Skyline stared wistfully. The driver was wearing a Ferrari polo shirt; his girlfriend's baseball cap was the Rosso Scuderia of Schumacher and Barrichello's F1 cars. They were on a petrolhead pilgrimage.

And there is Ferrari's quandary. They have probably the most evocative brand in the world, and not just the car world. The Ferrari name is exciting and glamorous and everyone wants a slice. That means keyrings, T-shirts, jackets, umbrellas and even teddy bears. But owning a Ferrari should feel special and that's »

'THE PRIVATE JET HAS 24 SEATS AND A
STEWARDESS NAMED SIMONE SCHUMACHER. BY
THE TIME SHE'S TEN SECONDS INTO THE SAFETY
DEMO, 24 BLOKES HAVE FALLEN IN LOVE'

Clockwise from left
Lunch at Ristorante
Montana, F1 team
favourite; Lancia Thesis
motorcade; helicopter
leaves Fiorano circuit...
and arrives at villa;
14th century building
has undergone massive
restoration

what this trip is all about. UK buyers of new Ferraris will automatically become members of Fiorano Ferrari, entitling them to free track time and tuition, gifts, VIP invitations to private events and entry to the Fiorano website. Or they can upgrade to Corse level, for their own Fiorano racing overalls, helmet, boots and access to a fleet of F430 and 360 Challenge cars at circuits around the world. Current owners will be able to do the same; non-owners won't. Crucially for customer satisfaction, it even counts while you're on the year-long waiting list. If it's successful, Fiorano Ferrari may be extended worldwide.

So for a couple of days I'm an honorary Ferrari owner. We'll fast-forward past the bit where I drive a nasty little hire car around the M25, and move straight to the departure lounge of Farnborough airport. No packed buses from faraway car parks, no queues, no-one unsavoury.

The private jet has 24 seats and a stewardess named Simone Schumacher. By the time she's ten seconds into the safety demonstration, 24 blokes have fallen in love.

Ninety minutes later we're swooning through passport control at Bologna airport, straight into The Italian Job: six sharp-suited, shades-toting drivers standing by six black Lancia saloons. Tinted windows and all. We glide through the traffic and, when it's all looking a little too Italian, the first Lancia blocks the junction and the others fly through without a break in the pace. No-one hoots.

Above
Private charter jet and
a stewardess named
Schumacher – can life
get any better?

First stop is Ristorante Montana, favoured eating spot of the Formula One team, where our table is overlooked by a larger-than-life photograph of Schumacher hugging the proprietress. Six courses later we hobble to the cars, to be ferried to the factory round the corner.

I think I'd subconsciously expected the place to ring with the sound of panelbeaters' hammers, punctuated by the occasional roar of an open exhaust, because my first reaction is disappointment that the two production lines, one for V8s, one for V12s, are so clean and efficient-looking. Now and again a warning sounds as notice that a line is to move again – twice as often for the V8s as for the V12s, because twice as many V8s are built. The other difference is that the mid-engined V8s head front-first down the line, the front-engined V12s rear-first.

We head deeper into the factory. To our left are the men and women who assemble the doors. They look as bored as anyone doing a tedious job would. But there's Latin temperament on display on the production lines to our right, with laughter, shouting and banter aplenty, and in the trim rooms a little further along the line, the women look up from their sewing machines and smile flirtatiously. Every item they sew is for a specific car, a specific customer, in his or her choice of leather, of piping, thread colour and even stitching style.

Behind them are the glueing bays, where bare door

trim panels are sprayed with adhesive and skinned with leather, and just past the trim shop are the leather cutters. We stand fascinated as a guy casually throws a full hide onto the horizontal cutting bed, then leaves another artisan to mark the imperfections and plan the cutting of each trim section around them, using laser templates to make best use of the hide. After a minute or so of experimentation he steps back and lets the machine do its job, its laser cutter flying across the leather. Then the freshly cut pieces are peeled off the suction bed and carted to the trim shop, while the waste is rolled up and thrown away. I'm not the only one who starts to make an involuntary movement towards the bin, to rescue a piece of Ferrari hide.

And so we move on, past the start of the production lines, where painted shells from Modena begin their short journey to completion, and back along the side of the V12 line. To our left there are just large, blank panels. Suddenly our group is halted by Ferrari GB managing director Massimo Fedeli who, with a flourish, slides back one of the panels to reveal the low-volume production area and the previously unseen FXX model – in the crudest terms, a €1.5-million track-day Enzo. The two PR guys are either utterly shocked or very good actors, and one whispers to me in apparent dismay: 'Car magazine have been phoning me every day to ask if they could see this!'

Top and above
V12 production line, but V8 F430 has crept in (foreground); fine dining, Italian style.

Massimo is loving it. 'We always show our customers something special!' he proclaims (indeed, Fiorano Ferrari members will be invited to new model launches before journalists). We're allowed to clamber all around it.

Then we're off to the engine plant, via the testing bay and a tantalising glimpse of a pre-production version of the next 612. The engine plant was built in 2002 and is said to be state of the art, temperature- and humidity-monitored, with an indoor garden and flooded with natural light. It's one of those places that apparently works with little in the way of human intervention, the polar opposite of the bustling production lines.

I stand alone for several minutes, fascinated, in front of a pedantically precise robot that dips tiny valve guides one at a time into liquid gas to shrink them before fitting them into the cylinder head. And then I join the rest of the group to gaze at the range of historic Ferraris lined up in a currently empty area of the plant.

Off again, this time out of the factory gates and through industrial areas where a Ferrari training college, social club and merchandise shops sit oddly alongside household goods manufacturers like AEG.

Through the gates of Fiorano circuit, past the Nissan Skyline, past Enzo's old house, where his office is still intact but other rooms are given over to the F1 drivers' gym equipment, and straight out to six helicopters. It's »

'I THINK I'D SUBCONSCIOUSLY
EXPECTED THE PLACE TO
RING TO THE SOUND OF
PANEL-BEATERS' HAMMERS,
PUNCTUATED BY THE
OCCASIONAL ROAR OF AN
OPEN EXHAUST'

an hour-and-a-half to the outskirts of Milan, where our helicopter, second in the MASH-style convoy, suddenly swoops up and around, banking tightly and down onto the lawns of one of the finest hotels I've ever seen.

This is Villa San Carlo Borromeo, built in the 14th century, ruined by the Nazis and finally restored during the 1980s and '90s. The ceilings are 30 feet high and fresco painted, and one wing houses a fantastic art gallery. Great meal, great booze (top-quality spumante from the Ferrari vineyard, unrelated to Enzo's bunch) and a long, deep sleep before we're off again, this time to Monza.

Yes, Monza, legendary Monza, frightening Monza, home of lethal banking, much steeper than Brooklands', scene of great victories by Fangio, Ascari et al. Today, wet Monza.

We're briefed by chief instructor Enrico Bertaggia, who tells us the usual stuff about safety plus a few handy driving tips, we kit out in race boots and overalls, and I find I'm in the first group out on the track. There are ten cars waiting, equally split between the 360 Challenge and the F430 road cars. I'm in the F430 first and my instructor is an affable guy in his 60s who introduces himself through the intercom as Richard. Fine.

Despite the lairy livery, the 430 is standard spec: 490bhp V8, six-speed paddle-shift transmission, e-differential, traction control, etc. It has a top speed of 196mph and a 0-60mph time of four seconds. I'm second onto the track,

Top and above
Ferrari and Maserati engine components are produced in new building, complete with trees; new FXX track car revealed

rain lashing down, Richard initially talking me through every gearchange, every braking point, every turn.

By circuit standards, Monza's relatively easy to learn. The last time a grand prix was run on the banking was 1961, and there are just six corners on the GP circuit, not including the hideous chicane on the start/finish straight that Richard finds it impossible to keep quiet about ('I just can't believe it's still here,' he mutters on every other lap) and I find impossible to master.

As for the car, well, it feels remarkably civilised. The air-con's on, the helmet is (sadly) muffling that zinging exhaust note, the controls are light and the paddle shift easy to master – the digital display on the dash means you can't not know which gear you're in. I actually feel a touch too relaxed, but then these are the opening laps and we're not meant to be hoofing it. I hit about 120mph down the main straight – a good 40mph off our expected top speed, but rain is limiting the fun.

After about eight laps we head for the pits. We jump out, Richard takes off his crash helmet and I get a shock. It's Richard Attwood! First man to win Le Mans for Porsche, survivor of the early days of the 917; a motorsport hero.

Off for refreshments and a chance to chat to those who have already been out too – those who were nervous are now much happier, and there's no-one who isn't excited at the prospect of further laps. My next session is in the 360 Challenge, which is the track version of the

'I ENTER PARABOLICA A GOOD 20MPH QUICKER THAN I'D DONE AT ANY OTHER TIME OF THE DAY. THE FRONT OF THE 430 BEGINS TO WASH OUT; WE'RE HEADING FOR THE GRAVEL TRAPS'

Clockwise from left
360 Challenge leads F430; laser-planning prior to cutting hide; F430 in race livery; 360 leaves Monza pits; chief instructor Enrico

now-obsolete 360, the predecessor to the F430. 400bhp, 183mph, 0-60mph in four seconds. Plus the Challenge has competition seats, harnesses, roll-cage and much less in the way of electronic aids. And no air-con.

I prefer this car on the track. It feels more urgent, the louder exhaust, firmer suspension and even the warmer cabin adding to the adrenalin rush. I immediately put in smoother, faster laps in the 360, topping 140mph, and I know that it's down to me concentrating harder.

Why am I concentrating harder? Because I have to! Where I now know that the 430 was keeping me in line with its incredibly subtle electronic intervention, the 360 will slither and scrabble for grip. It's exciting but on such powerful cars it would be naïve to say that the 430's electronics are a bad thing.

My instructor talks of braking so delicately that the pedal is controlled simply by clenching my toes, and of easing off the accelerator during changes just enough that the change doesn't bang in on the harsher set-up gearbox of the Challenge car. He insists on me backing off when crossing the streams of water that are now flooding the track; when I don't, the car jumps sideways and my lesson is learnt.

The Fiorano 360s are kitted out with on-board cameras and telemetry, so after my second session I'm hauled into a pit garage full of laptop-tapping boffins to be shown my performance around the track, compared against Enrico's

Above
Octane's David Lillywhite prepares for more tuition from Richard Attwood

laps in the dry. A bit unfair, methinks, but interesting all the same and, as should be expected from one of the only car journos on the trip, I was in the top three for lap times.

Maybe it went to my head, because my final session in the 430, back with Richard Attwood, was seriously ropey. We'd had a big lunch, got up at the crack of dawn two days in a row, concentrated hard in horrible conditions all day, but that's not much of an excuse when you're sat next to someone who's driven through the night in the 240mph lethal weapon that is a Porsche 917.

'Whoah, too fast, much too fast,' cries Richard as I enter Parabolica a good 20mph quicker than I'd done at any other time of the day and for no good reason that I can think of. The front of the 430 begins to wash out, we're heading for the gravel traps and I'm in full-on useless mode. But the car pulls out of it and, for a short, reality-defying moment, I think that I'm a little more skilled at handling a powerful supercar than I thought.

'You wouldn't have got round there without the electronics,' says Richard, matter-of-factly. Oh.

We head for Bergamo airport soon afterwards and smile tiredly at Simone on the plane. I drive the horrible hire car back round the M25 on the rev-limiter and settle weary-eyed on my settee with a beer to watch my in-car footage video. It's very good (I don't even look too stupid). Thank goodness it wasn't in the 430...

FERRARI CLASSICHE

Want to find out how original your classic Ferrari is, or does
it simply need a little fettling? Maranello is waiting to help…
Words: Harry Metcalfe Photography: Charlie McGee & David Shephard

Since its creation was announced by Ferrari

president Luca di Montezemolo back in July 2006, Ferrari Classiche has been a hive of activity. Housed in the same area around the Maranello factory's inner courtyard where Enzo Ferrari's original workshop used to be found, the sole purpose of this relatively new department is, as its name suggests, to serve the needs of owners of classic Ferraris.

The biggest demand comes from those wishing to check the authenticity of their historic Ferraris, something that is becoming more and more important as auction houses sell multi-million-dollar Ferraris on an increasingly regular basis. The process involves a team of engineers checking and photographing every important component on the car being inspected and confirming that the numbers on the chassis and engine are exactly as they would have been when the car first left the factory. If it is satisfied that everything is as it should be, Ferrari Classiche produces a record of the inspection in the form of the most exquisite hard-backed dossier (complete with a dummy metal chassis plate on the cover showing the details of the inspected car) together with a beautiful originality certificate signed by Ferrari vice president and son of Enzo, Piero Ferrari. The cost for all this work? Around 1200-5000 euros, depending on the model being inspected and how much work has to be done in order to prove its authenticity.

It's a service that has proved very popular. After all, if you get your car successfully Ferrari Classiche certified, its value is most definitely increased. However, it's not always good news. Ferrari Classiche boss Roberto

'If you get your car successfully Ferrari Classiche certified its value is most definitely increased'

Left: Harry (and his 330 GTC) with Davide Kluzer, Ferrari's press director (middle), and Roberto Vaglietti, head of Ferrari Classiche (right). Above: Dinos in the workshop and an example of a Ferrari Classiche authenticity report

Vaglietti says they have already uncovered a number of cars that were not as original as their owners had hoped they were, as well as finding several cars that had been stolen some years earlier only to re-appear with false numbers adorning the chassis (there's a silver Daytona currently languishing in the workshop that the police have impounded after Roberto discovered it wasn't the car its false chassis plates were claiming).

But it's not just this authentication process that takes place at the spotless, 950-square-metre workshop – Ferrari Classiche also offers a full restoration service. Using (of course) only Ferrari components, they will restore any Ferrari over 20 years old at a bargain workshop rate of just 65 euros an hour.

I must confess that I'm speaking from first-hand experience here, as in May 2007 I had my recently purchased 1966 Ferrari 330 GTC 2+2 taken to Ferrari Classiche for a little bit of TLC. Nothing major – new fuel pumps, new suspension bushes, that sort of thing – but the feeling of pride I get each time I walk through Ferrari's courtyard to inspect progress on the car is priceless. I have even enjoyed a 40-minute passenger ride in my car with a Ferrari test-driver of many years standing at the wheel taking us along exactly the same roads that Ferrari has used to test all its road cars for decades. If you want to see what your car can really do, this is the perfect way to find out.

But the day I'm really looking forward to arrives in a few weeks' time when I finally get to drive my re-fettled 330 GTC back through Ferrari's hallowed gates, some 41 years since it first did so. Now that's a moment I'm going to treasure forever. If you've got a classic Ferrari in need a little bit of attention then, thanks to Ferrari Classiche, you could experience that feeling one day too. △

It's a wonder that I've

ended up with such a long-term relationship with Ferrari. I succumbed easily to the charisma of the marque, although I was only seven at the time. I remember my first car being a Ferrari 625 GP racer in blue and yellow. It ran faultlessly, but then it was a die-cast Dinky so there was little to go wrong, apart from paint coming off the driver's helmet when it had the sort of massive accident only small children can engineer.

Later, in the late-'50s, I admired the cars in the paddock at Goodwood, but resisted any real plans for ownership due to the inevitable financial constraints placed on schoolboys. When fate decreed that I could finally indulge in spending on wine, women and singing, I foolishly frittered away much of it on cars. It was my own fault – I demanded a dealer and got Maranello Concessionaires instead of 'Terry the Pill'...

The best Ferraris go beyond the realm of being tools to become, if not art, at least high craft. Enzo Ferrari was a »

60 YEARS OF FERRARI

NICK MASON
on the 250GTO
(and the 275, the Daytona, the F40, the Enzo...)

What's it like to be a long-term Ferrari owner? Nick Mason reflects on some of the cars
he's been lucky enough to experience, and the passion they inspire

Photography courtesy Ten Tenths Ltd

wonderfully flawed human being but he cared passionately. He wasn't an Ettore Bugatti, a Bruce McLaren or a Gordon Murray – that is, he wasn't a designer, driver or ground-breaking engineer – and yet he produced such wonderful cars, as well as a few really rather average ones. If he had been in politics in the same period I suspect Italy would have won WW2.

For me, the 275GTB/4 seemed the perfect starter choice. As often happens with real car nuts, it never occurred to me to actually try the damned thing before buying it, and I'm rather proud (in a weird way) to say this technique has generally worked well over the years. In fact, I tend to look rather suspiciously on potential buyers of my cars who insist on driving them, and I liked the fine print on one dealer's receipt that suggested the car was simply sold as a collectors' item and any driving activity couldn't possibly be considered as being covered.

In a world that had only just begun to discover the commercial aspects of psychedelic music, the 275 had many of the looks of a GTO without the impossible price tag. It looked a million dollars and cost a lot less. The four-cam was, obviously, top of the range, and better than the two because it had a bigger number.

I can't now remember where the car came from, but it felt by miles the most serious car I had ever owned.

They say that the two best moments of owning a yacht are the day you buy it and the day you sell. And, by God, the same was true of that 275. The view from the cockpit was magnificent, with acres of beautiful bodywork to worry about, leather seats and lots and lots of gauges. There was even a leather-bound instruction book and the window catches hadn't yet fallen off.

The trouble was, the car was a disaster. Its two greatest faults were a tendency to wet its plugs, and brakes that at low speed with reduced servo aid were worse than a vintage Austin Chummy's. I became adept at parking on a hill to aid the bump start, and removing armloads of plugs that then had to be cleaned, or at least heated, over a gas stove. On one occasion when away from home the help of a rather smart Bristol hotel kitchen had to be enlisted to carry out this work. I was lucky they didn't come back with a pastry topping and a touch of garlic...

Those brakes tested nerve and leg muscles to the limit and were an early form of Pilates equipment for strengthening the legs. One of the most memorable experiences was taking the car **》**

Below and right:
275GTB/4 was Nick's first Ferrari, bought in the 1970s, but he never bonded with it as he did with its GTO replacement

'The 275 looked a million dollars... Trouble was, the car

'No car is perfect, but the GTO comes close.
In terms of forgiveness for the driver,
it should be sainted'

'The 512TR formed part of a package that morphed into a competition Daytona – which easily qualified as being far less practical'

to Maranello Concessionaires for some advice. The well-spoken man who greeted me decided that the best solution would be to drive the beast. Apparently the brakes were excellent – well of course they were, for the salesman was Mike Salmon and we never travelled at less than full revs. Mike clearly had no time for doodling around in traffic and couldn't imagine that I would either.

I later wrote to a titled bloke who I heard had had a mod done to sort out the problem. I got the most unhelpful letter back suggesting it might be a little complicated and pricey for the likes of me, but fortunately this turned out to be a unique experience. Like most enthusiasts' groups, Ferrari owners are usually only too eager to help. In fact, if I have a complaint, it's that any query frequently unlocks a raging torrent of advice.

Oddly, I don't remember my GTB/4 going, which probably shows that there wasn't that much love lost between us, but on the subject of 275s, I once had a friend in North London who used his as a builder's van. He manufactured a roof rack to carry plumbing fittings and kept the car in a side street. It looked terrible and he took great delight in giving short shrift to would-be purchasers who thought they had found a bargain. He knew exactly what it was worth, and most impressive of all did a total engine rebuild in his bathroom, using the bath to expand the crankcase while assembling the engine. It was also noticeable that he had some trouble holding down a long-term relationship... It is possible there is a connection here.

In the years since the GTB/4, I've inevitably become a bit of a GTO bore, having lived with mine long enough now to see my status as an owner change from new rich kid to sad old sausage. No car is perfect, but the GTO comes close. As a drivers' car it has an almost perfect balance between engine power, brakes and suspension, while in terms of forgiveness to the driver it should be sainted. It also makes a great noise and has a sense of history permeating the cockpit, with a view over the bonnet that is just begging to include those Mulsanne marker boards whisking by.

The body is simply stunning. Jess Pourret, whose book *The Ferrari Legend: 250GT Competition* is to GTO owners what the Constitution is to Americans, records that, contrary to popular mythology, it was designed in-house at Ferrari rather than by Pininfarina. Whatever, it's purposeful but exotic enough to make a lot of chisel-jawed, steely-eyed guys unable to resist touching it – particularly when it's warm. (Bugatti tail sections are also susceptible to this and, post-VSCC Silverstone, will frequently need remedial work to the mild indentations in their top surface.)

I have taken my children to school in the GTO on a snowy day when nothing else would start, and we even used it for my daughter's wedding – fortunately the vicar was a proper motor

Below
Nick collected his F40 new from the factory – 'perhaps the most exciting car for a first drive'.

enthusiast and felt that a side-exhaust Ferrari was by far the most suitable mode of transport for brides.

The car has generally been reliable. It dropped a valve on my first GTO rally in 1982, which was a bitter disappointment since they only occur every five years, but it's finished all the others – though on one occasion it needed support from Moët & Chandon's vineyard engineering facility to refit a prop shaft. Otherwise most problems have been self-induced. Overheating in traffic was the result of using a lightweight radiator in an attempt to get a little more speed on the track and make some inroads against those damned E-type Jaguars!

There's nothing like such talk to bring out the rather thin-lipped, self-righteous tone in those who disapprove of the over-development of historic racers. I belong firmly to the group that believes it's entirely wrong to do all this development on anyone else's car; it would only be OK if I could do more to mine, but sadly the 3-litre GTO engine doesn't lend itself to the opportunity offered by some other competitors.

Having achieved the Holy Grail of GTO ownership I ended up trying some other models in case I'd made a mistake. The closest competitor for me was the Daytona. It was terrific, and in a way I still miss it. Mine was a left-hand-drive example – and, just in case it's still around, it should have two speedos that could be rapidly interchanged to allow

'Rear vision was marginal, but the design ethic was that no-one would be overtaking you'

for kph or mph. The fact that this also kept the mileage down was an added bonus...

Although a real Tarzan car to park (but a doddle on the brake pressure required), it was great on the open road. I did a lot of miles in mine during a six-month period working in France. In between recording in the Alps Maritimes and exhausting a number of sets of Michelin tyres on the steep route up to the recording studios, it set some fairly politically incorrect times for Cannes to Le Mans, and Nice to Spa.

One great feature was the cabin size. It actually had a boot with room for some luggage, as well as space within for all those bits and pieces that accumulate on long journeys. The air-conditioning struggled a bit, but it was only after it had gone and I bought my very first new Ferrari from the factory that I realised just how civilised it was. In some ways the change was like moving from a manor house to an expensive but small flat.

After years of second-hand cars there was something very special about the factory visit. My dad had met Enzo, and even benefited from his friendship with the Commendatore when organising at short notice a drive and all the associated paperwork to co-pilot on the 1953 Mille Miglia. Although I came along too late to meet the great man, I did become friendly with probably the nearest person to him in the organisation.

Brenda Vernor is still the font of all Ferrari knowledge in Maranello. Not just the type numbers and history of the cars, but all the really good stuff about the drivers, the owners, their wives and girlfriends, and the machinations of Ferrari politics. There may be presidents and CEOs, but none would be as bold as Brenda in terms of the scurrilous gossip that helps transform the Ferrari experience from mechanical to human. If there are bodies buried, Brenda not only knows where they are, but what they are wearing.

It was unbelievably exciting to take my F40 – perhaps the most exciting car ever for a first drive – out of the factory gate and hammer up the autostrada. An over-long lunch had meant that Bob Houghton and myself hadn't quite bothered with the briefing about details like how to switch the dash lights on – or even the headlights, come to that. And a map wouldn't have been much use, as there wasn't a light to read it by.

The fitted luggage still delights me – a thin disc of leather suitable for an extra-large pizza or a low-rise sombrero, and a wedge-shaped briefcase that was clearly designed for a good chunk of Parmigiano-Reggiano. It's best either to pack light (that is, wear what you need) or to send the chauffeur ahead. Rear vision was marginal, too – the design ethic was clearly that no-one would be overtaking you anyway (I later had some better rear screens moulded). But despite these bugbears, in my opinion the F40 has made the transition from new supercar to genuine classic, which is not a journey that every design makes.

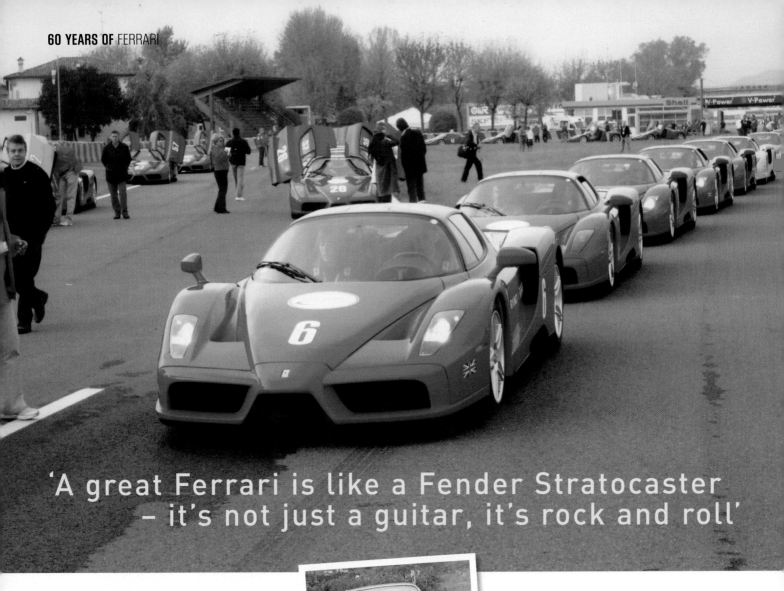

'A great Ferrari is like a Fender Stratocaster – it's not just a guitar, it's rock and roll'

I also bought a 512TR new from the factory, but it never really endeared itself to me. Luggage space was inadequate and the cockpit was a bit too cramped, and I wasn't mad about the visibility. I think I felt I'd already had enough of that sort of car, and it formed part of a package that morphed into a competition Daytona – which had even less luggage space, no air-conditioning and easily qualified as being far less practical.

I had a couple of Dinos, and I still have a great affection for them. The silliest thing I did with one of mine was to hit an ice patch at the top of my street and slide its nose into the rear of another of my cars, pushing that one into the back end of the nanny's car. I hadn't the nerve to fill in the insurer's accident claim form. I could imagine the headlines: 'Rock drummer in three-car pile up'...

The second silliest act was to exchange a Dino for a Lancia Stratos. If you believe that if it looks right, it is right, this car might change your philosophy. For a lunatic rally ace it's ideal; for the rest of us it's a rather frightening fairground ride. I spent a lot of time looking at the road ahead through the side windows. The rather natty suede seats were the best bit of the interior – I still remember the almighty thump as the window fell down inside the door panel.

Oh, and then there was a brief flirtation with a 412. Auto everything and magnolia hide. Three-speed 'box and full four-seat capacity. This was some crazed notion about practical family

Above:
Nick now regrets swapping his Dino for a Stratos – 'a rather frightening fairground ride'

motoring, I think, and it was soon packed off to a dealer.

Finally, there is the exquisitely impractical Enzo. I do have my differences with it. A really quick time around Fiorano is important, but Mr Schumacher should have taken it to the shops to discover that limited visibility at roundabouts creates just too much excitement, and too many insurance claims. And it is big – well, wide anyway. But it does go, and it has that sort of steering wheel you can enjoy even when you're not moving.

In fact, it's almost better when you're not moving. I was a little miffed to have it explained to me that, although the car had only done 740 miles, the new clutch that was already required was considered a consumable rather than a guarantee item.

Having said that, the car is now considered to have earned its keep after its appearance on *Top Gear* where, in return for the loan of the car, Jeremy's approach to the BBC's code of practice on advertising was ridden over rough-shod as he touted (or allowed me to tout) my then recently published book, *Inside Out*.

To my mind, a great Ferrari is a little like a Fender Stratocaster – it's not just a guitar, it's rock and roll, it's Hank Marvin, Eric Clapton or Jimi Hendrix. An instrument in the right hands to get the right results has to take on some element of romance. Gosh, the LSD's beginning to wear off, so hear endeth the sermon – if not on the mount, at least on the garage lift.

THE FUTURE'S

Ferrari reveals plans for its road cars: performance improvements to come from reduced size

'Millechili' concept (front) illustrates how Ferraris will shrink in size, and therefore weight, compared with current models (FXX behind).
Far right: Ferrari general manager Amedeo Felisa

LIGHT

and weight, not huge power increases

Words: Harry Metcalfe Pictures: Gus Gregory

It seems even

Ferrari isn't immune to concerns about the part its products play in an increasingly environmentally-aware world.

The company has been thinking long and hard about the effect future CO2 emissions regulations will have on its next generation of cars, and as part of its recent 60th birthday celebrations bosses took the unprecedented step of lifting the lid on just how it plans to face up to the conundrum of building eco-friendly supercars. And what the assembled press heard and saw was little short of revolutionary.

For example, if you thought the next Enzo-level Ferrari would be simply a road-legal development of the FXX then think again. As one Ferrari spokesman put it, a two-ton car with 1000bhp is not the future. But a one-ton car with 500-600bhp? Now that might be the answer...

Ferrari, it seems, thinks the biggest performance gains can be achieved by getting the best power density from its cars, and it illustrated this new drive for lightweight, efficient solutions with a number of technical displays, the centrepiece of which was the 'FXX Millechili' concept.

Looking like a cut-down Enzo, it's not an altogether serious engineering study – the vehicle on show featured a plastic and cardboard body – but it demonstrated Ferrari's intent to reduce size, and therefore weight, as did its name, 'Millechili' being Italian for 1000kg, the suggested weight for such a car. Meanwhile, away from the displays, a number of key Ferrari engineers talked us through the company's brave new vision, and they had quite a few revelations in store...

CARBONFIBRE WILL play an ever-larger part in road-going Ferraris, as the company is committed to transferring as much of its F1-derived expertise in this material to its road cars as possible. The most significant development is a new carbonfibre laminate that will be used instead of aluminium for the body panels. Lighter than aluminium, it is also a more flexible material to work with and has the added benefit of better crash characteristics.

Carbon suspension components are also on the cards, with F1-style 'flex joints' enabling wishbones to be bolted directly to the chassis, any suspension movement handled by the wishbone itself flexing rather than a conventional bush or joint (with its associated weight).

Another revelation is that the brake discs found on future Ferraris could be smaller than those fitted to today's cars thanks to the introduction of second-generation carbon-ceramic discs from Brembo. These new 'CCM-2' discs have a much higher coefficient of friction, allowing them to be smaller for the same braking power. Ferrari is also hoping that by using high-friction pads in conjunction with this new disc technology it will be able to do away with a servo, saving further weight as well as improving feel at the pedal. However, another avenue being explored is brake-by-wire technology, as this would allow the pads to be moved away from the discs electronically, improving efficiency by reducing drag on » the discs when the brakes aren't being used. Further sensors would recognise when the driver is about to brake and move the pads back close to the disc before the brake pedal is pushed.

The combination of smaller discs and less weight means that wheels and tyres can shrink in size too. As well as producing less drag, smaller tyres have a lower rolling resistance; tyre manufacturers are working on new construction techniques that could deliver a further 35 per cent saving on that front over the next five years or so.

ENGINE-WISE, huge leaps in power aren't on the agenda, so what is? Direct injection will come with the next generation of powerplants to improve efficiency. They'll also be able to run on bioethanol, giving another boost to performance thanks to the fuel's naturally higher octane rating.

Ferrari has looked at a number of other options – radical supercharged two-stroke engines, turbocharging and twin-crank engines – but it looks as if it will continue on a conventional, normally aspirated route. The only shock, particularly for fans of traditional Ferraris, is that the V12 configuration looks under threat – its internal friction makes it inherently more thirsty than a V10 or V8.

Ferrari is also talking about hybrid powertrains on its road cars by 2012, but this has less to do with reducing emissions and more to do with increasing performance by developing a road-going version of the system F1 cars will be forced to use from the 2009 season. On its road cars Ferrari is hoping to be able to store around 100kW of energy in special batteries that are much lighter than today's variants.

Meanwhile, instead of cutting gearshift times with a complex, DSG-style twin-clutch gearbox, Ferrari plans to use a compact, high-revving electric motor directly attached to the gearbox differential to deliver an instant slug of torque at the moment the clutch interrupts drive to the wheels, giving the driver the impression of seamless shifts. (While shift times have come down to 100ms on the 599 – and will be just 60ms on the hardcore Ferrari F430 Challenge Stradale being launched at Frankfurt this September – Ferrari can't get this below around 30ms.)

Perhaps more immediately obvious than all these under-the-skin changes will be Ferrari's radical rethink of its cabins. Fixed seats are on the cards, and these will be in a more reclined position, along the lines of an F1 car's seat, allowing designers to use a much lower roof line (dropping by around 80mm) and add more rake to the windscreen. Different sized drivers would, of course, be accommodated by a moveable pedal box and a fully adjustable steering wheel. The steering wheel itself is set to take on a new appearance, gaining a fixed hub that will contain all the controls that would normally be housed within a conventional dashboard.

Finally, returning to the outside of the car, Ferrari has been working with Imperial College London to develop trick 'synthetic jets'. These tiny devices, just 0.5mm in diameter, are in effect simple air valves that can be placed on strategic parts of the body. Each controlled via a tiny solenoid valve, they can dramatically affect the airflow across a car's structure. Used in conjunction with more familiar active aerodynamics (including moveable spoilers on the underside of the car), Ferrari thinks it will see a big reduction in drag coefficients on future cars.

Summing up, Ferrari's general manager Amedeo Felisa reckoned the overall weight saving of 300kg the company is hoping to achieve on a production version of a car like the Millechili would consist of a 100kg saving in the construction of the body, 100kg in the repackaging of the engine and transmission, 50kg from using carbon suspension components and 50kg from the revised interior.

Felisa says power will continue to increase slightly for any given engine size thanks to new technology allowing even higher revs than at present and ultra-efficient combustion control, but despite this, average CO2 figures for Ferraris will drop from the current 400g/km to around 250 by 2012.

'Ferrari has always given its new models better performance than their predecessors, and we will continue to do so,' says Felisa, 'but future Ferraris will also be more efficient.' In these challenging times for car makers it's reassuring to see Ferrari taking what some might call a more intelligent look at what will make a great performance car in the decade ahead. △

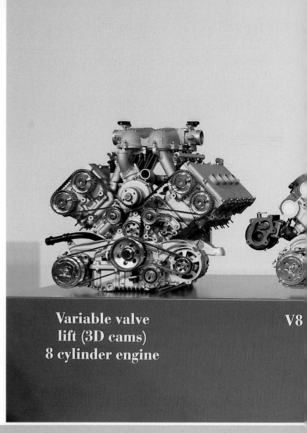

Clockwise from right: the various engine configurations Ferrari has explored; aerodynamics will play an important role in improving efficiency; shrinking computer components; FXX and Millechili; smaller, second-generation carbon brakes; numerous controls set to move to steering wheel hub

Variable valve lift (3D cams) 8 cylinder engine   **V8**

po engine

**Double cranckshaft
12 cylinder/6
combustion
chambers engine**

**In-line
three cylinder
two stroke engine**

**ELECTRONICS EVOLUTION FACTORS
AND APPLICATION ON F1 AND ROAD CARS**

1989

1987   1996

2007

EVERY FERRARI ROAD CAR

From the 64bhp 166 of 1947 to today's 612bhp 599 GTB Fiorano, here's the lowdown on every road-going Ferrari of the last 60 years

166 (1947)
The true Ferrari road cars started with the 166, which were developed from the 125 range of race-oriented cars. All manner of bodies were built by various coachbuilders for the leaf-sprung V12-powered 166 chassis.
Total: 71. Power: 64bhp. Top speed: 125mph

195 (1950)
With model designation derived from the capacity of a single cylinder, the 195s were similar to the 166s but with a 2341cc V12 instead of the 166's 2-litre. Again, bodies were by various coachbuilders in several styles.
Total: 27. Power: 180bhp. Top speed: 130mph

212 Inter, 212 Export (1951)
Bigger engine and more power, but the same basic chassis for the 212 Export, while the 212 Inter had a longer wheelbase. Coachbuilt bodies were created by Vignale, Ghia, Touring and Pinin Farina.
Total: 106. Power: 170bhp. Top speed: 140mph

340/342/375 America (1950)
Based on an evolution of the 166 chassis, the America series of cars used a 4.1-litre long-block V12 designed by Aurelio Lampredi. The 342 was more of a tourer, while the 375 was a 4.5-litre. Various body styles.
Total: 41. Power: 300bhp. Top speed: 149mph

250 Europa (1953)
The first Ferrari built specifically for road use rather than adapted from a competition car. It was the only 250 to use the Lampredi V12 (a short-block version) and was based on the 166 chassis. Various bodies, most by Farina.
Total: 17. Power: 200bhp. Top speed: 120mph

250 GT (1954)
The first volume Ferrari. It used the Colombo-designed V12, as used in the 166, and coil springs in place of the old transverse leaf springs. It was still a coachbuilt, with most versions made by Pininfarina.
Total: 130. Power: 220bhp. Top speed: 125mph

250 GT Tour de France (1955)

A special 250 GT to celebrate Ferrari's win in the Tour de France, with aluminium bodywork by Scaglietti and a tuned version of the Colombo V12. This is one of the all-time greats.
Total: 84. Power: 280bhp. Top speed: 137mph

410 Superamerica (1956)

To replace the 375 America, the Lampredi V12 was bored out to nearly 5 litres. The chassis was new and the brakes much improved. Coupe bodywork was by Farina, Ghia and Scaglietti.
Total: 38. Power: 400bhp. Top speed: 165mph

250 GT Cabriolet/California (1957)

Scaglietti built the open-top versions of the Pininfarina 250 GTs. The California had the Tour de France's tuned engine.
Total: 241/104. Power: 240bhp.
Top speed: 137mph

400 Superamerica (1959)

One of the last coachbuilt Ferraris, and powered by a Colombo V12 rather than a Lampredi. Most were built by Pininfarina in 'aerodynamic coupe' style. Disc brakes all-round, too.
Total: 54. Power: 400bhp. Top speed: 160mph

250 GT SWB (1960)

By cutting the 250 GT chassis down to a wheelbase of 2400mm, weight was reduced, cornering ability improved and the looks of the car made more aggressive. A true great.
Total: 167. Power: 280bhp. Top speed: 167mph

250 GT Coupé Pininfarina (1960)

Styled, as its name suggests, by Pininfarina, with a focus on comfort and convenience (there's no shortage of luggage space). Biggest seller yet.
Total: 350. Power: 240bhp.
Top speed: 126mph

250 GTE (1960)

The first production four-seater from Ferrari, although the rear seats were all but useless. The engine, gearbox and front seats were moved forward in the chassis to make space for the rear seats.
Total: 950. Power: 235bhp. Top speed: 120mph

250 GT Berlinetta Lusso (1962)

The road-going version of the legendary racing 250 GTO, the elegant Lusso is now one of the most sought-after Ferraris of all time. It used a three-carburettor version of the GTO's six-carb engine, making 250bhp.
Total: 350. Power: 250bhp. Top speed: 149mph

275 GTB/GTS and GTB/4 (1964)

Essentially the 2400mm 250 chassis with a larger, 3285cc engine and a new body. The open GTS was less ornate than the closed GTB. Four-cam version followed.
Total: 456/14/350. Power: 280bhp. Speed: 162mph

330 GT 2+2 (1964)

With much more sober styling than its stablemates, the 4-litre 2+2 330 GT is often overlooked now, but it was actually a strong seller. Odd-looking twin headlights on early versions were soon dropped.
Total: 1075. Power: 300bhp. Top speed: 152mph

500 Superfast (1964)

The replacement for the top-of-the-range 400 Superamerica, the 500 Superfast had a new 5-litre engine, the 330 GT's chassis and an aggressive swooping body style.
Lavish interior included air-con.
Total: 36. Power: 400bhp. Top speed: 174mph

330 GTC/GTS (1965)

Based on the 275 GTB and GTS, the 330 GTC and GTS (coupe and roadster) used the 300bhp 4-litre engine and, unusually for a Ferrari of the time, was available with alloy wheels rather than just the usual wire items.
Total: 600/100. Power: 300bhp. Top speed: 152mph

365 GTB/4 and GTS/4 'Daytona' (1968)
This was the replacement for the great 275 GTB/4. It surprised (and disappointed) many by eschewing the by-then fashionable mid-engined layout, but turned heads by dropping the traditional front grille for a radical droop-snoot look. Rare GTS 'Daytona Spider' was one dramatic-looking roadster.
Total: 1284/122. Power: 352bhp. Top speed: 174mph

365 California (1966)
The 365 California was aimed squarely at Ferrari's most elite customers, hence the tiny production number. It was based on the 2650mm chassis, with a 4390cc version of the V12 engine putting out well over 300bhp.
Total: 14. Power: 320bhp. Top speed: 152mph

365 GTC/GTS (1968)
These evolutions of the 330 GTC and GTS received the 4.4-litre V12, but were almost immediately made obsolete by the stunning (and technically much-improved) 365 GTB/4 Daytona.
Total: 150/20. Power: 320bhp. Top speed: 152mph

365 GT 2+2 (1968)
At over 16ft long and weighing nearly two tons, this is a big one! Along with its extra two seats, this 365 also had self-levelling rear suspension (a Ferrari first), air-con and electric windows.
Total: 800. Power: 320bhp. Top speed: 125mph

Dino 206 GT/246 GT/246 GTS (1970)
Never badged as a Ferrari, the Dino has slowly come of age, although the 2-litre, 180bhp 206 isn't nearly as sought-after as the 2.4-litre 246. Total: 152/2487/1274.
Power: 195bhp. Speed: 152mph

365 GTC/4 (1971)
Although less characterful in style than the Daytona, the 365 GTC/4 was much more civilised to drive than previous 365s. At the time the integrated bumpers were highly innovative.
Total: 500. Power: 340bhp. Top speed: 162mph

365 GT4 2+2 (1973)
The 365 GT4 2+2 was totally different again from other 365s and moved levels of Ferrari luxury up a notch or two. Thanks to the efficient use of the 2700mm chassis, four people could travel in comfort in this 2+2.
Total: 525. Power: 340bhp. Top speed: 152mph

365 GT4/BB 'Boxer' (1973)
It took a long time for Ferrari to produce a mid-engined grand tourer, but when the BB eventually appeared it impressed pundits with its clean, modern lines and the performance from its 4.4-litre V12.
Total: 387. Power: 380bhp. Top speed: 188mph

308 GT4 2+2 (1974)
Styled, unusually, by Bertone, the GT4 was originally badged as a Dino, not a Ferrari. A 208 version, inspired by fuel-crisis tax laws in Italy, had a mere 2 litres. The GT4 was never as sought after as the following 308s.
Total: 2826. Power: 255bhp. Top speed: 147mph

308 GTB/GTS/GTBi/GTSi/GTB QV/GTS QV (1976)
A mid-engined classic from Pininfarina. GTS had a targa roof, 'i' versions got Bosch fuel injection, QVs had four valves per cylinder.
Total: 2897/3219/494/1743/748/3042.
Power: 255bhp. Top speed: 152mph

400 GT (1976) and 400i (1979)
A 4.8-litre V12 turned the 365 GT/4 into the 400, with few aesthetic changes other than a front spoiler. Bosch fuel injection replaced carbs on 400i. First Ferrari available as an automatic.
Total: 501 (354 auto)/1294 (873 auto).
Power: 340bhp. Speed: 152mph

BB 512 (1976) and 512i (1981)
By upgrading the 365 GT/4 BB with a 4.9-litre engine, and tweaking the styling slightly with a small front spoiler and NACA ducts in the sills, a true classic was created. Became the 512i when fuel injection was added in 1981.
Total: 929/1007. Power: 360bhp. Top speed: 188mph

Mondial 8 (1981) and Mondial QV/Cabriolet QV (1984)
Cleverly incorporated four seats into a sporty design, but looked unbalanced and needed more than 214bhp. Four-valve QV improved matters.
Total: 703/1145/629. Power: 240bhp. Speed: 149mph

Testarossa (1984)
Name came from the 1950s Testa Rossa (Italian for 'red head'); outrageous styling from the excesses of the 1980s. Was a massive 1975mm wide. Five roadsters were built.
Total: 7177. Power: 390bhp. Top speed: 180mph

Mondial 3.2/Cabriolet (1985)
A 3.2-litre V8 (up from 3 litres) gave the Mondial some much-needed extra power to overcome its weight. Got Testarossa-style pop-up headlights at the same time.
Total: 987/810. Power: 270bhp. Top speed: 188mph

288 GTO (1984)
Another true great, and definitely worthy of the GTO name. The 288 GTO shape was based around the 308's body, but with a larger front spoiler, broader wings and a kicked-up tail. With light weight and 400bhp from the turbocharged 2.8-litre V8, it was seriously quick. Intended to go racing, changes to Group B regulations meant it never saw competitive action.
Total: 272. Power: 400bhp. Top speed: 190mph

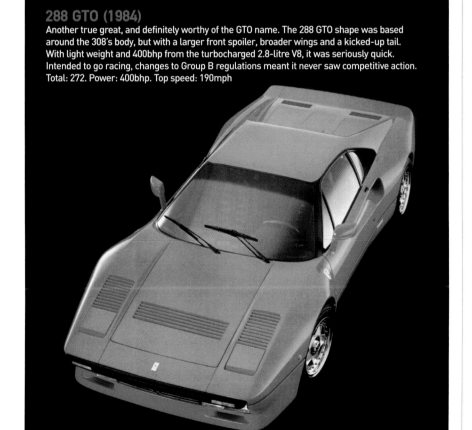

412 GT/Auto (1985)
The 400 GT grows up, getting a 4.9-litre engine, fuel injection and new ignition systems, and a still more luxurious engine with twin air-con plants, one for the front, one for the rear. Styling barely changed, though.
Total: 576 (306 auto). Power: 340bhp. Speed: 155mph

328 GTB/GTS (1985)
A neat evolution of the 308, with subtly updated styling and the capacity of its mid-mounted V8 raised to 3185cc, giving an extra 30bhp. As with the 308 there was also a GTS version with a removable targa-type roof panel.
Total: 1344/6068. Power: 270bhp. Top speed: 163mph

F40 (1987)
The 40th anniversary of Ferrari was celebrated with the launch of the wonderful F40, an extreme road-going supercar with a 3-litre twin turbo V8, composite chassis and bodywork and a truly Spartan interior. While not as sophisticated as rival Porsche's fiendishly complex 959, the F40 seemed the more passionate machine and also trumped it for top speed, being the first road-going Ferrari to top 200mph.
Total: 1315. Power: 478bhp. Max speed: 201mph

512 TR (1992)
The 512TR was a Testarossa with extra power, thanks to fuel injection, and revised styling to the front grille and pop-up headlights.
Total: 2280. Power: 428bhp. Top speed: 195mph

348 Spider (1993)
Aimed fair and square at the US market, the Spider was a pure roadster, with strengthened body to compensate for the lack of roof.
Total: 1090. Power: 300bhp. Top speed: 171mph

Mondial t/Cabriolet t (1989)
The Mondial range was updated in '89 with the 't' versions, which saw the transverse V8 engine turned 90 degrees to be mounted longitudinally, forming a T-shape with the gearbox.
Total: 840/1010. 300bhp. Top speed: 158mph

348 tb/ts/GTB/GTS (1989)
The 348 tb and the removable-roof ts were replacements for the 328GTB and GTS. Testarossa-style side vents cooled the engine.
Totals: 2895/4230/252/137
Power: 300bhp. Top speed: 174mph (GTB)

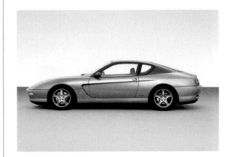

456 GT (1994)
Undoubtedly one of the best-looking 2+2s ever made, the 5.5-litre V12-engined 456 was available with manual gearbox (GT) and as an auto (GTA).
Total: 1936. Power: 442bhp. Top speed: 186mph

F355B/GTS (1994)
As a successor to the V8 line of 308, 328 and 348, the 355 had plenty to live up to – and did so admirably. The F1 version had F1-style paddle-operated sequential gearchange.
Total: 4915/434. Power: 380bhp. Speed: 183mph

F512M (1995)
This third evolution of the Testarossa, was the last Ferrari to have a flat-12. Power was upped, and there was a new look: headlights no longer pop-up, new front grille and revised rear end.
Total: 500. Power: 440bhp. Top speed: 196mph

F355 Spider (1995)
Converting the coupe 355 into a roadster was a big success. The hood featured a semi-automatic lowering and raising mechanism, synchronizing movement of the hood, seats and windows.
Total: 3714. Power: 380bhp. Top speed: 183mph

F50 (1996)
The idea of the V12 F50 was to produce the closest possible thing to a practical road-going Formula One car, so the F50 was built as a carbonfibre monocoque, with ground-effect aerodynamics and sequential gearbox.
Total: 349. Power: 520bhp. Top speed: 202mph

550 Maranello (1997)
A return to front-engined supercars with front-mounted V12, long bonnet and coupe styling. Electronic dampers and traction control were firsts on a Ferrari road car.
Total: 3083. Power: 485bhp. Top speed: 199mph

456M GT/GTA (1998)
Despite appearances, the 456M was quite different from the 456. Although the V12 engine was unchanged, the suspension was heavily revised and electronically managed to work with the ABS.
Total: 3289. Power: 442bhp. Top speed: 186mph

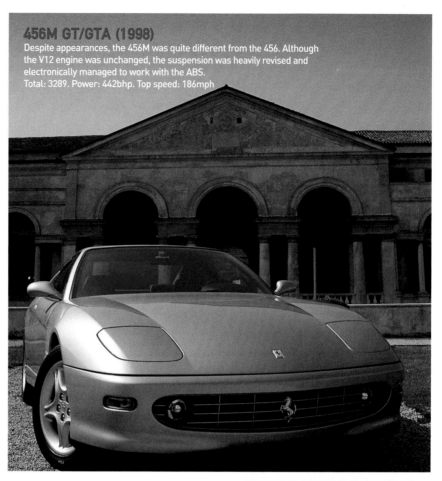

360 Modena/F1 (1999)
To counter the trend of ever-heavier new cars, Ferrari made great efforts to keep the V8-powered 360 as light as possible, with aluminium body and spaceframe chassis.
Total: 2630/6170 F1s. 400bhp. Top speed: 186mph

360 Spider (2000)
Hood down, the 360 Spider harks back to classic 1950s barchettas, with twin roll hoops and fairings behind driver's and passenger's heads. But it's loaded with modern goodies, too, including a fully automatic roof raising and lowering system.
Totals: 2115 / 5450 F1s. Power: 400bhp. Top speed: 186mph

550 Barchetta Pininfarina (2001)
After the strong reaction to the 360 Spider, Ferrari produced the 550 Barchetta with the same twin hoops and fairings as the 360. The difference, of course, is that the 550 had a front-engined V12 instead of mid-engined V8.
Total: 448. Power: 485bhp. Top speed: 186mph

575M (2002)

Subtle styling changes, such as a smaller front grille, distinguish the 575 from the 550, but it's the bigger engine (5748cc), F1-type transmission and adaptive suspension that are the big changes.
Total: 246/1810 F1s. 515bhp. Top speed: 202mph

360 Challenge Stradale (2003)

The one-make racers in the 360 Challenge series inspired this fabulous road-racer, known as the Challenge Stradale (Italian for street). It had reduced weight and much of the character of the racers. A modern classic.
Total: 378. Power: 425bhp. Top speed: 186mph

Enzo (2002)

The ultimate! Like the F50 before it, the Enzo made great use of F1 technology, with composite construction, electronically controlled transmission (changes in 150 milliseconds) and the same output from its V12 as an F1 car.
Total: 399. Power: 650bhp. Top speed: 217mph-plus

612 Scaglietti (2004)

To commemorate the historic links between Ferrari and the Scaglietti coachbuilding company, the V12-powered 612 Scaglietti was created. Ironically it isn't one of Pininfarina's best shapes.
Total: n/a. Power: 540bhp. Top speed: 199mph

F430 (2004)

The successor to the 360 is a technical tour de force, with (for the first time on a road car) an electronically controlled diff, plus F1 sequential gearbox and the usual traction control, etc.
Total: n/a. Power: 490bhp. Top speed: 196mph

Superamerica (2005)

The name Superamerica has always been associated with the most prestigious Ferraris. This front-engined V12 was no exception, with a glass roof that can be electronically dimmed.
Total: n/a. Power: 540bhp. Top speed: 199mph

F430 Spider (2005)

No surprise that an open F430 would appear, and it's as good-looking as you'd expect. Strengthening added about 70kg to the weight.
Total: n/a. Power: 490bhp. Top speed: 193mph

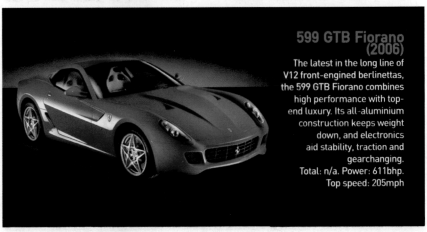

599 GTB Fiorano (2006)

The latest in the long line of V12 front-engined berlinettas, the 599 GTB Fiorano combines high performance with top-end luxury. Its all-aluminium construction keeps weight down, and electronics aid stability, traction and gearchanging.
Total: n/a. Power: 611bhp. Top speed: 205mph